america's war

About the National Endowment for the Humanities: Created in 1965 as an independent federal agency, the National Endowment for the Humanities supports learning in history, literature, philosophy and other areas of the humanities. NEH grants enrich classroom learning, create and preserve knowledge and bring ideas to life through public television, radio, new technologies, exhibitions and programs in libraries, museums and other community places. Additional information about NEH and its grant programs is available at www.neh.gov.

About the American Library Association: The American Library Association, founded in 1876, is the oldest and largest national library association in the world. The Association's mission is to provide leadership for the development, promotion, and improvement of library and information services and the profession of librarianship in order to enhance learning and ensure access to information for all. Through its Public Programs Office, ALA promotes cultural and community programming as an essential part of library service in all types and sizes of libraries. Additional information about ALA is available at www.ala.org.

ISBNs: 978-0-8389-8580-9 (print); 978-0-8389-9309-5 (PDF); 978-0-8389-9310-1 (Mobi); 978-0-8389-9311-8 (Kindle); 978-0-8389-9312-5 (ePub)

Library of Congress Cataloging-in-Publication Data
America's war : talking about the Civil War and emancipation on their 150th anniversaries / edited by Edward L. Ayers.
    p.   cm.
    Includes bibliographical references.
    ISBN 978-0-8389-8580-9 (pbk. : alk. paper)—ISBN 978-0-8389-9309-5 (pdf)—
ISBN 978-0-8389-9312-5 (epub)—ISBN 978-0-8389-9310-1 (mobi)—
ISBN 978-0-8389-9311-8 (kindle)
    1. United States—History—Civil War, 1861–1865—Sources. 2. Slaves—Emancipation—United States—Sources. I. Ayers, Edward L., 1953–
    E464.A45 2011
    973.7—dc23   2011021388

Cover image: *Feeding the Squirrel Rifles,* courtesy of the Becker Collection.
Book design by Karen Sheets de Gracia in Chapparal and Shannon.

Printed in the United States of America.

america's war

Talking About the
Civil War and
Emancipation
on Their
150th
Anniversaries

Edited by
Edward L. Ayers

Co-published by the
American Library Association
and the
National Endowment for the Humanities

Dedication of a Monument to the Memory of the Heroes of the New Hampshire
Regiment Killed in the Battle of Winchester, April 10, 1865 (detail) by James E. Taylor

contents

Part 3 · Making Sense of Shiloh

Part 4 · The Shape of War

acknowledgments

THE AMERICAN LIBRARY ASSOCIATION (ALA) would like to thank the individuals and organizations that have so generously contributed their time, talents, and resources to the publication of this anthology, *America's War: Talking About the Civil War and Emancipation on Their 150th Anniversaries.*

As one of three companion works for the national reading and discussion program *Let's Talk About It: Making Sense of the American Civil War*, this anthology will serve as a focus of discussion in hundreds of communities throughout the sesquicentennial period. We owe great thanks to the National Endowment for the Humanities (NEH) for making this project possible, sparking exploration, reflection, conversation, and greater understanding about this pivotal period in our nation's history through its support of humanities programming for public library audiences. Funding from NEH has supported all aspects of this anthology's production, as well as distribution of more than 6,000 copies for circulation in public, academic, community, and special libraries in 48 states and the District of Columbia.

We have been proud to count NEH as a partner and supporter of the library-based *Let's Talk About It* program model since it was launched on a nationwide level nearly thirty years ago. On this model, participants read a common series of books selected by a nationally known scholar; discuss them in the context of a larger, overarching theme; and explore that theme through the lens of the humanities. Information about the program model, including a list of libraries offering Civil War discussion programs through 2015, is available online at www.programminglibrarian.org/ltai.

We also wish to thank the editor and national project scholar, Edward L. Ayers. His role has gone far beyond material selection and editing for *America's War;* rather, he has been an invaluable partner in all phases of the project, from concept to creation to implementation.

And finally, we are grateful to the historians, librarians, state humanities council representatives, and staff of the University of Richmond, NEH, and ALA Public Programs Office who have helped shape *America's War* in ways large and small. These individuals include Jane Aikin, Kathryn Ames, Douglas Arnold, Frannie Ashburn, Colleen Barbus, Judith Bookbinder, Eva Caldera, Erik Cameron, Lainie Castle, Carrie Caumont, Mary Davis Fournier, Gary Gallagher, Peter Gilbert, Larry Grieco, Joe Kelly, Sofiana Krueger, Jim Leach, Esther Mackintosh, Carolyn Martin, Michael McDonald, Julia Nguyen, Thomas Phelps, Dwight Pitcaithley, Malcolm Richardson, Deb Robertson, Leah Ducato Rudolph, Amanda Rychener, Joel Schwartz, David Skinner, Robert K. Sutton, Ann Thompson, Angela Thullen, Patti Van Tuyl and Carole Watson.

Keith Michael Fiels, Executive Director
American Library Association

preface

IN THE YEARS 2011 THROUGH 2015, people across the United States will observe the 150th anniversary of the American Civil War. The memory of this war takes us back to a time in American history when civility ruptured and the nation split in two.

The war was on a scale so devastating that nobody could have imagined it beforehand. In the first engagement in Virginia's verdant countryside, people carried picnic baskets to watch from hilltops as regiments engaged in battles, as if they were sporting events.

Four years later, more than 620,000 soldiers had died in a war that grimly tested American values and mettle. Few Americans were left untouched by the ravages of conflict. The long and complex drama featured politicians and generals, but the greatest story remains that of the farmers and craftsmen, merchants and bricklayers who wore the blue and gray. In battle after battle, they marched to the beat of two different drummers with contrasting senses of patriotism.

The cataclysm of a war that divided families as well as states is also the story of those left behind and those fought over—the women of every social stratum who tended the wounded and worked alone to nourish their children and sustain family livelihoods; the enslaved men and women forced to take desperate measures, including roles in combat, to secure their freedom. In the end, the war settled two issues: that slavery is incompatible with democratic values, and that these United States are indivisible, inseparable from one another.

As this anthology's subtitle makes plain, emancipation is the central theme of "America's War." In declaring that "all men are created equal," our founders had asserted a principle they considered to be self-evident and universal. Nonetheless, the country so uniquely founded on their dreams and ideals did not embody at its birth a full equalitarian sense of justice. For the sake of unity, the contentious issue of slavery had been set aside.

The constitutional processes put in place were meant to sustain democracy in a nation destined to grow geographically, demographically, technologically, and in wisdom. To counter kingly despotism and ensure democratic accountability, our founders recognized the frailty of human nature and thus divided and decentralized political power. Power separation with competitive overlaps between and within branches and levels of government precipitated a never-ending creative tension. The transformation of this tension into unified political energy is a constant challenge. In over two centuries of experimentation with democratic governance, our gravest constitutional test came when the North and the South could not reconcile divided views on states' rights as they affected human dignity in the mid nineteenth century.

Martin Luther King Jr. eloquently observed that the arc of the moral universe is long, but it bends toward justice. American history vindicates King's observation. But as unequivocal as our founders were in their affirmation of individual rights, progress was tragically slow in advancing equality for all. It took two centuries of struggle, including the Civil War, abolitionist and suffragist movements, and courageous civil rights leadership to bring to maturity the values embedded in the Declaration of Independence.

In 1863, at the midpoint of the Civil War, President Abraham Lincoln gave the most memorable address in American history, reading from notes jotted on the back of an envelope at the site where so many young men had given what he so profoundly described as "the last full measure of devotion."

Lincoln reminded his countrymen, then and now, that "[i]t is for us, the living" to be dedicated "to the unfinished work which they who have fought here have thus far so nobly advanced." It is for us the living, Lincoln affirmed, to resolve that "government of the people, by the people, for the people, shall not perish from the earth."

History can sometimes be more controversial than current events. Public memory of the Civil War is not uniform. Its causes and effects are still being probed and debated. This volume, supported by the National Endowment for the Humanities (NEH), is designed to contribute to the public dialogue. Skillfully selected and framed by Edward L. Ayers, distinguished historian and president of the University of Richmond, the speeches, diaries, memoirs and short stories within it represent a broad range of perspectives from a large cast of characters.

The Ayers anthology is meant to be read in combination with the creative voice of Gwendolyn Brooks in her novel *March* and the historical perspective of James McPherson in his scholarly treatise *Crossroads of Freedom: Antietam*. These three books form the basis of discussion programs taking place over the next four years in libraries across the country about the Civil War, its causes, and its legacy.

NEH is proud to have the American Library Association as its partner in this nationwide reading and discussion program on the Civil War. Civil discourse—the respectful willingness to consider other views and place them in the context of history, philosophy, and life experiences—is an ancient virtue of civilized society. Just as democracy demands equality, civilization requires civility. And there may be no institution more civil than the public library—a center of learning that offers a welcoming space where members of the public can learn about the history we share and express different points of view in an ethos of openness and mutual respect.

The sesquicentennial of the Civil War and emancipation is a time for America to take stock, to reflect on who we are as a people, what we have overcome, and whether there are lessons that can be gleaned from our history. Taking time to reflect together about the causes and ramifications of our greatest internal conflict is one of the most appropriate ways for "us the living" to renew the American spirit in these still-troubled times.

Jim Leach, Chairman
National Endowment for the Humanities

introduction

YOU ARE LIKELY TO BE surprised by some of what you find in this collection. The cast of characters, the range of perspectives, and the number of interesting questions about the Civil War have expanded to a remarkable extent over the last few decades. While the key questions and characters endure, we now have the exciting opportunity to see through the eyes of many people neglected in earlier generations. A hundred and fifty years after the pivotal event in our nation's history, we are still discovering its meanings.

The purpose of these selections is to give people interesting things to talk about. The American Civil War is intrinsically interesting, though it has often been buried in cliché and overfamiliarity. The global significance of the war seems different than it did fifty years ago, at the time of the centennial, when its major consequence seemed to be the unification of a nation that would stand against communism. Today, the Civil War seems to matter, too, because it brought an end to the most powerful system of slavery in the modern world. If the themes of union and freedom give the war the meanings we wish to see, however, we have also come to acknowledge that the war reveals humans' capacity for killing one another in vast numbers.

From the moment Americans found themselves pulled into a civil war of unimaginable scale and consequence, they tried desperately to make sense of what was happening to them. From the secession crisis into the maelstrom of battle, from the nightmare of slavery into the twilight of emancipation, Americans of all kinds made up narratives that tried to order the chaos. Because the need to understand that war endured long after the end of fighting, people have told stories about the Civil War for the last century-and-a-half—and they always will.

Whatever their origin or timing, all these stories tell more than appears on the surface. They speak, often in spite of themselves, of purposes and patterns larger than their immediate subject. They often belie or undercut their original purpose, too obviously reveal their wishful thinking and self-deception. The histories we write today strive for balance and inclusion, but we, too, tell ourselves stories, new and old, for our own reasons. The only way we can understand those stories is to read them together to explore their similarities and differences.

Each of the readings in this collection adds a crucial voice to our understanding, a perspective we need in order to see the whole. The silences or anger or hatred or idealism that separate the voices are as important as their commonalities. The American Civil War was not a single thing, a simple thing. It changed shape from the beginning to the end. The war's full significance, incomplete in 1865, continues to unfold all around us.

The selections in this book range from the 1850s through the first decade of the twenty-first century. They reflect the perspectives of Americans—from an enslaved man to the president of the United States, from a teenage girl to veterans recalling battles fought decades earlier, from diary writers caught in the terror of the moment to novelists imagining events that unfolded generations before their own time. Whatever their sources, the selections here convey unique and distinctive voices.

The clearest example of the difference between the people of the nineteenth century and those of the twenty-first lies in the representation of African Americans. Any student of the Civil War era must confront the callous and stereotyped portrayals of black people by whites in the writings of the time. A disregard of the full humanity of black Americans seemed all too natural. The flashes of empathy and concern that sometimes emerged stand as the exceptions.

Other themes stretch across these selections. Though we have grown accustomed to thinking of the years before the Civil War as prelude to a war people knew was coming, they did not in fact have that knowledge. People expected, as Abraham Lincoln put it, that some kind of "tug" had to come, but they did not expect a cataclysmic war that would sacrifice their sons, brothers, and fathers and devastate a generation. People expected some kind of struggle over slavery, but they did not expect the full emancipation of four million people within a few years. If Americans had known of these things, many would not have fought. And if we are to understand their actions, we must set aside our own knowledge of how events turned out.

People have found turning points around one event after another, especially between 1862 and 1864. In fact, the very profusion of these turning points should make us wary of the concept, for the war continually turned. The future of slavery, the relationship of the states to the federal government, the fate of African Americans, and the degree of postwar reconciliation between the North and the South could each have followed different trajectories at many points throughout the conflict and beyond.

The selections show, too, that the United States and the Confederacy held sharp conflicts within their own borders. Despite sentimental images of soldiers in blue and gray marching off to war with their communities cheering them on, many struggles divided the North and the South. In the United States, people squabbled over the very purposes of the war from start to finish, some arguing that only a war for union was worth fighting, others arguing that only a war for freedom deserved such sacrifice, and still others arguing that nothing justified such a bloodletting. Furious dissidents against the inequities of the draft rioted in the streets of New York. In the South, leaders of states raged that the Confederacy exercised tyranny in its draft and taxation. Women rallied in the streets of Richmond against the inequities of sacrifice and hunger. Border areas fell into their own civil wars, chaotic, bloody, and destined to fester for generations.

The selections that follow show that Northerners and Southerners believed passionately in the justice of their cause. They urged themselves and their families to ever-greater sacrifice. Before the war's outbreak, only a relatively few self-appointed spokesmen called for a new Southern republic based on slavery. Within weeks of its creation, though, people declared themselves willing to die for that republic—and they did die, in staggering numbers. The Confederacy was a brand-new nation, built out of the materials at hand: an edited United States Constitution, the apparent sanction of the Old Testament, movements for independence in Greece and Italy, and a determination to protect a system of slavery of global economic importance. The United States was a few decades older, but it, too, was untested, the idea of perpetual union only recently and imperfectly defined.

The experience of fighting was as alien and surprising as the coming of the war itself. The United States had only a tiny army and navy, with an anemic tradition of a professional military. The states that would become the Confederacy possessed virtually no military resources. Yet, within a matter of months, both sides amassed enough men and military material to fight a war across an enormous expanse of space and time. In one horrific battle after another, they killed each other in proportions that would only be equaled sixty years later on the fields of Europe in the Great War.

The experience of African Americans varied greatly. For the four million held in slavery, war sometimes meant they were sent to work on fortifications, sometimes sent to battle with young masters, and sometimes removed as far from the presence of Union troops as possible. Enslaved people seized opportunities to make themselves free, risking their lives to travel to Union camps or to follow Union troops. Over 200,000 African American men, some free before the war and some enslaved, joined the United States Army and Navy. Only small numbers of black men willingly picked up arms for the Confederacy. Most enslaved people, laboring far from the battle-front, remained on the farms and plantations where they had lived before the war, praying for freedom and taking whatever steps they could to make that freedom real.

Within each section of this collection, the writings are organized as a kind of conversation. In some cases, they are ordered by the dates when they were written, in others by the order of the events they evoked. Both of these organizing principles are important, so it would be good to think about both. People could see things in the 1870s they could not have seen in the 1850s, but the reverse is also true. We do not necessarily grow collectively wiser with time, though new experiences and new kinds of writing reveal things invisible to people at an earlier time.

The selections of *America's War* build on the remarkable scholarship of the last several decades. Historians and literary scholars have carefully gathered and edited the works of writers, famous and otherwise, setting their words in context, clarifying issues of controversy, and presenting important writings that few general readers would be able to find on their own. Readers will discover a wide range of usages, spelling, and documentation in the works that follow; each reflects the original document and time and purposes for which it was written. Gathering to talk about these powerful voices from the past is the best way to understand them. It is also a useful way to understand ourselves a hundred and fifty years after this war descended on the United States.

Edward L. Ayers, President
University of Richmond

PART 1

Imagining War

The United States General Hospital at Georgetown, D.C., Formerly the Union Hotel,
from *Frank Leslie's Illustrated Newspaper*, July 6, 1861.

As mentioned in the Preface, *America's War* has been published in support of a five-part reading and discussion series planned for libraries and other organizations across the country. Each section of this anthology was developed to serve as the focus of a single discussion group meeting, inspiring five thematic conversations about the Civil War. In addition to *America's War*, there are two other companion works included in the series: Geraldine Brooks's *March*, which is meant to be part of the first conversation, and James McPherson's *Crossroads of Freedom: Antietam*, meant to be part of the fourth.

The first conversation begins with a novel of our own times, a work that imagines our way into the past. Brooks's *March*, which appeared in 2005, tells its story through the characters of another novel: *Little Women*, Louisa May Alcott's story of sisters and a mother, published in 1868, only three years after Appomattox. Brooks tells the story of the father and husband of those women, the Reverend March, who in Alcott's story is significant mainly for his absence.

In *March*, we see the story through his eyes, eyes that do not always comprehend clearly what they perceive. We travel with the chaplain into places where he is not wanted, where his values bring ridicule and contempt. The harsh world of slavery, men, and war challenges everything the March family members believe in, including one another. Brooks's novel is a powerful and humane meditation on America as it descended into the chaos of war.

The 2006 paperback edition of *March* appends eight interesting and useful questions that should make a good foundation for the first discussion in this series. In fact, those questions—about the war's purpose, about the moral underpinnings of people's actions, about the ways the war changed people—provide good questions to keep in mind while you read the other selections.

The anthology opens with a reading selected to accompany the discussion of *March*—a brief selection of Louisa May Alcott's own journal of her experience as a nurse for the Union in 1862. In this remarkably frank document, the unmarried 30-year-old tells of her determination to find a purpose for her life by helping in the hospitals of Washington, D.C., an important setting in Brooks's novel. Alcott experiences horror, satisfaction, and deep personal trials during her time with the wounded, diseased, and dying men. Her journal allows us to compare fiction and firsthand testimony, and to think about what we can learn from each.

To understand the context in which the traditions of Civil War fiction emerged, a good place to start is Alice Fahs, *The Imagined Civil War*, from 2001, which provides a helpful overview of the writing produced in the North and the South during the war itself. Edmund Wilson's *Patriotic Gore*, published during the opening years of the war's centennial in 1961, is a characteristically fiery and powerful interpretation of key texts of the war.

The fiction of the Civil War has a rich tradition and remains vital today. While any listing of Civil War novels is bound to leave off favorites, the following recommendations offer some good places to start. The novel that established a moral framework for much of the Union purpose is Harriet Beecher Stowe's *Uncle Tom's Cabin*, published in 1852. It also provided the basis for the most popular play in nineteenth-century America, a play performed countless times across the country both before and after the war. The first modern novel of the war was Stephen Crane's *Red Badge of Courage*, published in 1895 by a young author born after the war's end. A mainstay of high school classrooms, Crane's novel introduces a note of human failing and doubt that has become a motif in most Civil War fiction. Margaret Mitchell's *Gone with the Wind*, appearing in 1936, defined the way the war would be remembered in the twentieth century and beyond, especially once it became simplified in the 1939 film based on its story. With its strong female central character, racial stereotyping, romanticizing of the slave South, and demonizing of the Yankees and Reconstruction, *Gone with the Wind* has fed, and limited, Americans' imagination for generations. It has also inspired many people's interest in the Civil War and its profoundly human struggles.

The most popular novel of the Civil War written since World War II is Michael Shaara's *The Killer Angels*, published in 1974. Exploring the war through the eyes of key officers in both the United States and Confederate armies at Gettysburg, Shaara's novel compresses central issues of the war into a powerful story. Since Shaara, popular Civil War novels have included Charles Frazier's *Cold Mountain* (1997), Howard Bahr's *The Black Flower* (1997), Russell Banks's *Cloudsplitter* (1998), and E. L. Doctorow's *The March* (2006). All of those novels, and many more published in recent decades, strike notes more ambiguous than either *Gone with the Wind* on one hand, or *Killer Angels* on the other.

1

LOUISA MAY ALCOTT

Journal kept at the hospital, Georgetown, D.C.

1862

NOVEMBER. — THIRTY YEARS OLD. Decided to go to Washington as nurse if I could find a place. Help needed, and I love nursing, and *must* let out my pent-up energy in some new way. Winter is always a hard and a dull time, and if I am away there is one less to feed and warm and worry over.

I want new experiences, and am sure to get 'em if I go. So I've sent in my name, and bide my time writing tales, to leave all snug behind me, and mending up my old clothes, for nurses don't need nice things, thank Heaven!

December. — On the 11th I received a note from Miss H. M. Stevenson telling me to start for Georgetown next day to fill a place in the Union Hotel Hospital. Mrs. Ropes of Boston was matron, and Miss Kendall of Plymouth was a nurse there, and though a hard place, help was needed. I was ready, and when my commander said "March!" I marched. Packed my trunk, and reported in B. that same evening.

We had all been full of courage till the last moment came; then we all broke down. I realized that I had taken my life in my hand, and might never see them all again. I said, "Shall I stay, Mother?" as I hugged her close. "No, go! and the Lord be with you! " answered the Spartan woman; and till I turned the corner she bravely smiled and waved her wet handkerchief on the door-step. Shall I ever see that dear old face again?

So I set forth in the December twilight, with May and Julian Hawthorne as escort, feeling as if I was the son of the house going to war.

Friday, the 12th, was a very memorable day, spent in running all over Boston to get my pass, etc., calling for parcels, getting a tooth filled, and buying a veil, — my only purchase. A. C. gave me some old clothes; the dear Sewalls money for myself and boys, lots of love and help; and at 5 p.m., saying "good-by" to a group of tearful faces at the station, I started on my long journey, full of hope and sorrow, courage and plans.

A most interesting journey into a new world full of stirring sights and sounds, new adventures, and an ever-growing sense of the great task I had undertaken.

I said my prayers as I went rushing through the country white with tents, all alive with patriotism, and already red with blood. A solemn time, but I'm glad to live in it; and am sure it will do me good whether I come out alive or dead.

All went well, and I got to Georgetown one evening very tired. Was kindly welcomed, slept in my narrow bed with two other roommates, and on the morrow began my new life by seeing a poor man die at dawn, and sitting all day between a boy with pneumonia and a man shot through the lungs. A strange day, but I did my best; and when I put mother's little black shawl round the boy while he sat up panting for breath, he smiled and said, "You are real motherly, ma'am." I felt as if I was getting on. The man only lay and stared with his big black eyes, and made me very nervous. But all were well behaved; and I sat looking at the twenty strong faces as they looked back at me, — the only new thing they had to amuse them, — hoping that I looked "motherly" to them; for my thirty years made me feel old, and the suffering round me made me long to comfort every one.

January, 1863. Union Hotel Hospital, Georgetown, D. C. — I never began the year in a stranger place than this: five hundred miles from home, alone, among strangers, doing painful duties all day long, and leading a life of constant excitement in this great house, surrounded by three or four hundred men in all stages of suffering, disease, and death. Though often homesick, heartsick, and worn out, I like it, find real pleasure in comforting, tending, and cheering these poor souls who seem to love me, to feel my sympathy though unspoken, and acknowledge my hearty good-will, in spite of the ignorance, awkwardness, and bashfulness which I cannot help showing in so new and trying a situation. The men are docile, respectful, and affectionate, with but few exceptions; truly lovable and manly many of them. John Sulie, a Virginia blacksmith, is the prince of patients; and though what we call a common man in education and condition, to me is all I could expect or ask from the first gentleman in the land. Under his plain speech and unpolished manner I seem to see a noble character, a heart as warm and tender as a woman's, a nature fresh and frank as any child's. He is about thirty, I think, tall and handsome, mortally wounded, and dying royally without reproach, repining, or remorse. Mrs. Ropes and myself love him, and feel indignant that such a man should be so early lost; for though he might never distinguish himself before the world, his influence and example cannot be without effect, for real goodness is never wasted.

Monday, 4th. — I shall record the events of a day as a sample of the days I spend: — Up at six, dress by gaslight, run through my ward and throw up the windows, though the men grumble and shiver; but the air is bad enough to breed a pestilence; and as no notice is taken of our frequent appeals for better ventilation, I must do what I can. Poke up the fire, add blankets, joke, coax, and command; but continue to open doors and windows as if life depended upon it. Mine does, and doubtless many another, for a more perfect pestilence-box than this house I never saw, — cold, damp, dirty, full of vile odors from wounds, kitchens, wash-rooms, and stables. No competent head, male or female, to right matters, and a jumble of good, bad, and indifferent nurses, surgeons, and attendants, to complicate the chaos still more.

After this unwelcome progress through my stifling ward, I go to breakfast with what appetite I may; find the uninvitable fried beef, salt butter, husky bread, and washy coffee; listen to the clack of eight women and a dozen men, the first silly, stupid, or possessed of one idea; the last absorbed with their breakfast and themselves to a degree that is both ludicrous and provoking, for all the dishes are ordered down the table *full* and returned *empty;* the conversation is entirely among themselves, and each announces his opinion with an air of importance that frequently causes me to choke in my cup, or bolt my meals with undignified speed lest a laugh betray to these famous beings that a "chiel's amang them takin' notes."

Till noon I trot, trot, giving out rations, cutting up food for helpless "boys," washing faces, teaching my attendants how beds are made or floors are swept, dressing wounds, taking Dr. F. P.'s orders (privately wishing all the time that he would be more gentle with my big babies), dusting tables, sewing bandages, keeping my tray tidy, rushing up and down after pillows, bed-linen, sponges, books, and directions, till it seems as if I would joyfully pay down all I possess for fifteen minutes' rest. At twelve the big bell rings, and up comes dinner for the boys, who are always ready for it and never entirely satisfied. Soup, meat, potatoes, and bread is the bill of fare. Charley Thayer, the attendant, travels up and down the room serving out the rations, saving little for himself, yet always thoughtful of his mates, and patient as a woman with their helplessness. When dinner is over, some sleep, many read, and others want letters written. This I like to do, for they put in such odd things, and express their ideas so comically, I have great fun interiorly, while as grave as possible exteriorly. A few of the men word their paragraphs well and make excellent letters. John's was the best of all I wrote. The answering of letters from friends after some one had died is the saddest and hardest duty a nurse has to do.

Supper at five sets every one to running that can run; and when that flurry is over, all settle down for the evening amusements, which consist of newspapers, gossip, the doctor's last round, and, for such as need them, the final doses for the night. At nine the bell rings, gas is turned down, and day nurses go to bed. Night nurses go on duty, and sleep and death have the house to themselves.

My work is changed to night watching, or half night and half day, — from twelve to twelve. I like it, as it leaves me time for a morning run, which is what I need to keep well; for bad air, food, and water, work and watching, are getting to be too much for me.

I trot up and down the streets in all directions, sometimes to the Heights, then half way to Washington, again to the hill, over which the long trains of army wagons are constantly vanishing and ambulances appearing. That way the fighting lies, and I long to follow.

Ordered to keep my room, being threatened with pneumonia. Sharp pain in the side, cough, fever, and dizziness. A pleasant prospect for a lonely soul five hundred miles from home! Sit and sew on the boys' clothes, write letters, sleep, and read; try to talk and keep merry, but fail decidedly, as day after day goes, and I feel no better. Dream awfully, and wake unrefreshed, think of home, and wonder if I am to die here, as Mrs. R., the matron, is likely to do. Feel too miserable to care much what becomes of me. Dr. S. creaks up twice a day to feel my pulse, give me doses, and ask if I am at all consumptive, or some other cheering question. Dr. O. examines my lungs and looks sober. Dr. J. haunts the room, coming by day and night with wood, cologne, books, and messes, like a motherly little man as he is. Nurses fussy and anxious, matron dying, and everything very gloomy. They want me to go home, but I *won't* yet.

January 16th. — Was amazed to see Father enter the room that morning, having been telegraphed to by order of Mrs. R. without asking leave. I was very angry at first, though glad to see him, because I knew I should have to go. Mrs. D. and Miss Dix came, and pretty Miss W., to take me to Willard's to be cared for by them. I wouldn't go, preferring to keep still, being pretty ill by that time.

On the 21st I suddenly decided to go home, feeling very strangely, and dreading to be worse. Mrs. R. died, and that frightened the doctors about me; for my trouble was the same, — typhoid pneumonia. Father, Miss K., and Lizzie T. went with me. Miss Dix brought a basket full of bottles of wine, tea, medicine, and cologne, besides a little blanket and pillow, a fan, and a testament. She is a kind old soul, but very queer and arbitrary.

Was very sorry to go, and "my boys" seemed sorry to have me. Quite a flock came to see me off; but I was too sick to have but a dim idea of what was going on.

Had a strange, excited journey of a day and night, — half asleep, half wandering, just conscious that I was going home; and, when I got to Boston, of being taken out of the car, with people looking on as if I was a sight. I daresay I was all blowzed, crazy, and weak. Was too sick to reach Concord that night, though we tried to do so. Spent it at Mr. Sewall's; had a sort of fit; they sent for Dr. H., and I had a dreadful time of it.

Next morning felt better, and at four went home. Just remember seeing May's shocked face at the depot, Mother's bewildered one at home, and getting to bed in the firm belief that the house was roofless, and no one wanted to see me.

As I never shall forget the strange fancies that haunted me, I shall amuse myself with recording some of them.

The most vivid and enduring was the conviction that I had married a stout, handsome Spaniard, dressed in black velvet, with very soft hands, and a voice that was continually saying, "Lie still, my dear!" This was Mother, I suspect; but with all the comfort I often found in her presence, there was blended an awful fear of the Spanish spouse who was always coming after me, appearing out of closets, in at windows, or threatening me dreadfully all night long. I appealed to the Pope, and really got up and made a touching plea in something meant for Latin, they tell me. Once I went to heaven, and found it a twilight place, with people darting through the air in a queer way, — all very busy, and dismal, and ordinary. Miss Dix, W. H. Channing, and other people were there; but I thought it dark and "slow," and wished I hadn't come.

PART 2

....

Choosing Sides

Squirrel Rifles: Sketch at the Depot in Xenia, Ohio, by Henri Lovie

The second conversation in the collection takes us directly into the world Geraldine Brooks imagined. We see through the eyes of people who had to decide for themselves where justice, honor, duty, and loyalty lay. The readings for this conversation are primary documents, direct testimony from the past. As a result, they are less conveniently packaged than fiction but possess a unique kind of power. Readers will need to set aside contemporary expectations about word choice, pacing, and detail, for the nineteenth century valued different standards than have become common today. Such effort is more than compensated for, however, by the excitement of seeing people struggle in real time with issues of the most profound importance and consequence. The writing in this section is some of the most powerful ever produced by Americans.

Since struggles over slavery underpinned America's Civil War, the section opens with a searing speech by Frederick Douglass from 1852. Asked by people much like the March family and their abolitionist friends to deliver a speech in Rochester, New York, on the Fourth of July, Douglass gave them more than they asked for. His speech stripped away any illusions white Americans may have had about their innocence, confronting them directly with the hypocrisy of a nation dedicated to freedom and built on slavery. Striking a similar note, Henry David Thoreau (who also appears as a character in *March*), confronted his friends with a blistering defense of John Brown after the aborted 1859 raid on the armory at Harpers Ferry. While much of the nation rushed to denounce and ridicule Brown, Thoreau celebrated him and all that he stood for. Such defenses confirmed the worst suspicions of white Southerners.

Abraham Lincoln, elected the year after Harpers Ferry, had to confront disunion even before he took office. By the time he delivered his first inaugural address, presented here, the seven states of the Deep South had already formed the Confederate States of America. His speech was an attempt to reassure the voters who had elected him that he would not betray their trust by allowing the nation to be divided. In that speech, he tried to reassure the white South that he would not drive them away.

Alexander Stephens of South Carolina, the vice president of the new Confederacy, defended secession as an undeniable right and celebrated slavery as the very cornerstone of the new nation. With the alternatives so starkly drawn between Lincoln and the new Confederacy, a convention in Virginia debated, week after week, what course that state should take. Priding itself on being the birthplace of George Washington and Thomas Jefferson, Virginia knew that the decision of whether to join the Confederacy or to remain with the Union would change everything that followed.

Robert Montague and Chapman Stuart crystallized what many had been saying: Secessionists argued that they had no choice but to defend themselves; Unionists argued that choices did indeed remain, that the country must be saved. Reasoned debate collapsed, however, as soon as the guns fired at Fort Sumter, and Lincoln called for militia from Virginia and other states to put down the rebellion. The convention in Virginia, which had voted for union only weeks before, now voted for secession, albeit with a third of the delegates refusing to support the decision. Soon, North Carolina, Tennessee, and Arkansas followed Virginia's lead. Maryland, Kentucky, and Missouri—slave states—stayed uneasily in the Union.

Robert E. Lee embodied the agony of disunion. A former commandant of West Point, a man who had lived his adult life in the United States Army, Lee traveled from his posting in Texas to his Virginia home, just outside Washington, D.C., to confront the decision. Elizabeth Brown Pryor, in a subtle work of modern scholarship, reconstructs the tortured days in which Lee struggled with the decision of whether to follow his oath to the United States—indeed, to command its armies—or to follow Virginia on a course he had opposed and dreaded. Pryor's fascinating postscript, composed for this volume, reveals how our understanding of history is continually being enriched by the discovery of new materials. In this case, her own interpretation of Lee turns out to have more complications than even she realized.

Mark Twain tells, with his characteristic self-deflating humor, of his own wayward path in the confusing early days of the war. Along with other boys of his Missouri neighborhood, Twain joined the Confederacy, only to decide that he had no real stake in the war and to head west. By doing so, Twain escaped the moral anguish, bloody sacrifice, and lost years exacted by the Civil War. He was not alone, for the western territories and states boomed during the war, laying the foundations for the Old West of cowboys and Indians and railroads and homesteaders, developments that overlapped the struggles of the Civil War and Reconstruction.

This conversation ends with a diary by a young woman about the same age as Mark Twain. Sarah Morgan, an 18-year-old resident of Baton Rouge, Louisiana, had been, like her father, a staunch Unionist. But in the first nine months of the war, her town already occupied by the United States Army, Morgan alternated between defiant glorification of the Confederacy and deep doubt about the war and her own role in it. Like the March girls, her contemporaries in the North, Morgan found herself surrounded by a war she felt herself powerless to alter.

The issues addressed in this session's conversations embrace some of the most contentious issues in the writing of American history. What role did slavery play in the war's origins and why do we keep debating that role? Why were Americans unsuccessful in finding peaceful compromise? What did Americans expect to happen at the beginning of the war? With people of the time disagreeing so vehemently about the war, how do we decide who deserves the most credibility?

Historians have narrowed the range of debate about the Civil War in some ways—agreeing, virtually unanimously, albeit with significant differences of emphasis, that slavery drove all the central conflicts that culminated in the war—but they have broadened the cast of characters and issues considerably. A good place to start is David Potter's *The Impending Crisis* (1977), a balanced narrative. On Abraham Lincoln's evolution, Eric Foner's *The Fiery Trial* (2010) is the best place to gain a full understanding. I have attempted to weave together the struggles confronted by people in the North and South in *In the Presence of Mine Enemies* (2003), a study of two communities near the Mason-Dixon Line. For a good overview of the historical literature, see James M. McPherson and William J. Cooper Jr., *Writing the Civil War: The Quest to Understand* (1999).

2

FREDERICK DOUGLASS

"What To the Slave Is the Fourth of July?"*

July 5, 1852

The oration, "What To the Slave Is the Fourth of July?", delivered before a packed house at the Corinthian Hall in Rochester, New York on July 5, 1852, is the most famous antislavery speech Douglass ever gave. Published in pamphlet form under the title *Oration, Delivered in Corinthian Hall, Rochester, July 5th, 1852* (Rochester: Lee & Mann, 1852), the speech has always been a favorite of editors and anthologists because it exhibits so many of Douglass's strengths as a speaker—in particular, his ability to combine incisive social analysis with compelling argumentative skills and an adroit use of rhetoric. One of the most outstanding features of his mature style, showcased in "What To the Slave Is the Fourth of July?", is his self-conscious use of classical figures of speech, such as antithesis, hyperbole, metaphor, irony, and personification.

More than likely Douglass's effective experimentation with these rhetorical figures was what led some of his early listeners to doubt that he had ever been a slave. Douglass tried to answer the skeptics with his 1845 *Narrative*, in which he exploited all his favorite figures of speech while providing extensive details designed to prove that he was who he claimed to be, a self-taught fugitive slave. But after returning from his triumphal British speaking tour in the spring of 1847, Douglass began to see two diverging roles for himself as a speaker in the antislavery movement. On the one hand, he could continue to play the part he was best known for, that of the former slave who spoke autobiographically about the outrages of slavery. On the other hand, he could adopt a new persona who talked less about himself and his former bondage and more about the current condition of African Americans in the North within the context of the larger antislavery struggle. "What To the Slave Is the Fourth of July?", with its measured references to Douglass's personal experience in slavery, its ruthless dissection of the Fugitive Slave Law, and its thorough unmasking of the North's racial hypocrisies, displays Douglass successfully bridging the dual, and by 1852 the increasingly conflicted, roles available to him as an antislavery speaker and social reformer.

The nineteenth-century lecture platform was a stage on which ideas were not merely expounded—they were dramatized through picturesque language, bodily gesture, tone of voice, and pace of delivery. No orator of that era was more at home in this immensely popular arena of public performance than Frederick Douglass. His style and manner of self-presentation on the platform were carefully designed to reinforce the great theme of his speeches: the dignity and humanity of the African American. Douglass's sophistication in marshaling figurative language along with literary allusions and a ready supply of examples from American and European history helped to establish a reputation for oratorical genius that ensured demand for him on the lyceum circuit long after the social cause for which he had first become a speaker—the abolition of slavery—had been won.

MR. PRESIDENT, FRIENDS AND FELLOW Citizens: He who could address this audience without a quailing sensation, has stronger nerves than I have. I do not remember ever to have appeared as a speaker before any assembly more shrinkingly, nor with greater distrust of my ability, than I do this day. A feeling has crept over me, quite unfavorable to the exercise of my limited powers of speech. The task before me is one which requires much previous thought and study for its proper performance. I know that apologies of this sort are generally considered flat and unmeaning. I trust, however, that mine will not be so considered. Should I seem at ease, my appearance would much misrepresent me. The little experience I have had in addressing public meetings, in country school houses, avails me nothing on the present occasion.

The papers and placards say, that I am to deliver a 4th [of] July oration. This certainly, sounds large, and out of the common way, for me. It is true that I have often had the privilege to speak in this beautiful Hall, and to address many who now honor me with their presence. But neither their familiar faces, nor the perfect gage I think I have of Corinthian Hall, seems to free me from embarrassment.

The fact is, ladies and gentlemen, the distance between this platform and the slave plantation, from which I escaped, is considerable—and the difficulties to be overcome in getting from the latter to the former, are by no means slight. That I am here to-day, is, to me, a matter of astonishment as well as of gratitude. You will not, therefore, be surprised, if in what I have to say, I evince no elaborate preparation, nor grace my speech with any high sounding exordium. With little experience and with less learning, I have been able to throw my thoughts hastily and imperfectly together; and trusting to your patient and generous indulgence, I will proceed to lay them before you.

This, for the purpose of this celebration, is the 4th of July. It is the birthday of your National Independence, and of your political freedom. This, to you, is what the Passover was to the emancipated people of God. It carries your minds back to the day, and to the act of your great deliverance; and to the signs, and to the wonders, associated with that act, and that day. This celebration also marks the beginning of another year of your national life; and reminds you that the Republic of America is now 76 years old. I am glad, fellow-citizens, that your nation is so young. Seventy-six years, though a good old age for a man, is but a mere speck in the life of a nation. Three score years and ten is the allotted time for individual men; but nations number their years by thousands. According to this fact, you are, even now only in the beginning of your national career, still lingering in the period of childhood. I repeat, I am glad this is so. There is hope in the thought, and hope is much needed, under the dark clouds which lower above the horizon. The eye of the reformer is met with angry flashes, portending disastrous times; but his heart may well beat lighter at the thought that America is young, and that she is still in the impressible stage of her existence. May he not hope that high lessons of wisdom, of justice and of truth, will yet give direction to her destiny? Were the nation older, the patriot's heart might be sadder, and the reformer's brow heavier. Its future might be shrouded in gloom, and the hope of its prophets go out in sorrow. There is consolation in the thought, that America is young.—Great streams are not easily turned from channels, worn deep in the course of ages. They may sometimes rise in quiet and stately majesty, and inundate the land, refreshing and fertilizing the earth with their mysterious properties. They may also rise in wrath and fury, and bear away, on their angry waves, the accumulated wealth of years of toil and hardship. They, however, gradually flow back to the same old channel, and flow on as serenely as ever. But, while the river may not be turned aside, it may dry up, and leave nothing behind but the withered branch, and the unsightly rock, to howl in the abyss-sweeping wind, the sad tale of departed glory. As with rivers so with nations.

Fellow-citizens, I shall not presume to dwell at length on the associations that cluster about this day. The simple story of it is, that, 76 years ago, the people of this country were British subjects. The style and title of your "sovereign people" (in which you now glory) was not then born. You were under the British Crown. Your fathers esteemed the English Government as the home government; and England as the fatherland. This home government, you know, although a considerable distance from your home, did, in the exercise of its parental prerogatives, impose upon its colonial children, such restraints, burdens and limitations, as, in its mature judgment, it deemed wise, right and proper.

But, your fathers, who had not adopted the fashionable idea of this day, of the infallibility of government, and the absolute character of its acts, presumed to differ from the home government in respect to the wisdom and the justice of some of those burdens and restraints. They went so far in their excitement as to pronounce the measures of government unjust, unreasonable, and oppressive, and altogether such as ought not to be quietly submitted to. I scarcely need say, fellow-citizens, that my opinion of those measures fully accords with that of your fathers. Such a declaration of agreement on my part, would not be worth much to anybody. It would, certainly, prove nothing, as to what part I might have taken, had I lived during the great controversy of 1776. To say *now* that America was right, and England wrong, is exceedingly easy. Everybody can say it; the dastard, not less than the noble brave, can flippantly discant on the tyranny of England towards the American Colonies. It is fashionable to do so; but there was a time when, to pronounce against England, and in favor of the cause of the colonies, tried men's souls. They who did so were accounted in their day, plotters of mischief, agitators and rebels, dangerous men. To side with the right, against the wrong, with the weak against the strong, and with the oppressed against the oppressor! *here* lies the merit, and the one which, of all others, seems unfashionable in our day. The cause of liberty may be stabbed by the men who glory in the deeds of your fathers. But, to proceed.

Feeling themselves harshly and unjustly treated, by the home government, your fathers, like men of honesty, and men of spirit, earnestly sought redress. They petitioned and remonstrated; they did so in a decorous, respectful, and loyal manner. Their conduct was wholly unexceptionable. This, however, did not answer the purpose. They saw themselves treated with sovereign indifference, coldness and scorn. Yet they persevered. They were not the men to look back.

As the sheet anchor takes a firmer hold, when the ship is tossed by the storm, so did the cause of your fathers grow stronger, as it breasted the chilling blasts of kingly displeasure. The greatest and best of British statesmen admitted its justice, and the loftiest eloquence of the British Senate came to its support. But, with that blindness which seems to be the unvarying characteristic of tyrants, since Pharoah and his hosts were drowned in the Red sea, the British Government persisted in the exactions complained of.

The madness of this course, we believe, is admitted now, even by England; but we fear the lesson is wholly lost on our present rulers.

Oppression makes a wise man mad. Your fathers were wise men, and if they did not go mad, they became restive under this treatment. They felt themselves the victims of grievous wrongs, wholly incurable in their colonial capacity. With brave men there is always a remedy for oppression. Just here, the idea of a total separation of the colonies from the crown was born! It was a startling idea, much more so, than we, at this distance of time, regard it. The timid and the prudent (as has been intimated) of that day, were, of course, shocked and alarmed by it.

Such people lived then, had lived before, and will, probably, ever have a place on this planet; and their course, in respect to any great change, (no matter how great the good to be attained, or the wrong to be redressed by it), may be calculated with as much precision as can be the course of the stars. They hate all changes, but silver, gold and copper change! Of this sort of change they are always strongly in favor.

These people were called tories in the days of your fathers; and the appellation, probably, conveyed the same idea that is meant by a more modern, though a somewhat less euphonious term, which we often find in our papers, applied to some of our old politicians.

Their opposition to the then dangerous thought was earnest and powerful; but, amid all their terror and affrighted vociferations against it, the alarming and revolutionary idea moved on, and the country with it.

On the 2d of July, 1776, the old Continental Congress, to the dismay of the lovers of ease, and the worshippers of property, clothed that dreadful idea with all the authority of national sanction. They did so in the form of a resolution; and as we seldom hit upon resolutions, drawn up in our day, whose transparency is at all equal to this, it may refresh your minds and help my story if I read it.

> Resolved, That these united colonies *are*, and of right, ought to be free and Independent States; that they are absolved from all allegiance to the British Crown; and that all political connection between them and the State of Great Britain is, and ought to be, dissolved.

Citizens, your fathers made good that resolution. They succeeded; and to-day you reap the fruits of their success. The freedom gained is yours; and you, therefore, may properly celebrate this anniversary.

The 4th of July is the first great fact in your nation's history—the very ring-bolt in the chain of your yet undeveloped destiny.

Pride and patriotism, not less than gratitude, prompt you to celebrate and to hold it in perpetual remembrance. I have said that the Declaration of Independence is the RING-BOLT to the chain of your nation's destiny; so, indeed, I regard it. The principles contained in that instrument are saving principles. Stand by those principles, be true to them on all occasions, in all places, against all foes, and at whatever cost.

From the round top of your ship of state, dark and threatening clouds may be seen. Heavy billows, like mountains in the distance, disclose to the leeward huge forms of flinty rocks! That *bolt* drawn, that *chain* broken, and all is lost. *Cling to this day—cling to it,* and to its principles, with the grasp of a storm-tossed mariner to a spar at midnight.

The coming into being of a nation, in any circumstances, is an interesting event. But, besides general considerations, there were peculiar circumstances which make the advent of this republic an event of special attractiveness.

The whole scene, as I look back to it, was simple, dignified and sublime.

The population of the country, at the time, stood at the insignificant number of three millions. The country was poor in the munitions of war. The population was weak and scattered, and the country a wilderness unsubdued. There were then no means of concert and combination, such as exist now. Neither stream nor lightning had then been reduced to order and discipline. From the Potomac to the Delaware was a journey of many days. Under these, and innumerable other disadvantages, your fathers declared for liberty and independence and triumphed.

Fellow Citizens, I am not wanting in respect for the fathers of this republic. The signers of the Declaration of Independence were brave men. They were great men too—great enough to give fame to a great age. It does not often happen to a nation to raise, at one time, such a number of truly great men. The point from which I am compelled to view them is not, certainly, the most favorable; and yet

I cannot contemplate their great deeds with less than admiration. They were statesmen, patriots and heroes, and for the good they did, and the principles they contended for, I will unite with you to honor their memory.

They loved their country better than their own private interests; and, though this is not the highest form of human excellence, all will concede that it is a rare virtue, and that when it is exhibited, it ought to command respect. He who will, intelligently, lay down his life for his country, is a man whom it is not in human nature to despise. Your fathers staked their lives, their fortunes, and their sacred honor, on the cause of their country. In their admiration of liberty, they lost sight of all other interests.

They were peace men; but they preferred revolution to peaceful submission to bondage. They were quiet men; but they did not shrink from agitating against oppression. They showed forbearance; but that they knew its limits. They believed in order; but not in the order of tyranny. With them, nothing was *"settled"* that was not right. With them, justice, liberty and humanity were *"final;"* not slavery and oppression. You may well cherish the memory of such men. They were great in their day and generation. Their solid manhood stands out the more as we contrast it with these degenerate times.

How circumspect, exact and proportionate were all their movements! How unlike the politicians of an hour! Their statesmanship looked beyond the passing moment, and stretched away in strength into the distant future. They seized upon eternal principles, and set a glorious example in their defence. Mark them!

Fully appreciating the hardship to be encountered, firmly believing in the right of their cause, honorably inviting the scrutiny of an onlooking world, reverently appealing to heaven to attest their sincerity, soundly comprehending the solemn responsibility they were about to assume, wisely measuring the terrible odds against them, your fathers, the fathers of this republic, did, most deliberately, under the inspiration of a glorious patriotism, and with a sublime faith in the great principles of justice and freedom, lay deep, the cornerstone of the national superstructure, which has risen and still rises in grandeur around you.

Of this fundamental work, this day is the anniversary. Our eyes are met with demonstrations of joyous enthusiasm. Banners and pennants wave exultingly on the breeze. The din of business, too, is hushed. Even mammon seems to have quitted his grasp on this day. The ear-piercing fife and the stirring drum unite their accents with the ascending peal of a thousand church bells. Prayers are made, hymns are sung, and sermons are preached in honor of this day; while the quick martial tramp of a great and multitudinous nation, echoed back by all the hills, valleys and mountains of a vast continent, bespeak the occasion one of thrilling and universal interest—a nation's jubilee.

Friends and citizens, I need not enter further into the causes which led to this anniversary. Many of you understand them better than I do. You could instruct me in regard to them. That is a branch of knowledge in which you feel, perhaps, a much deeper interest than your speaker. The causes which led to the separation of the colonies from the British crown have never lacked for a tongue. They have all been taught in your common schools, narrated at your firesides, unfolded from your pulpits, and thundered from your legislative halls, and are as familiar to you as household words. They form the staple of your national poetry and eloquence.

I remember, also, that, as a people, Americans are remarkably familiar with all facts which make in their own favor. This is esteemed by some as a national trait—perhaps a national weakness. It is a fact, that whatever makes for the wealth or for the reputation of Americans, and can be had *cheap!* will be found by Americans. I shall not be charged with slandering Americans, if I say I think the American side of any question may be safely left in American hands.

I leave, therefore, the great deeds of your fathers to other gentlemen whose claim to have been regularly descended will be less likely to be disputed than mine!

The Present

My business, if I have any here to-day, is with the present. The accepted time with God and his cause is the ever-living now.

"Trust no future, however pleasant,
    Let the dead past bury its dead;
Act, act in the living present,
    Heart within, and God overhead."

We have to do with the past only as we can make it useful to the present and to the future. To all inspiring motives, to noble deeds which can be gained from the past, we are welcome. But now is the time, the important time. Your fathers have lived, died, and have done their work, and have done much of it well. You live and must die, and you must do your work. You have no right to enjoy a child's share in the labor of your fathers, unless your children are to be blest by your labors. You have no right to wear out and waste the hard-earned fame of your fathers to cover your indolence. Sydney Smith tells us that men seldom eulogize the wisdom and virtues of their fathers, but to excuse some folly or wickedness of their own. This truth is not a doubtful one. There are illustrations of it near and remote, ancient and modern. It was fashionable, hundreds of years ago, for the children of Jacob to boast, we have "Abraham to our father," when they had long lost Abraham's faith and spirit. That people contented themselves under the shadow of Abraham's great name, while they repudiated the deeds which made his name great. Need I remind you that a similar thing is being done all over this country to-day? Need I tell you that the Jews are not the only people who built the tombs of the prophets, and garnished the sepulchres of the righteous? Washington could not die till he had broken the chains of his slaves. Yet his monument is built up by the price of human blood, and the traders in the bodies and souls of men, shout—"We have Washington to *our father*." Alas! that it should be so; yet so it is.

"The evil that men do, lives after them,
    The good is oft' interred with their bones."

Fellow-citizens, pardon me, allow me to ask, why am I called upon to speak here to-day? What have I, or those I represent, to do with your national independence? Are the great principles of political freedom and of natural justice, embodied in that Declaration of Independence, extended to us? and am I, therefore, called upon to bring our humble offering to the national altar, and to confess the benefits and express devout gratitude for the blessings resulting from your independence to us?

Would to God, both for your sakes and ours, that an affirmative answer could be truthfully returned to these questions! Then would my task be light, and my burden easy and delightful. For *who* is there so cold, that a nation's sympathy could not warm him? Who so obdurate and dead to the claims of gratitude, that would not thankfully acknowledge such priceless benefits? Who so stolid and selfish, that would not give his voice to swell the hallelujahs of a nation's jubilee, when the chains of servitude had been torn from his limbs? I am not that man. In a case like that, the dumb might eloquently speak, and the "lame man leap as an hart."

But, such is not the state of the case. I say it with a sad sense of the disparity between us. I am not included within the pale of this glorious anniversary! Your high independence only reveals the immeasurable distance between us. The blessings in which you, this day, rejoice, are not enjoyed in common.—The rich inheritance of justice, liberty, prosperity and independence, bequeathed by your fathers, is shared by you, not by me. The sunlight that brought life and healing to you, has brought stripes and death to me. This Fourth [of] July is *yours*, not *mine*. *You* may rejoice, *I* must mourn. To drag a man in fetters into the grand illuminated temple of liberty, and call upon him to join you in joyous anthems, were inhuman mockery and sacrilegious irony. Do you mean, citizens, to mock me, by asking me to speak to-day? If so, there is a parallel to your conduct. And let me warn you that it is dangerous to copy the example of a nation whose crimes, towering up to heaven, were thrown down by the breath of the Almighty, burying that nation in irrecoverable ruin! I can to-day take up the plaintive lament of a peeled and woe-smitten people!

"By the rivers of Babylon, there we sat down. Yea! we wept when we remembered Zion. We hanged our harps upon the willows in the midst thereof. For there, they that carried us away captive, required of us a song; and they who wasted us required of us mirth, saying, Sing us one of the songs of Zion. How can we sing the Lord's song in a strange land? If I forget thee, O Jerusalem, let my right hand forget her cunning. If I do not remember thee, let my tongue cleave to the roof of my mouth."

Fellow-citizens; above your national, tumultous joy, I hear the mournful wail of millions! whose chains, heavy and grievous yesterday, are, to-day, rendered more intolerable by the jubilee shouts that reach them. If I do forget, if I do not faithfully remember those bleeding children of sorrow this day, "may my right hand forget her cunning, and may my tongue cleave to the roof of my mouth!" To forget them, to pass lightly over their wrongs, and to chime in with the popular theme, would be treason most scandalous and shocking, and would make me a reproach before God and the world. My subject, then, fellow-citizens, is AMERICAN SLAVERY. I shall see, this day, and its popular characteristics, from the slave's point of view. Standing, there, identified with the American bondman, making his wrongs mine, I do not hesitate to declare, with all my soul, that the character and conduct of this nation never looked blacker to me than on this 4th of July! Whether we turn to the declarations of the past, or to the professions of the present, the conduct of the nation seems equally hideous and revolting. America is false to the past, false to the present, and solemnly binds herself to be false to the future. Standing with God and the crushed and bleeding slave on this occasion, I will, in the name of humanity which is outraged, in the name of liberty which is fettered, in the name of the constitution and the Bible, which are disregarded and trampled upon, dare to call in question and to denounce, with all the emphasis I can command, everything that serves to perpetuate slavery—the great sin and shame of America! "I will not equivocate; I will not excuse;" I will use the severest language I can command; and yet not one word shall escape me that any man, whose judgment is not blinded by prejudice, or who is not at heart a slaveholder, shall not confess to be right and just.

But I fancy I hear some one of my audience say, it is just in this circumstance that you and your brother abolitionists fail to make a favorable impression on the public mind. Would you argue more, and denounce less, would you persuade more, and rebuke less, your cause would be much more likely to succeed. But, I submit, where all is plain there is nothing to be argued. What point in the anti-slavery creed would you have me argue? On what branch of the subject do the people of this country need light? Must I undertake to prove that the slave is a man? That point is conceded already. Nobody doubts it. The slave holders themselves acknowledge it in the enactment of laws for their government. They acknowledge it when they punish disobedience on the part of the slave. There are seventy-two crimes in the State of Virginia, which, if committed by a black man, (no matter how ignorant he be,) subject him to the punishment of death; while only two of the same crimes will subject a white man to the like punishment.—What is this but the acknowledgement that the slave is a moral, intellectual and responsible being? The manhood of the slave is conceded. It is admitted in the fact that Southern statute books are covered with enactments forbidding, under severe fines and penalties, the teaching of the slave to read or to write.—When you can point to any such laws, in reference to the beasts of the field, then I may consent to argue the manhood of the slave. When the dogs in your streets, when the fowls of the air, when the cattle on your hills, when the fish of the sea, and the reptiles that crawl, shall be unable to distinguish the slave from a brute, *then* will I argue with you that the slave is a man!

For the present, it is enough to affirm the equal manhood of the negro race. Is it not astonishing that, while we are ploughing, planting and reaping, using all kinds of mechanical tools, erecting houses, constructing bridges, building ships, working in metals of brass, iron, copper, silver and gold; that, while we are reading, writing and cyphering, acting as clerks, merchants and secretaries, having among us lawyers, doctors, ministers, poets, authors, editors, orators and teachers; that, while we are engaged in all manner of enterprises common to other men, digging gold in California, capturing the whale in the Pacific, feeding sheep and cattle on the hill-side, living, moving, acting, thinking, planning, living in families as husbands, wives and children, and, above all, confessing and worshipping the Christian's God, and looking hopefully for life and immortality beyond the grave, we are called upon to prove that we are men!

Would you have me argue that man is entitled to liberty? that he is the rightful owner of his own body? You have already declared it. Must I argue the wrongfulness of slavery? Is that a question for Republicans? Is it to be settled by the rules of logic and argumentation, as a matter beset with great difficulty, involving a doubtful application of the principle of justice, hard to be understood? How should I look today, in the presence of Americans, dividing, and subdividing a discourse, to show that men have a natural right to freedom? speaking of it relatively, and positively, negatively, and affirmatively. To do so, would be to make myself ridiculous, and to offer an insult to your understanding.—There is not a man beneath the canopy of heaven, that does not know that slavery is wrong *for him.*

What, am I to argue that it is wrong to make men brutes, to rob them of their liberty, to work them without wages, to keep them ignorant of their relations to their fellow men, to beat them with sticks, to flay their flesh with the lash, to load their limbs with irons, to hunt them with dogs, to sell them at auction, to sunder their families, to knock out their teeth, to burn their flesh, to starve them into obedience and submission to their masters? Must I argue that a system thus marked with blood, and stained with pollution, is *wrong?* No! I will not. I have better employments for my time and strength, than such arguments would imply.

What, then, remains to be argued? Is it that slavery is not divine; that God did not establish it; that our doctors of divinity are mistaken? There is blasphemy in the thought. That which is inhuman, cannot be divine! *Who* can reason on such a proposition? They that can, may; I cannot. The time for such argument is past.

At a time like this, scorching irony, not convincing argument, is needed. O! had I the ability, and could I reach the nation's ear, I would, to-day, pour out a fiery stream of biting ridicule, blasting reproach, withering sarcasm, and stern rebuke. For it is not light that is needed, but fire; it is not the gentle shower, but thunder. We need the storm, the whirlwind, and the earthquake. The feeling of the nation must be quickened; the conscience of the nation must be roused; the propriety of the nation must be startled; the hypocrisy of the nation must be exposed; and its crimes against God and man must be proclaimed and denounced.

What, to the American slave, is your 4th of July? I answer; a day that reveals to him, more than all other days in the year, the gross injustice and cruelty to which he is the constant victim. To him, your celebration is a sham; your boasted liberty, an unholy license; your national greatness, swelling vanity; your sounds of rejoicing are empty and heartless; your denunciations of tyrants, brass fronted impudence; your shouts of liberty and equality, hollow mockery; your prayers and hymns, your sermons and thanksgivings, with all your religious parade, and solemnity, are, to him, mere bombast, fraud, deception, impiety, and hypocrisy—a thin veil to cover up crimes which would disgrace a nation of savages. There is not a nation on the earth guilty of practices, more shocking and bloody, than are the people of these United States, at this very hour.

Go where you may, search where you will, roam through all the monarchies and despotisms of the old world, travel through South America, search out every abuse, and when you have found the last, lay your facts by the side of the every day practices of this nation, and you will say with me, that, for revolting barbarity and shameless hypocrisy, America reigns without a rival.

3

HENRY D. THOREAU

"A Plea for Captain John Brown"

1859

Read to the citizens of Concord, Mass., Sunday Evening, October 30, 1859. Also as the fifth lecture of the Fraternity Course in Boston, November 1; and at Worcester, November 3.

I TRUST THAT YOU WILL pardon me for being here. I do not wish to force my thoughts upon you, but I feel forced myself. Little as I know of Captain Brown, I would fain do my part to correct the tone and the statements of the newspapers, and of my countrymen generally, respecting his character and actions. It costs us nothing to be just. We can at least express our sympathy with, and admiration of, him and his companions, and that is what I now propose to do.

First, as to his history.

I will endeavor to omit, as much as possible, what you have already read. I need not describe his person to you, for probably most of you have seen and will not soon forget him. I am told that his grandfather, John Brown, was an officer in the Revolution; that he himself was born in Connecticut about the beginning of this century, but early went with his father to Ohio. I heard him say that his father was a contractor who furnished beef to the army there, in the war of 1812; that he accompanied him to the camp, and assisted him in that employment, seeing a good deal of military life, more, perhaps, than if he had been a soldier, for he was often present at the councils of the officers. Especially, he learned by experience how armies are supplied and maintained in the field—a work which, he observed, requires at least as much experience and skill as to lead them in battle. He said that few persons had any conception of the cost, even the pecuniary cost, of firing a single bullet in war. He saw enough, at any rate, to disgust him with a military life, indeed to excite in him a great abhorrence of it; so much so, that though he was tempted by the offer of some petty office in the army, when he was about eighteen, he not only declined that, but he also refused to train when warned, and was fined for it. He then resolved that he would never have anything to do with any war, unless it were a war for liberty.

When the troubles in Kansas began, he sent several of his sons thither to strengthen the party of the Free State men, fitting them out with such weapons as he had; telling them that if the troubles should increase, and there should be need of him, he would follow to assist them with his hand and counsel. This, as you all know, he soon after did; and it was through his agency, far more than any other's, that Kansas was made free.

For a part of his life he was a surveyor, and at one time he was engaged in wool-growing, and he went to Europe as an agent about that business. There, as every where, he had his eyes about him, and made many original observations. He said, for instance, that he saw why the soil of England was so rich, and that of Germany (I think it was) so poor, and he thought of writing to some of the crowned heads about it. It was because in England the peasantry live on the soil which they cultivate, but in Germany they are gathered into villages, at night. It is a pity that he did not make a book of his observations.

I should say that he was an old-fashioned man in his respect for the Constitution, and his faith in the permanence of this Union. Slavery he deemed to be wholly opposed to these, and he was its determined foe.

He was by descent and birth a New England farmer, a man of great common sense, deliberate and practical as that class is, and tenfold more so. He was like the best of those who stood at Concord

Bridge once, on Lexington Common, and on Bunker Hill, only he was firmer and higher principled than any that I have chanced to hear of as there. It was no abolition lecturer that converted him. Ethan Allen and Stark, with whom he may in some respects be compared, were rangers in a lower and less important field. They could bravely face their country's foes, but he had the courage to face his country herself, when she was in the wrong. A Western writer says, to account for his escape from so many perils, that he was concealed under a "rural exterior;" as if, in that prairie land, a hero should, by good rights, wear a citizen's dress only.

He did not go to the college called Harvard, good old Alma Mater as she is. He was not fed on the pap that is there furnished. As he phrased it, "I know no more of grammar than one of your calves." But he went to the great university of the West, where he sedulously pursued the study of Liberty, for which he had early betrayed a fondness, and having taken many degrees, he finally commenced the public practice of Humanity in Kansas, as you all know. Such were *his humanities*, and not any study of grammar. He would have left a Greek accent slanting the wrong way, and righted up a falling man.

He was one of that class of whom we hear a great deal, but, for the most part, see nothing at all—the Puritans. It would be in vain to kill him. He died lately in the time of Cromwell, but he reappeared here. Why should he not? Some of the Puritan stock are said to have come over and settled in New England. They were a class that did something else than celebrate their forefathers' day, and eat parched corn in remembrance of that time. They were neither Democrats nor Republicans, but men of simple habits, straightforward, prayerful; not thinking much of rulers who did not fear God, not making many compromises, nor seeking after available candidates.

"In his camp," as one has recently written, and as I have myself heard him state, "he permitted no profanity; no man of loose morals was suffered to remain there, unless, indeed, as a prisoner of war. 'I would rather,' said he, 'have the small-pox, yellow fever, and cholera, all together in my camp, than a man without principle. . . . It is a mistake, sir, that our people make, when they think that bullies are the best fighters, or that they are the fit men to oppose these

Southerners. Give me men of good principles,—God-fearing men,— men who respect themselves, and with a dozen of them I will oppose any hundred such men as these Buford ruffians.'" He said that if one offered himself to be a soldier under him, who was forward to tell what he could or would do, if he could only get sight of the enemy, he had but little confidence in him.

He was never able to find more than a score or so of recruits whom he would accept, and only about a dozen, among them his sons, in whom he had perfect faith. When he was here, some years ago, he showed to a few a little manuscript book,—his "orderly book" I think he called it,—containing the names of his company in Kansas, and the rules by which they bound themselves; and he stated that several of them had already sealed the contract with their blood. When some one remarked that, with the addition of a chaplain, it would have been a perfect Cromwellian troop, he observed that he would have been glad to add a chaplain to the list, if he could have found one who could fill that office worthily. It is easy enough to find one for the United States army. I believe that he had prayers in his camp morning and evening, nevertheless.

He was a man of Spartan habits, and at sixty was scrupulous about his diet at your table, excusing himself by saying that he must eat sparingly and fare hard, as became a soldier or one who was fitting himself for difficult enterprises, a life of exposure.

A man of rare common sense and directness of speech, as of action; a transcendentalist above all, a man of ideas and principles,—that was what distinguished him. Not yielding to a whim or transient impulse, but carrying out the purpose of a life. I noticed that he did not overstate any thing, but spoke within bounds. I remember, particularly, how, in his speech here, he referred to what his family had suffered in Kansas, without ever giving the least vent to his pent-up fire. It was a volcano with an ordinary chimney-flue. Also referring to the deeds of certain Border Ruffians, he said, rapidly paring away his speech, like an experienced soldier, keeping a reserve of force and meaning, "They had a perfect right to be hung." He was not in the least a rhetorician, was not talking to Buncombe or his constituents any where, had no need to invent any thing, but to tell the simple truth, and communicate his own resolution; therefore he appeared incomparably strong, and eloquence in Congress and elsewhere seemed to me at a discount. It was like the speeches of Cromwell compared with those of an ordinary king.

As for his tact and prudence, I will merely say, that at a time when scarcely a man from the Free States was able to reach Kansas by any direct route, at least without having his arms taken from him, he, carrying what imperfect guns and other weapons he could collect, openly and slowly drove an ox-cart through Missouri, apparently in the capacity of a surveyor, with his surveying compass exposed in it, and so passed unsuspected, and had ample opportunity to learn the designs of the enemy. For some time after his arrival he still followed the same profession. When, for instance, he saw a knot of the ruffians on the prairie, discussing, of course, the single topic which then occupied their minds, he would, perhaps, take his compass and one of his sons, and proceed to run an imaginary line right through the very spot on which that conclave had assembled, and when he came up to them, he would naturally pause and have some talk with them, learning their news, and, at last, all their plans perfectly; and having thus completed his real survey, he would resume his imaginary one, and run on his line till he was out of sight.

When I expressed surprise that he could live in Kansas at all, with a price set upon his head, and so large a number, including the authorities, exasperated against him, he accounted for it by saying, "It is perfectly well understood that I will not be taken." Much of the time for some years he has had to skulk in swamps, suffering from poverty and from sickness, which was the consequence of exposure, befriended only by Indians and a few whites. But though it might be known that he was lurking in a particular swamp, his foes commonly did not care to go in after him. He could even come out into a town where there were more Border Ruffians than Free State men, and transact some business, without delaying long, and yet not be molested; for said he, "No little handful of men were willing to undertake it, and a large body could not be got together in season."

As for his recent failure, we do not know the facts about it. It was evidently far from being a wild and desperate attempt. His enemy, Mr. Vallandigham, is compelled to say, that "it was among the best planned and executed conspiracies that ever failed."

Not to mention his other successes, was it a failure, or did it show a want of good management, to deliver from bondage a dozen human beings, and walk off with them by broad daylight, for weeks if not months, at a leisurely pace, through one State after another, for half the length of the North, conspicuous to all parties, with a price set upon his head, going into a court room on his way and telling what he had done, thus convincing Missouri that it was not profitable to try to hold slaves in his neighborhood?—and this, not because the government menials were lenient, but because they were afraid of him.

Yet he did not attribute his success, foolishly, to "his star," or to any magic. He said, truly, that the reason why such greatly superior numbers quailed before him, was, as one of his prisoners confessed, because they *lacked a cause*—a kind of armor which he and his party never lacked. When the time came, few men were found willing to lay down their lives in defence of what they knew to be wrong; they did not like that this should be their last act in this world.

But to make haste to *his* last act, and its effects.

The newspapers seem to ignore, or perhaps are really ignorant of the fact, that there are at least as many as two or three individuals to a town throughout the North, who think much as the present speaker does about him and his enterprise. I do not hesitate to say that they are an important and growing party. We aspire to be something more than stupid and timid chattels, pretending to read history and our bibles, but desecrating every house and every day we breathe in. Perhaps anxious politicians may prove that only seventeen white men and five negroes were concerned in the late enterprise, but their very anxiety to prove this might suggest to themselves that all is not told. Why do they still dodge the truth? They are so anxious because of a dim consciousness of the fact, which they do not distinctly face, that at least a million of the free inhabitants of the United States would have rejoiced if it had succeeded. They at most only criticise the tactics. Though we wear no crape, the thought of that man's position and probable fate is spoiling many a man's day here at the North for other thinking. If any one who has seen him here can pursue successfully any other train of thought, I do not know what he is made of. If there is any such who gets his usual allowance of sleep, I will warrant him to fatten easily under any circumstances which do not touch his body or purse. I put a piece of paper and a pencil under my pillow, and when I could not sleep, I wrote in the dark.

[...]

I read all the newspapers I could get within a week after this event, and I do not remember in them a single expression of sympathy for these men. I have since seen one noble statement, in a Boston paper, not editorial. Some voluminous sheets decided not to print the full report of Brown's words to the exclusion of other matter. It was as if a publisher should reject the manuscript of the New Testament, and print Wilson's last speech. The same journal which contained this pregnant news, was chiefly filled, in parallel columns, with the reports of the political conventions that were being held. But the descent to them was too steep. They should have been spared this contrast, been printed in an extra at least. To turn from the voices and deeds of earnest men to the *cackling* of political conventions! Office seekers and speechmakers, who do not so much as lay an honest egg, but wear their breasts bare upon an egg of chalk! Their great game is the game of straws, or rather that universal aboriginal game of the platter, at which the Indians cried *hub, hub!* Exclude the reports of religious and political conventions, and publish the words of a living man.

But I object not so much to what they have omitted as to what they have inserted. Even the *Liberator* called it "a misguided, wild, and apparently insane . . . effort." As for the herd of newspapers and magazines, I do not chance to know an editor in the country who will deliberately print anything which he knows will ultimately and permanently reduce the number of his subscribers. They do not believe that it would be expedient. How then can they print truth? If we do not say pleasant things, they argue, nobody will attend to us. And so they do like some travelling auctioneers, who sing an obscene song in order to draw a crowd around them. Republican editors, obliged to get their sentences ready for the morning edition, and accustomed to look at every thing by the twilight of politics, express no admiration, nor true sorrow even, but call these men "deluded fanatics"— "mistaken men"—"insane," or "crazed." It suggests what a *sane* set of editors we are blessed with, *not* "mistaken men"; who know very well on which side their bread is buttered, at least.

A man does a brave and humane deed, and at once, on all sides, we hear people and parties declaring, "I didn't do it, nor countenance *him* to do it, in any conceivable way. It can't be fairly inferred from my past career." I, for one, am not interested to hear you define your position. I don't know that I ever was, or ever shall be. I think it is mere egotism, or impertinent at this time. Ye needn't take so much pains to wash your skirts of him. No intelligent man will ever be convinced that he was any creature of yours. He went and came, as he himself informs us, "under the auspices of John Brown and nobody else." The Republican party does not perceive how many his *failure* will make to vote more correctly than they would have them. They have counted the votes of Pennsylvania &. Co., but they have not correctly counted Captain Brown's vote. He has taken the wind out of their sails, the little wind they had, and they may as well lie to and repair.

What though he did not belong to your clique! Though you may not approve of his method or his principles, recognize his magnanimity. Would you not like to claim kindredship with him in that, though in no other thing he is like, or likely, to you? Do you think that you would lose your reputation so? What you lost at the spile, you would gain at the bung.

If they do not mean all this, then they do not speak the truth, and say what they mean. They are simply at their old tricks still.

"It was always conceded to him," *says one who calls him crazy,* "that he was a conscientious man, very modest in his demeanor, apparently inoffensive, until the subject of Slavery was introduced, when he would exhibit a feeling of indignation unparalleled."

The slave-ship is on her way, crowded with its dying victims; new cargoes are being added in mid ocean; a small crew of slaveholders,

countenanced by a large body of passengers, is smothering four millions under the hatches, and yet the politician asserts that the only
proper way by which deliverance is to be obtained, is by "the quiet
diffusion of the sentiments of humanity," without any "outbreak."
As if the sentiments of humanity were ever found unaccompanied
by its deeds, and you could disperse them, all finished to order, the
pure article, as easily as water with a watering-pot, and so lay the
dust. What is that that I hear cast overboard? The bodies of the dead
that have found deliverance. That is the way we are "diffusing" humanity, and its sentiments with it.

[. . .]

I am here to plead his cause with you. I plead not for his life, but
for his character—his immortal life; and so it becomes your cause
wholly, and is not his in the least. Some eighteen hundred years ago
Christ was crucified; this morning, perchance, Captain Brown was
hung. These are the two ends of a chain which is not without its
links. He is not Old Brown any longer; he is an Angel of Light.

I see now that it was necessary that the bravest and humanest
man in all the country should be hung. Perhaps he saw it himself. I
almost fear that I may yet hear of his deliverance, doubting if a prolonged life, if any life, can do as much good as his death.

"Misguided"! "Garrulous"! "Insane"! "Vindictive"! So ye write in
your easy chairs, and thus he wounded responds from the floor of
the Armory, clear as a cloudless sky, true as the voice of nature is:
"No man sent me here; it was my own prompting and that of my
Maker. I acknowledge no master in human form."

And in what a sweet and noble strain he proceeds, addressing
his captors, who stand over him: "I think, my friends, you are guilty
of a great wrong against God and humanity, and it would be perfectly right for any one to interfere with you so far as to free those
you wilfully and wickedly hold in bondage."

And referring to his movement: "It is, in my opinion, the greatest service a man can render to God."

"I pity the poor in bondage that have none to help them; that
is why I am here; not to gratify any personal animosity, revenge,

or vindictive spirit. It is my sympathy with the oppressed and the wronged, that are as good as you, and as precious in the sight of God."

You don't know your testament when you see it.

"I want you to understand that I respect the rights of the poorest and weakest of colored people, oppressed by the slave power, just as much as I do those of the most wealthy and powerful."

"I wish to say, furthermore, that you had better, all you people at the South, prepare yourselves for a settlement of that question, that must come up for settlement sooner than you are prepared for it. The sooner you are prepared the better. You may dispose of me very easily. I am nearly disposed of now; but this question is still to be settled—this negro question, I mean; the end of that is not yet."

I foresee the time when the painter will paint that scene, no longer going to Rome for a subject; the poet will sing it; the historian record it; and, with the Landing of the Pilgrims and the Declaration of Independence, it will be the ornament of some future national gallery, when at least the present form of Slavery shall be no more here. We shall then be at liberty to weep for Captain Brown. Then, and not till then, we will take our revenge.

4

ABRAHAM LINCOLN

First Inaugural Address

March 4, 1861

FELLOW CITIZENS OF THE UNITED STATES:

In compliance with a custom as old as the government itself, I appear before you to address you briefly, and to take, in your presence, the oath prescribed by the Constitution of the United States, to be taken by the President "before he enters on the execution of his office."

I do not consider it necessary, at present, for me to discuss those matters of administration about which there is no special anxiety, or excitement.

Apprehension seems to exist among the people of the Southern States, that by the accession of a Republican Administration, their property, and their peace, and personal security, are to be endangered. There has never been any reasonable cause for such apprehension. Indeed, the most ample evidence to the contrary has all the while existed, and been open to their inspection. It is found in nearly all the published speeches of him who now addresses you. I do but quote from one of those speeches when I declare that "I have no purpose, directly or indirectly, to interfere with the institution of slavery in the States where it exists. I believe I have no lawful right to do so, and I have no inclination to do so." Those who nominated and elected me did so with full knowledge that I had made this, and many similar declarations, and had never recanted them. And more than this, they placed in the platform, for my acceptance, and as a law to themselves, and to me, the clear and emphatic resolution which I now read:

"*Resolved,* That the maintenance inviolate of the rights of the States, and especially the right of each State to order and control its own domestic institutions according to its own judgment exclusively, is essential to that balance of power on which the perfection and endurance of our political fabric depend; and we denounce the lawless invasion by armed force of the soil of any State or Territory, no matter under what pretext, as among the gravest of crimes."

I now reiterate these sentiments: and in doing so, I only press upon the public attention the most conclusive evidence of which the case is susceptible, that the property, peace and security of no section are to be in anywise endangered by the now incoming Administration. I add too, that all the protection which, consistently with the Constitution and the laws, can be given, will be cheerfully given to all the States when lawfully demanded, for whatever cause—as cheerfully to one section, as to another.

There is much controversy about the delivering up of fugitives from service or labor. The clause I now read is as plainly written in the Constitution as any other of its provisions:

"No person held to service or labor in one State, under the laws thereof, escaping into another, shall, in consequence of any law or regulation therein, be discharged from such service or labor, but shall be delivered up on claim of the party to whom such service or labor may be due."

It is scarcely questioned that this provision was intended by those who made it, for the reclaiming of what we call fugitive slaves; and the intention of the law-giver is the law. All members of Congress swear their support to the whole Constitution—to this provision as much as to any other. To the proposition, then, that slaves whose cases come within the terms of this clause, "shall be delivered up," their oaths are unanimous. Now, if they would make the effort in good temper, could they not, with nearly equal unanimity, frame and pass a law, by means of which to keep good that unanimous oath?

There is some difference of opinion whether this clause should be enforced by national or by state authority; but surely that difference is not a very material one. If the slave is to be surrendered, it can be of but little consequence to him, or to others, by which authority it is done. And should any one, in any case, be content that his oath shall go unkept, on a merely unsubstantial controversy as to *how* it shall be kept?

Again, in any law upon this subject, ought not all the safeguards of liberty known in civilized and humane jurisprudence to be introduced, so that a free man be not, in any case, surrendered as a slave? And might it not be well, at the same time, to provide by law for the enforcement of that clause in the Constitution which guarranties that "The citizens of each State shall be entitled to all previleges and immunities of citizens in the several States?"

I take the official oath to-day, with no mental reservations, and with no purpose to construe the Constitution or laws, by any hypercritical rules. And while I do not choose now to specify particular acts of Congress as proper to be enforced, I do suggest, that it will be much safer for all, both in official and private stations, to conform to, and abide by, all those acts which stand unrepealed, than to violate any of them, trusting to find impunity in having them held to be unconstitutional.

It is seventy-two years since the first inauguration of a President under our national Constitution. During that period fifteen different and greatly distinguished citizens, have, in succession, administered the executive branch of the government. They have conducted it through many perils; and, generally, with great success. Yet, with all this scope for precedent, I now enter upon the same task for the brief constitutional term of four years, under great and peculiar difficulty. A disruption of the Federal Union heretofore only menaced, is now formidably attempted.

I hold, that in contemplation of universal law, and of the Constitution, the Union of these States is perpetual. Perpetuity is implied, if not expressed, in the fundamental law of all national governments. It is safe to assert that no government proper, ever had a provision in its organic law for its own termination. Continue to execute all the express provisions of our national Constitution, and the Union will endure forever—it being impossible to destroy it, except by some action not provided for in the instrument itself.

Again, if the United States be not a government proper, but an association of States in the nature of contract merely, can it, as a contract, be peaceably unmade, by less than all the parties who made it? One party to a contract may violate it—break it, so to speak; but does it not require all to lawfully rescind it?

Descending from these general principles, we find the proposition that, in legal contemplation, the Union is perpetual, confirmed by the history of the Union itself. The Union is much older than the Constitution. It was formed in fact, by the Articles of Association in 1774. It was matured and continued by the Declaration of Independence in 1776. It was further matured and the faith of all the then thirteen States expressly plighted and engaged that it should be perpetual, by the Articles of Confederation in 1778. And finally, in 1787, one of the declared objects for ordaining and establishing the Constitution, was *to form a more perfect union.*"

But if destruction of the Union, by one, or by a part only, of the States, be lawfully possible, the Union is *less* perfect than before the Constitution, having lost the vital element of perpetuity.

It follows from these views that no State, upon its own mere motion, can lawfully get out of the Union,—that *resolves* and *ordinances* to that effect are legally void; and that acts of violence, within any State or States, against the authority of the United States, are insurrectionary or revolutionary, according to circumstances.

I therefore consider that, in view of the Constitution and the laws, the Union is unbroken; and, to the extent of my ability, I shall take care, as the Constitution itself expressly enjoins upon me, that the laws of the Union be faithfully executed in all the States. Doing this I deem to be only a simple duty on my part; and I shall perform it, so far as practicable, unless my rightful masters, the American people, shall withhold the requisite means, or, in some authoritative manner, direct the contrary. I trust this will not be regarded as a menace, but only as the declared purpose of the Union that it *will* constitutionally defend, and maintain itself.

In doing this there needs to be no bloodshed or violence; and there shall be none, unless it be forced upon the national authority. The power confided to me, will be used to hold, occupy, and possess the property, and places belonging to the government, and to collect the duties and imposts; but beyond what may be necessary for these objects, there will be no invasion—no using of force against, or among the people anywhere. Where hostility to the United States, in any interior locality, shall be so great and so universal, as to prevent competent resident citizens from holding the Federal offices, there will be no attempt to force obnoxious strangers among the people for that object. While the strict legal right may exist in the government to enforce the exercise of these offices, the attempt to do so would be so irritating, and so nearly impracticable with all, that I deem it better to forego, for the time, the uses of such offices.

The mails, unless repelled, will continue to be furnished in all parts of the Union. So far as possible, the people everywhere shall have that sense of perfect security which is most favorable to calm thought and reflection. The course here indicated will be followed, unless current events, and experience, shall show a modification, or change, to be proper; and in every case and exigency, my best discretion will be exercised, according to circumstances actually existing, and with a view and a hope of a peaceful solution of the national troubles, and the restoration of fraternal sympathies and affections.

That there are persons in one section, or another who seek to destroy the Union at all events, and are glad of any pretext to do it, I will neither affirm or deny; but if there be such, I need address no word to them. To those, however, who really love the Union, may I not speak?

Before entering upon so grave a matter as the destruction of our national fabric, with all its benefits, its memories, and its hopes, would it not be wise to ascertain precisely why we do it? Will you hazard so desperate a step, while there is any possibility that any portion of the ills you fly from, have no real existence? Will you, while the certain ills you fly to, are greater than all the real ones you fly from? Will you risk the commission of so fearful a mistake?

All profess to be content in the Union, if all constitutional rights can be maintained. Is it true, then, that any right, plainly written in the Constitution, has been denied? I think not. Happily the human mind is so constituted, that no party can reach to the audacity of doing this. Think, if you can, of a single instance in which a plainly written provision of the Constitution has ever been denied. If, by the mere force of numbers, a majority should deprive a minority of any clearly written constitutional right, it might, in a moral point of view, justify revolution—certainly would, if such right were a vital one. But such is not our case. All the vital rights of minorities, and of individuals, are so plainly assured to them, by affirmations and negations, guarranties and prohibitions, in the Constitution, that controversies never arise concerning them. But no organic law can ever be framed with a provision specifically applicable to every question which may occur in practical administration. No foresight can anticipate, nor any document of reasonable length contain express provisions for all possible questions. Shall fugitives from labor be surrendered by national or by State authority? The Constitution does not expressly say. *May* Congress prohibit slavery in the territories? The Constitution does not expressly say. *Must* Congress protect slavery in the territories? The Constitution does not expressly say.

From questions of this class spring all our constitutional controversies, and we divide upon them into majorities and minorities. If the minority will not acquiesce, the majority must, or the government must cease. There is no other alternative; for continuing the government, is acquiescence on one side or the other. If a minority, in such case, will secede rather than acquiesce, they make a precedent which, in turn, will divide and ruin them; for a minority of their own will secede from them, whenever a majority refuses to be controlled by such minority. For instance, why may not any portion of a new confederacy, a year or two hence, arbitrarily secede again, precisely as portions of the present Union now claim to secede from it. All who cherish disunion sentiments, are now being educated to the exact temper of doing this. Is there such perfect identity of interests among the States to compose a new Union, as to produce harmony only, and prevent renewed secession?

Plainly, the central idea of secession, is the essence of anarchy. A majority, held in restraint by constitutional checks, and limitations, and always changing easily, with deliberate changes of popular opinions and sentiments, is the only true sovereign of a free people. Whoever rejects it, does, of necessity, fly to anarchy or to despotism. Unanimity is impossible; the rule of a minority, as a permanent arrangement, is wholly inadmissable; so that, rejecting the majority principle, anarchy, or despotism in some form, is all that is left.

I do not forget the position assumed by some, that constitutional questions are to be decided by the Supreme Court; nor do I deny that such decisions must be binding in any case, upon the parties to a suit, as to the object of that suit, while they are also entitled to very high respect and consideration, in all paralel cases, by all other departments of the government. And while it is obviously possible that such decision may be erroneous in any given case, still the evil effect following it, being limited to that particular case, with the chance that it may be over-ruled, and never become a precedent for other cases, can better be borne than could the evils of a different practice. At the same time the candid citizen must confess that if the policy of the government, upon vital questions, affecting the whole people, is to be irrevocably fixed by decisions of the Supreme Court, the instant they are made, in ordinary litigation between parties, in personal actions, the people will have ceased, to be their own rulers, having, to that extent, practically resigned their government, into the hands of that eminent tribunal. Nor is there, in this view, any assault upon the court, or the judges. It is a duty, from which they may not shrink, to decide cases properly brought before them; and it is no fault of theirs, if others seek to turn their decisions to political purposes.

One section of our country believes slavery is *right*, and ought to be extended, while the other believes it is *wrong*, and ought not to be extended. This is the only substantial dispute. The fugitive slave clause of the Constitution, and the law for the suppression of the foreign slave trade, are each as well enforced, perhaps, as any law can ever be in a community where the moral sense of the people imperfectly supports the law itself. The great body of the people abide by the dry legal obligation in both cases, and a few break over in each. This, I think, cannot be perfectly cured; and it would be worse in both cases *after* the separation of the sections, than before. The foreign slave trade, now imperfectly suppressed, would be ultimately revived without restriction, in one section; while fugitive slaves, now only partially surrendered, would not be surrendered at all, by the other.

Physically speaking, we cannot separate. We cannot remove our respective sections from each other, nor build an impassable wall between them. A husband and wife may be divorced, and go out of the presence, and beyond the reach of each other; but the different parts of our country cannot do this. They cannot but remain face to face; and intercourse, either amicable or hostile, must continue between them. Is it possible then to make that intercourse more advantageous, or more satisfactory, *after* separation than *before?* Can aliens make treaties easier than friends can make laws? Can treaties be more faithfully enforced between aliens, than laws can among friends? Suppose you go to war, you cannot fight always; and when, after much loss on both sides, and no gain on either, you cease fighting, the identical old questions, as to terms of intercourse, are again upon you.

This country, with its institutions, belongs to the people who inhabit it. Whenever they shall grow weary of the existing government, they can exercise their *constitutional* right of amending it, or their *revolutionary* right to dismember, or overthrow it. I can not be ignorant of the fact that many worthy, and patriotic citizens are desirous of having the national constitution amended. While I make no recommendation of amendments, I fully recognize the rightful authority of the people over the whole subject, to be exercised in either of the modes prescribed in the instrument itself; and I should, under existing circumstances, favor, rather than oppose, a fair oppertunity being afforded the people to act upon it.

I will venture to add that, to me, the convention mode seems preferable, in that it allows amendments to originate with the people themselves, instead of only permitting them to take, or reject, propositions, originated by others, not especially chosen for the purpose, and which might not be precisely such, as they would wish to either accept or refuse. I understand a proposed amendment to the Constitution—which amendment, however, I have not seen, has passed Congress, to the effect that the federal government, shall never interfere with the domestic institutions of the States, including that of persons held to service. To avoid misconstruction of what I have said, I depart from my purpose not to speak of particular amendments, so far as to say that, holding such a provision to now be implied constitutional law, I have no objection to its being made express, and irrevocable.

The Chief Magistrate derives all his authority from the people, and they have conferred none upon him to fix terms for the separation of the States. The people themselves can do this also if they choose; but the executive, as such, has nothing to do with it. His duty is to administer the present government, as it came to his hands, and to transmit it, unimpaired by him, to his successor.

Why should there not be a patient confidence in the ultimate justice of the people? Is there any better, or equal hope, in the world? In our present differences, is either party without faith of being in the right? If the Almighty Ruler of nations, with his eternal truth and justice, be on your side of the North, or on yours of the South, that truth, and that justice, will surely prevail, by the judgment of this great tribunal, the American people.

By the frame of the government under which we live, this same people have wisely given their public servants but little power for mischief; and have, with equal wisdom, provided for the return of that little to their own hands at very short intervals.

While the people retain their virtue, and vigilence, no administration, by any extreme of wickedness or folly, can very seriously injure the government, in the short space of four years.

My countrymen, one and all, think calmly and well, upon this whole subject. Nothing valuable can be lost by taking time. If there be an object to *hurry* any of you, in hot haste, to a step which you would never take *deliberately,* that object will be frustrated by taking time; but no good object can be frustrated by it. Such of you as are now dissatisfied, still have the old Constitution unimpaired, and, on the sensitive point, the laws of your own framing under it; while the new administration will have no immediate power, if it would, to change either. If it were admitted that you who are dissatisfied, hold the right side in the dispute, there still is no single good reason for precipitate action. Intelligence, patriotism, Christianity, and a firm reliance on Him, who has never yet forsaken this favored land, are still competent to adjust, in the best way, all our present difficulty.

In your hands, my dissatisfied fellow countrymen, and not in *mine,* is the momentous issue of civil war. The government will not assail *you.* You can have no conflict, without being yourselves the aggressors. *You* have no oath registered in Heaven to destroy the government, while *I* shall have the most solemn one to "preserve, protect and defend" it.

I am loth to close. We are not enemies, but friends. We must not be enemies. Though passion may have strained, it must not break our bonds of affection. The mystic chords of memory, streching from every battle-field, and patriot grave, to every living heart and hearthstone, all over this broad land, will yet swell the chorus of the Union, when again touched, as surely they will be, by the better angels of our nature.

5

ALEXANDER H. STEPHENS

"Cornerstone" Speech

March 21, 1861

Several weeks after Lincoln refused to recognize secession, Alexander H. Stephens (1812–83), a former US Senator from Georgia and the recently chosen vice-president of the Confederacy, celebrated the resolve of white southerners and the distinctiveness of southern civilization. Although he was a fervent advocate of state sovereignty, Stephens had opposed secession until early 1861. In the impromptu speech he delivered before an enthusiastic audience in Savannah on March 21, 1861, he argues that the "cornerstone" of southern greatness lay in slavery and white supremacy. Portraying African Americans as members of an inherently inferior race who benefited from enslavement, Stephens asserts unequivocally that white southerners had the resources and will to form a powerful new nation. Science and experience, he claims, had proved wrong the principle asserted in the Declaration of Independence that all men were created equal.

... WE ARE IN THE MIDST of one of the greatest epochs in our history. The last ninety days will mark one of the most memorable eras in the history of modern civilization. ... Seven States have within the last three months thrown off an old government and formed a new. This revolution has been signally marked, up to this time, by the fact of its having been accomplished without the loss of a single drop of blood.

This new constitution, or form of government, constitutes the subject to which your attention will be partly invited. In reference to it, I make this first general remark. . . . All the essentials of the old constitution, which have endeared it to the hearts of the American people, have been preserved and perpetuated. Some changes have been made. . . .

Allow me briefly to allude to some of these improvements. The question of building up class interests, or fostering one branch of industry to the prejudice of another under the exercise of the revenue power, which gave us so much trouble under the old constitution, is put at rest. . . . This old thorn of the tariff, which was the cause of so much irritation in the old body politic, is removed forever from the new.

Again, the subject of internal improvements, under the power of Congress to regulate commerce, is put at rest under our system. The power claimed by construction under the old constitution, was at least a doubtful one—it rested solely upon construction. We of the South, generally apart from considerations of constitutional principles, opposed its exercise upon rounds of its inexpediency and injustice. . . .

Another feature to which I will allude, is that the new constitution provides that cabinet ministers and heads of departments may have the privilege of seats upon the floor of the Senate and House of Representatives—may have the right to participate in the debates and discussions upon the various subjects of administration. . . .

Another change in the constitution relates to the length of the tenure of the presidential office. In the new constitution it is six years instead of four, and the President rendered ineligible for a re-election. This is certainly a decidedly conservative change. It will remove from the incumbent all temptation to use his office or exert the powers confided to him for any objects of personal ambition. . . .

But not to be tedious in enumerating the numerous changes for the better, allow me to allude to one other—though last, not least. The new constitution has put at rest, forever, all the agitating questions relating to our peculiar institution—African slavery as it exists amongst us—the proper status of the negro in our form of civilization. This was the immediate cause of the late rupture and present revolution. Jefferson in his forecast, had anticipated this, as the "rock upon which the old Union would split." He was right. What was conjecture with him, is now a realized fact. But whether he fully comprehended the great truth upon which that rock stood and stands, may be doubted. The prevailing ideas entertained by him and most of the leading statesmen at the time of the formation of the old constitution, were that the enslavement of the African was in violation of the laws of nature; that it was wrong in principle, socially, morally, and politically. It was an evil they knew not well how to deal with, but the general opinion of the men of that day was that, somehow or other in the order of Providence, the institution would be evanescent and pass away. This idea, though not incorporated in the constitution, was the prevailing idea at that time. The constitution, it is true, secured every essential guarantee to the institution while it should last, and hence no argument can be justly urged against the constitutional guarantees thus secured, because of the common sentiment of the day. Those ideas, however, were fundamentally wrong. They rested upon the assumption of the equality of races. This was an error. It was a sandy foundation, and the government built upon it fell when the "storm came and the wind blew."

Our new government is founded upon exactly the opposite idea; its foundations are laid, its corner-stone rests upon the great truth, that the negro is not equal to the white man; that slavery—subordination to the superior race—is his natural and normal condition. . . . This, our new government, is the first, in the history of the world, based upon this great physical, philosophical, and moral truth. This truth has been slow in the process of its development, like all other truths in the various departments of science. It has been so even amongst us. Many who hear me, perhaps, can recollect well, that this truth was not generally admitted, even within their day. The errors of the past generation still clung to many as late as twenty years ago. Those at the North, who still cling to these errors, with a zeal above knowledge, we justly denominate as fanatics. All fanaticism springs from an aberration of the mind—from a defect in reasoning. It is a species of insanity. One of the most striking characteristics of insanity, in many instances, is forming correct conclusions from fancied or erroneous premises; so with the anti-slavery fanatics; their conclusions are right if their premises were. They assume that the negro is equal, and hence conclude that he is entitled to equal privileges and rights with the white man. If their premises were correct, their conclusions would be logical and just—but their premise being wrong, their whole argument fails. I recollect once of having heard a gentleman from one of the northern States, of great power and ability, announce in the House of Representatives, with imposing effect, that we of the South would be compelled, ultimately, to yield upon this subject of slavery, that it was as impossible to war successfully against a principle in politics, as it was in physics or mechanics. That the principle would ultimately prevail. That we, in maintaining slavery as it exists with us, were warring against a principle, a principle founded in nature, the principle of the equality of men. The reply I made to him was, that upon his own grounds, we should, ultimately, succeed, and that he and his associates, in this crusade against our institutions, would ultimately fail. The truth announced, that it was as impossible to war successfully against a principle in politics as it was in physics and mechanics, I admitted; but told him that it was he, and those acting with him, who were warring against a principle. They were attempting to make things equal which the Creator had made unequal.

In the conflict thus far, success has been on our side, complete throughout the length and breadth of the Confederate States. It is upon this, as I have stated, our social fabric is firmly planted; and I cannot permit myself to doubt the ultimate success of a full recognition of this principle throughout the civilized and enlightened world.

As I have stated, the truth of this principle may be slow in development, as all truths are and ever have been, in the various branches of science. It was so with the principles announced by Galileo—it was so with Adam Smith and his principles of political economy. It was so with Harvey, and his theory of the circulation of the blood. It is stated that not a single one of the medical profession, living at the time of the announcement of the truths made by him, admitted them. Now, they are universally acknowledged.

May we not, therefore, look with confidence to the ultimate universal acknowledgment of the truths upon which our system rests? It is the first government ever instituted upon the principles in strict conformity to nature, and the ordination of Providence, in furnishing the materials of human society. Many governments have been founded upon the principle of the subordination and serfdom of certain classes of the same race; such were and are in violation of the laws of nature. Our system commits no such violation of nature's laws. With us, all of the white race, however high or low, rich or poor, are equal in the eye of the law. Not so with the negro. Subordination is his place. He, by nature, or by the curse against Canaan, is fitted for that condition which he occupies in our system. The architect, in the construction of buildings, lays the foundation with the proper material—the granite; then comes the brick or the marble. The substratum of our society is made of the material fitted by nature for it, and by experience we know that it is best, not only for the superior, but for the inferior race, that it should be so. It is, indeed, in conformity with the ordinance of the Creator. It is not for us to inquire into the wisdom of his ordinances, or to question them. For his own purposes, he has made one race to differ from another, as he has made "one star to differ from another star in glory."

The great objects of humanity are best attained when there is conformity to his laws and decrees, in the formation of governments as well as in all things else. Our confederacy is founded upon principles in strict conformity with these laws. This stone which was rejected by the first builders "is become the chief of the corner"— the real "corner-stone"—in our new edifice. . . .

I have been asked, what of the future? It has been apprehended by some that we would have arrayed against us the civilized world. I care not who or how many they may be against us, when we stand upon the eternal principles of truth, if we are true to ourselves and the principles for which we contend, we are obliged to, and must triumph.

[...]

But to pass on: Some have propounded the inquiry whether it is practicable for us to go on with the confederacy without further accessions? Have we the means and ability to maintain nationality among the powers of the earth? On this point I would barely say, that as anxiously as we all have been, and are, for the border States, with institutions similar to ours, to join us, still we are abundantly able to maintain our position, even if they should ultimately make up their minds not to cast their destiny with us. That they ultimately will join us—be compelled to do it—is my confident belief; but we can get on very well without them, even if they should not.

We have all the essential elements of a high national career. The idea has been given out at the North, and even in the border States, that we are too small and too weak to maintain a separate nationality. This is a great mistake. In extent of territory we embrace five hundred and sixty-four thousand square miles and upward. This is upward of two hundred thousand square miles more than was included within the limits of the original thirteen States. It is an area of country more than double the territory of France or the Austrian empire. . . . It is greater than all France, Spain, Portugal, and Great Britain, including England, Ireland, and Scotland, together. In population we have upward of five millions, according to the census of 1860; this includes white and black. The entire population, including white and black, of the original thirteen States, was less than four millions in 1790, and still less in '76, when the independence of our fathers was achieved. If they, with a less population, dared maintain their independence against the greatest power on earth, shall we have any apprehension of maintaining ours now?

In point of material wealth and resources, we are greatly in advance of them. The taxable property of the Confederate States cannot be less than twenty-two hundred millions of dollars! This, I think I venture but little in saying, may be considered as five times more than the colonies possessed at the time they achieved their independence. . . . With such an area of territory as we have—with such an amount of population—with a climate and soil unsurpassed by any on the face of the earth—with such resources already at our command—with productions which control the commerce of the world, who can entertain any apprehensions as to our ability to succeed, whether others join us or not?

It is true, I believe I state but the common sentiment, when I declare my earnest desire that the border States should join us. The differences of opinion that existed among us anterior to secession, related more to the policy in securing that result by co-operation than from any difference upon the ultimate security we all looked to in common. . . .

In this connection I take this occasion to state, that I was not without grave and serious apprehensions that if the worst came to the worst, and cutting loose from the old government should be the only remedy for our safety and security, it would be attended with much more serious ills than it has been as yet. Thus far we have seen none of those incidents which usually attend revolutions. No such material as such convulsions usually throw up has been seen. Wisdom, prudence, and patriotism, have marked every step of our progress thus far. This augurs well for the future, and it is a matter of sincere gratification to me, that I am enabled to make the declaration. Of the men I met in the Congress at Montgomery, I may be pardoned for saying this, an abler, wiser, a more conservative, deliberate, determined, resolute, and patriotic body of men, I never met in my life.

6

ROBERT MONTAGUE

Speech for Secession of Virginia

April 1–2, 1861

Lieutenant Governor Robert Latané Montague, forty-one years old in 1861, represented the Tidewater's Mathews and Middlesex counties (together 48.4 percent enslaved). This descendant of one of Virginia's first families was one of the convention's few large planters and its highest-ranking current officeholder (Governor Henry Wise and U.S. President John Tyler being former holders of their higher positions). In 1859 Montague had defeated Waitman Willey for his state post. He would serve later in the Confederate House of Representatives and as a postwar Virginia state legislator and judge.*

. . . WHEN THIS CONFEDERATION WAS FORMED, . . . two great prominent ideas lay at the foundation of the whole system. . . . First, . . . to combine the common forces of the country for the purpose of repelling foreign invasion. . . . Second, . . . [to establish] commercial, social, and political equality between the States . . . and prevent any invasion . . . of one State upon the rights of another. . . .

How stands Virginia to-day, when you apply that [second] principle to her condition? She has been invaded by citizens of her

---

* Introductory material from *Showdown in Virginia: The 1861 Convention and the Fate of the Union*, edited by William W. Freehling and Craig M. Simpson. Copyright ©2010 by William W. Freehling and Craig M. Simpson. Reprinted by permission of the University of Virginia Press.

sister States. That invasion cost your State between $300,000 and $400,000. . . . Your Legislature, last winter, appropriated $500,000 for the construction of an armory to manufacture arms and munitions of war. Your Legislature, at the present session, has appropriated $1,000,000 for arming your State. Here, then, is a tax of $2,000,000 imposed upon a people already ground down by a debt of $40,000,000. And for what, I ask? For what? Why, sir, to put your State in a position to defend herself against the members of her own family; to defend her equality; to protect herself against her sister States; or against the Federal Government, which is the common agent of all the States. Can this state of things last?

Sir, your Government rests in the affections of the people. Its abiding place must be in the honest hearts of the great masses of the people. And when those hearts become perverted, and when hate and malignity take the place of affection and regard, your whole system is a failure, and it becomes the part of wisdom and prudence to organize another that will cure these defects. . . .

My able and distinguished friend from Augusta [Mr. BALDWIN] . . . made . . . the most remarkable [point] that I ever heard fall from the lips of a Virginia statesman. He declared that . . . to settle this question, and to give peace, and quiet, and tranquility to the country for ever, he would not sanction, by way of amendments to the Constitution, what was called guarantees of power, because that would admit the right of the minority, and not of the majority, to control the government, and that this was a government of majorities.

Mr. BALDWIN: My statement on that subject, was, that our government has its foundation in the virtue and intelligence of the people; that the administrative force of the government must be lodged necessarily in the hands of the majority; . . . and that any attempt to build the administration of the Government on any narrower foundation than the virtue, and intelligence, and power of a majority of the people would lead to its overthrow.

Mr. MONTAGUE: Exactly. I did not misunderstand my friend. . . . But, sir, I utterly deny that proposition. It is entirely at war with the theory and practice of the government. . . . The very aim, and end, and object of a government, is to protect

the minority against the majority. A majority can always protect itself. If you give to the minority no guarantee of power
to protect itself, against the aggressions of the majority, then
your government is but a despotism of numbers, the worst of
all despotisms—a government of strength and not a government of right. If my friend will turn to the Constitution, he
will find that a minority of the people can break up the government whenever they please.... They have the power; and ...
the power shows that our government is not one of majorities....

Only one gentleman, so far as I remember, had attempted during the progress of our deliberations to make an argument against
this right [of secession] ... Other gentlemen have sneered at it ...
as ridiculous and absurd, ... [or] denounced in open and bold terms
all of us who ... act upon it as traitors, and inquired if there was not
such a thing as hemp for us.... While we have been denounced as
traitors, while our doctrine has been denounced as ridiculous, while
the doctrine of the fathers of the Republic is held up to the scorn of
the world, I trust I shall be excused if I attempt to put this great doctrine on a foundation from which I think it cannot be overthrown.

Virginia was the first State on this Continent that ever exercised the great doctrine of secession. When did Virginia do that?
On the 15th of May, 1776—prior to your Declaration of Independence. She did not go about to consult border States, to see what
they would do. In the plenitude of her sovereignty, and in the
depth of her patriotism, she severed her connection with the British Government....

Old Virginia, who adopted the first act of secession on this
continent, was the first to ... bring about another great measure
of secession. In January 1786, Virginia, by her Legislature proposed
a Convention, of Delegates from the States.... That Convention
recommended that all the States should appoint commissioners to
meet at Philadelphia, on the second Monday of May, 1787.... That
Convention met and formed our Constitution....

Now, what sort of government is this? ... Just take up the celebrated report of Mr. Madison, which has been the political law of
Virginia for sixty years, and ... you will see that it is declared to be

a compact between sovereign States. . . . Being a compact between sovereign States, the States who are parties to it can alone judge of its infraction, and of the mode and manner of redress. . . . "On what principle [Mr. Madison asked in the *Federalist* #43,]

> [can] a compact among the States . . . be superseded without the unanimous consent of the parties to it? This question is answered at once by recurring to the absolute necessity of the case; to the great principle of self-preservation; to the transcendent law of nature and of nature's God, which declares that the safety and happiness of society are the objects at which all political institutions aim, and to which all such institutions must be sacrificed. . . .
>
> A compact between independent sovereigns . . . can pretend to no higher validity than a league or treaty between the parties. . . . A breach of any one article is a breach of the whole treaty . . . A breach committed by either of the parties, absolves the others, and authorizes them, if they please, to pronounce the compact *violated and void*. . . .

The old articles of Confederation declared that the Union which they formed should be *perpetual*, and that it could not be altered or abolished without the consent of *all the States*. Yet the fact is, that nine States, upon the principles laid down by Mr. Madison above, did secede from that Union and form another—Virginia advised and started it, and this is her second act of secession. . . .

The right to secede is . . . Virginia's own doctrine. . . . I hope all true sons of Virginia will stand . . . [behind] one of the blessed doctrines of our glorious old mother, . . . [originating] in that high spirit of liberty which developed itself in Williamsburg in 1776 . . . If I am to be hung, if I am to be denounced as a traitor, . . . let it be for standing up and maintaining, in all their vigor and purity, the doctrines of the fathers of Virginia's immortal principles of civil liberty. [Applause.] . . .

Nobody will pretend that any force was resorted to by any power, of carrying the States into the Union. Now, sir, I ask, as it is admitted they went into the Union voluntarily, if there is anything in the Constitution which gives Congress or any department of the Federal Government the power to use force to keep them in? If there is, point it out. If any gentleman here shows me one word in the Constitution which gives Congress, or any department of the Federal Government, the power to keep a State in the Federal Union by force, I will yield the point. No, sir, it is not in the Constitution. You cannot find it there—*it is not there.* . . .

You gentlemen who belong to the Adams' school of politicians, hear what that great man, Mr. [John Quincy] Adams, said upon this question, and then, if you think proper, denounce the doctrine as "absurd and ridiculous." Will my friend read the extract for me? It is from an address delivered before the New York Historical Society in 1839, at the jubilee of the Constitution.

Mr. HOLCOMBE, of Albemarle, read the extract as follows:

> Nations acknowledge no judge between them upon earth. And their Governments, from necessity, must, in their intercourse with each other, decide when the failure of one party to a contract to perform its obligations absolves the other from the reciprocal fulfillment of his own. . . . We may admit the same right as vested in the people of every State in the Union, with reference to the General Government, which was exercised by the people of the United Colonies with reference to the supreme head of the British Empire, of which they formed a part. . . .
>
> Thus stands the *right.* But the indissoluble link of union between the people of the several States of this confederated nation is, after all, not in the *right,* but in the *heart.* If the day should ever come (may Heaven avert it!) when the affections of the people of these States shall be alienated from each other; when the fraternal spirit shall give way to cold indifference, or collisions of interest shall fester into hatred, the bands of political association will not long hold together parties no longer attracted by the magnetism of conciliated interests and kindly sympathies; and far better will it be for

the people of the disunited States to part in friendship from
each other, than to be held together by constraint. Then will
be the time for reverting to the precedent, which occurred
at the formation and adoption of the Constitution, to form
again a more perfect Union, by dissolving that which could
no longer bind, and to leave the separated parts to be re-
united by the law of political gravitation, to the centre. . . .

Mr. Adams . . . says we have had two precedents—one when
we seceded from England, and the other when we seceded from the
articles of Confederation; and when the day comes that the hearts
of these people are divided, when the Government no longer rests
upon kindly sympathies and affections, then it is time for them, as
Abraham and Lot did, to separate in peace. Adams men present, listen to the voice of your father. Come up now; you cannot shut your
eyes to the fact that the period has arrived when kindly sympathies
no longer exist, and instead of keeping Virginia in a free-soil Confederacy, and keeping her down as a mere political dependency upon
that central empire at Washington, use your efforts to bring about
a peaceable separation of people that can no longer live together in
peace and harmony. . . .

The gentleman from Monongalia [Mr. WILLEY] brought forward
here one argument against the exercise of this right which I was extremely surprised to hear. . . . The gentleman says that Florida cost
millions of dollars, that Texas cost millions of dollars, that Louisiana
cost millions of dollars, and asks whether we shall now permit them
to secede after having paid this large amount of money for them. . . .

I scout this argument. With perfect respect, I say to the gentleman that it is unworthy the consideration of any Virginian, to
measure sovereignty, to measure the great question of self-govern-
ment, and the great eternal principles of civil liberty, by dollars and
cents. I repeat, sir, . . . such an argument . . . should not be used
upon this floor. . . .

I will now . . . give one or two reasons why, in my judgment,
Virginia ought at this time, ought to-day, to resort to the exercise
of this right. I dissent from the gentleman from Augusta [Mr.

BALDWIN] . . . that slavery is stronger to-day than it had ever been. It is stronger with its friends—it is stronger in the States where it exists; but everywhere else it has infinitely more enemies to-day than it ever had. The whole world is against you; the whole civilized world, including three-fourths of your own country—including every power in Europe, except Spain, and every power upon this continent, except Brazil—is against you. And with these facts staring the gentleman in the face, he gets up and proclaims that slavery is stronger to-day than ever.

If that were so, how can he reconcile it with the history of our own government? That government is seventy-five years old. In its beginning, slavery existed in nearly every State; and if slavery is stronger to-day than ever before, how happens it that your government is for the first time in the hands of the enemies of slavery? How did it get there? . . .

In 1790 petitions were sent from Philadelphia and New York to Congress asking them to abolish slavery. . . . In 1792 petitions came again. In 1797 they came. In 1805 they came. In 1817 they came. In 1819 . . . we had the war upon the Missouri question. In 1827 petitions came again. In 1831 they came again. In 1835 the war regularly begun upon the right of petition, and it was waged there until it was shifted . . . to a war upon the territories. . . .

In 1840 for the first time this anti-slavery element entered into the Presidential election. Twenty years ago [James] Birney, as their candidate, received 7,000 votes. In 1844 he again received, as the candidate of the anti-slavery party, 62,140 votes. In 1848 [Martin] Van Buren and Gerrit Smith received 296,233 votes. In 1852 [John P.] Hale received 157,296 votes. In 1856 . . . John C. Fremont received 1,324,812 votes, showing an increase in sixteen years of over 1,300,000 votes. In 1860 Abraham Lincoln got votes enough to elect him President. . . .

These facts show that there has been a persistent war from the very first session of the First Congress down to the present moment, made upon you and upon your interests. . . . [Can] any sensible man . . . arrive at the conclusion that these people, who have been contending now for nearly seventy-five years for the accomplishment of one object, will relinquish it, give it up, just when successful, and go back to where they started?

Answer that point, gentlemen. Can it be answered upon any principle of human reason, upon any principle that governs human nature? If it cannot, these facts show you that your existence as a free people, that your existence as a slaveholding people depends upon your separation from this Government, where, if you remain, you will be crushed out; you will become degraded outcasts among the nations of the earth. . . .

The generation that now governs the North have grown up in the last 30 years, and [almost] every man . . . believes in their hearts, honestly before God, that slavery is a sin. Judge Story, Chancellor Kent, and Daniel Webster, in his great argument before the Supreme Court of the United States have taught them the fallacious doctrine that this is a Government of one people and . . . that one section must be in part responsible for the sins of the other section. . . . Judge Story's book is a text-book in all their Colleges. Dr. Wayland, a great theologian, . . . has written a book upon Moral Philosophy; . . . his book is a text-book in all their Colleges; and . . . a whole chapter [is] put forth to show that slavery is a sin. Then, sir, there is Peter Parley, useful and instructive as his books are—yet . . . you will find pervading the whole works an anti-slavery feeling. . . .

Here, then, you have the masses indoctrinated with Parley's doctrine, and the educated young man indoctrinated with Webster, Kent, Story and Wayland's doctrine. Then you have—and I defy any gentleman here to deny it—a union of the masses, . . . to strike down an institution which they believe is sinful, . . . with the educated men and political leaders; and I again defy any gentleman here to point me to an instance in the history of the world, when the masses have united with the leaders for a given purpose, that they ever ceased from their efforts until that purpose had been accomplished, or they themselves have been destroyed in their efforts to accomplish it. . . .

Look again at the way in which these Northern people have been educated. They have had anti-slavery catechisms, anti-slavery priests, antislavery lectures; they have anti-slavery everything. Their whole system is pervaded with anti-slavery feeling and anti-slavery sentiment. And yet Virginia statesmen get up here and talk about the overwhelming tide that is to destroy the anti-slavery feeling of the North, by paper guarantees attached to the Constitution. You may just as well attempt to dam up the tumbling waters of the Niagara, with your little finger, as to attempt any such thing. . . . I must state to you, Mr. Chairman, that I was startled, astounded to hear gentlemen . . . crying, "wait, wait," "delay, delay," when every day, every hour, brings the event these Northern people desire to accomplish nearer to your door.

Can we live with people like these? . . . Is there so corrupt a Government upon God's earth as your present Government at Washington? . . . It has lived seventy-five years, and now you have to wipe it out and begin afresh or it will end in despotism; and those men who will not vilely and slavishly submit to that despotism will be slaughtered upon some battle field fighting in defence of the rights and principles that have been handed down to us from our ancestors. . . . I believe in God, I believe in His Providence, I believe in His direction, and I believe, as a moral, Christian man, it is my duty to do what I can to separate my State from these people at the North, who are striving day and night to destroy one of God's institutions. . . .

We are told that about 1620 there was a storm at sea, and that . . . God, in His providence and mercy, to save a ship from being engulfed in the ocean, led her into a safe haven at Hampton Roads. . . . She put out twenty odd savage Africans. Our people assembled. They were amazed. They saw there a simple-hearted, docile people that might be elevated to a high standard of Christian civilization. . . . Virginia responded, . . . and in consequence of her response these twenty odd savage Africans have grown to be four millions of civilized men now upon your continent.

As Virginia was thus the great pioneer of the institution and its great author, would it not be the rankest cowardice, the most disgraceful scene ever acted on the theatre of the world, for her, in this hour of distress and extremity of that institution which she has imposed on the land, to turn her back upon it and to permit

Northern fanatics to exterminate it from the face of the earth? I do not believe that God will permit that to be done. You may talk about National Conventions, and Border Conferences, and you may send your committees to Washington every other day to confer with Mr. Lincoln, and to know when he is going to hit us: you may read letters from Secretary [of War Simon] Cameron, and Colonel Somebody, and Major Somebody else, each contradicting the other, to show that they are not going to remove guns from this city, but all will have no effect. God means, through the instrumentality of African slavery, to accomplish His great purpose of Christianizing and civilizing that race. You may throw impediments in the way, and thereby bring down punishment on your own hands, but you cannot stop it. . . . Every consideration of duty, of interest, of high Christian moral obligation, conspires to make us cause Virginia to secede at once, settle our difficulties peaceably afterwards, if we can—and if we cannot, forcibly.

If I find that you will not go with me, if you are determined to wait, wait, wait, . . . I will . . . go with you for the next plan which I think will best promote the great object I have in view. . . . I mean to stand by my principles and doctrines to the bitter end. If that day shall come—which God in his mercy avert—when you and I will have to be exiled or yield to this horde of Northern Vandals, . . . I will not be exiled. . . . I will stand on the shores of my own native Rappahannock, and there I will fall. . . . I will die in Virginia, and trust to God and to posterity to vindicate what is just and what is right. [Applause on the floor and gallery.]

7

CHAPMAN STUART

Speech for Virginia Remaining in the Union

April 5, 1861

. . . [D]isunionist orators dominated the convention's proceedings during the final days before the war. But during this increasingly tense period, Unionists still possessed the numerical advantage. Chapman Johnson Stuart's brief outburst summed up a crucial reason for the secessionists' continued shortfall.

Chapman Stuart, not to be confused with Alexander H. H. Stuart from the Valley's Augusta County, represented the Trans-Allegheny's Tyler and Doddridge counties (together containing only fifty-two slaves). Although one of the few convention speakers who owned no slaves, the forty-year-old Stuart professed utter loyalty to slavery—and prescient conviction that secession would devastate the east's peculiar institution.*

. . . I SAID YESTERDAY THAT MY constituents were ready and willing to stand up in defence of the rights and institutions of the people of the Eastern portion of the State. In saying so, I did not wish to be understood as meaning that the people of the West were willing to take the course pressed by those whom we call the ultra men of the Eastern portion of the State, but that the people of the West are

* Introductory material from *Showdown in Virginia: The 1861 Convention and the Fate of the Union*, edited by William W. Freehling and Craig M. Simpson. Copyright ©2010 by William W. Freehling and Craig M. Simpson. Reprinted by permission of the University of Virginia Press.

sound on the question of slavery, and are willing, at all hazards, to demand and have secured to you your rights; but I do not wish to be understood as being in favor of secession, or the constitutional right of secession.

We believe in the right of revolution. We believe that when the Constitution has been perverted to our injury and oppression, we have the right to throw off the shackles and appeal to our natural rights. But revolution presupposes, in my opinion, a remedy, and if the fact of dissevering our connection from the Federal Government would be a remedy for the evils of which we complain, then we would be in favor of it.

But I cannot see for my life how, under present circumstances, secession or revolution would be a remedy for the evils of which you complain. Will it relieve us from any of them? If we had to complain of the perversion of the Constitution by the Federal Government, to our injury and oppression, then revolution, if successful, would be a complete remedy. But if the complaint is in regard to the action of separate States, then secession from the General Government would be no remedy. If it were even successful, we would still find ourselves in identically the same position in which we now are. The institutions and laws of those States derogatory of the rights of the South, would still remain on their statute books.

The people of my district . . . all stand up as one solid mass . . . to contend and fight for our rights in the Union. We believe that secession, instead of being a remedy for the evils complained of, would be an aggravation of those evils. The great question that has given rise to complaint is the slavery question. And I have told you that although we have no direct interest in that question, we were loyal and true to the interests of the people of the eastern portion of the State.

We take the position that slavery is right, legally, morally, and in every sense of the word. But the Convention will recollect that the sentiment of the whole civilized world, at this day, is arrayed against the institution of slavery, and it is nothing but the prestige and power of the General Government now that guarantees to the slaveholder his right. We find a large portion of the people of the

Northern States standing up also to vindicate and support our rights. I believe that at this day there is a majority of the people of the free States in favor of the right of the Southern portion of the Confederacy to the institution of slavery.

They appeal to us to come to the rescue and help them to save the Union. They have fought for our rights in days gone by, and now they appeal to us as friends, for whose rights they have ever stood firm and true, to come to their aid and help them to save the Union. If we pursue the course indicated here by the secession party, we will cut ourselves loose from our friends in the free States, and array them against us and our institutions. If we say to those in the North, who have heretofore stood up for our rights, "We will have nothing more to do with you," can you expect or hope to retain the good will and kind feeling of that people? No, sir. By pursuing this course, you will, in my humble opinion, drive from us our heretofore best and truest friends, and unite them in one solid mass against our institutions. Then we will have the whole world arrayed in sentiment against our institutions, with a power right on our borders three times our strength, made our enemies by our own acts. Can we expect our friends in the North to stand by us after we destroyed our common Government and brought ruin upon them? It is hopeless to expect so. Then I hold that secession or revolution is no remedy for the evils complained of, but will tend as an aggravation of them, and will, if persisted in, lead to the extermination of slavery. . . .

8

ELIZABETH BROWN PRYOR

Excerpt from *Reading the Man: A Portrait of Robert E. Lee Through His Private Letters*

2007

LEE, SHOCKED AT THE THOUGHT of dismantling the nation, maintained that disunion was "anarchy" and that "secession is nothing but revolution."[1] (Exasperated with extremists both north and south, he decried equally the "aggressions" of the former and "selfish & dictatorial bearing" of the latter. Long after the "fire-eaters" were manipulating public emotion, he clung to the fantasy that secession could be peaceably reversed.[2] "I trust there is wisdom, patriotism enough in the Country to save them, for I cannot anticipate so great a calamity to the nation as a dissolution of the Union," he told one of his favorite nieces.[3] Lee's distress was so acute that it fractured the correct demeanor he normally cultivated. Not only did he startle his colleagues by exploding with rage when secessionists tried prematurely to force his resignation, he broke down when he heard that Texas had actually left the Union. "I shall never forget his look of astonishment . . . his lips trembling and his eyes full of tears," a friend wrote of that bleak February day.[4]

From the start of the crisis Lee knew that his destiny was to follow the fortunes of Virginia. If his state chose to stay in the Union, so would he; if it withdrew, his actions would follow suit. He was candid about this with everyone who asked him and never changed his conviction that this was the only respectable course. He hoped the crisis would abate, he explained to [Martha Custis Lee], but acknowledged that if it continued he would "go back in sorrow to my people & share the misery of my native state & save in her defence there will be one soldier less in the world than now."[5] As he left San Antonio, a fellow officer shouted after the ambulance he was riding in, "Colonel, do you intend to go South or remain North?" Lee stuck his head out and replied: "I shall never bear arms against the United States,—but it may be necessary for me to carry a musket in defence of my native State, Virginia, in which case I shall not prove recreant to my duty."[6]

It is clear that the nation's emergency had imposed a personal crisis on Lee. He never wavered in his determination to link his actions to Virginia's, but he was less clear about his reasons for it. "While I wish to do what is right," he declared in a moment of supreme confliction, "I am unwilling to do what is not, either at the bidding of the South or North."[7] He told a friend, Charles Anderson, that even though he saw little justification for secession, he had been educated to believe that his "loyalty to Virginia ought to take precedence over that which is due to the Federal Government." Anderson, recalling the legacy of Lee's brother Henry, who had railed against the primacy of states' rights, and Light-Horse Harry's passionate belief in Washington's nationalist principles, recalled: "I sadly asked myself: *whence was this education?*"[8] Light-Horse Harry Lee had led an army to stymie the first challenge to federal authority during the Whiskey Rebellion, and though he was once heard to declare that Virginia was his "country"—which he felt bound to "obey"—he had ultimately concluded that "our happiness depends entirely on maintaining our union" and that "in point of right, no state can withdraw itself from the union."[9]

Another part of Robert Lee's dilemma was that although he was convinced that the framers of the Constitution had never intended the right of secession, he strongly agreed with the secessionists on virtually every other policy.[10] He believed in racial supremacy and could not envision an egalitarian society; he thought the nation had been founded on "perpetual union," but admitted that if the bond could "only be maintained by the sword and bayonet, instead of brotherly Love & friendship . . . its existence will lose all interest with me.'[11] He spoke out for the Crittenden compromise, which would have guaranteed the permanent existence of slavery and permitted its extension into the territories, maintaining that this cornerstone of proslavery thought deserved "the support of every patriot."[12] Above all, Lee "resented" aggressive badgering by the North and feared southern political impotence under the rule of its majority population.[13]

The way Lee envisioned his own role in the conflict was particularly convoluted. Here his pronouncements often appear at odds not only with themselves but with realistic expectation. He could not raise his sword against the United States—but if called on to carry a musket for Virginia, he would not shirk. He would take to planting corn, and there would be one less soldier in the world—"save in defence of my native state." None of this seems plausible; yet it would not be the last time Lee retreated to a dream world of subsistence farming and revolutionary imagery. One of the more intricate steps in this psychic Virginia reel is the word "defence."[14] It appears Lee thought that if he stayed in the old army, he might be able to maintain a position that resisted offensive operations; and that if Virginia seceded, he could restrict himself to actions that checked aggression. Apparently this belief was bolstered by General Scott, who showed him cabinet papers that denounced war and maintained that any mobilization was solely for the protection of the capital. Indeed he clung to this vision of reactive defense until well after the first battle of Manassas.[15]

The only way out of this corner was for Virginia to remain in the Union so that Lee could both uphold the United States and defend his natal ground. Lee was open in his hope that this would be the case. "I am particularly anxious that Virginia should keep right," he advised [Eleanor "Agnes" Lee], "as she was chiefly instrumental in the formation & inauguration of the Constitution, so I would wish that she might be able to maintain it, to save the union."[16] One of the haunting questions of these anxious months is why he did not use his influence to guide Virginia's decision. In this, the most critical moment of his life, it seems he fell back on his old passivity. Lee's name was not yet a household word, but his reputation from the Mexican War was widely appreciated, and his part in the peaceful termination of the John Brown affair was celebrated throughout the South. Neighbors and relatives waited to follow his lead: one recalled that "for some the question 'What will Colonel Lee do?' was only second in interest to 'What will Virginia do:'"[17] It was well known that he had the ear of General Scott and that his opinion might sway the lawmakers in Washington. Harper's Ferry had also given him special access in Richmond. His standing there was such that Confederate vice president Alexander Stephens admitted "a look, or even intonation of voice" by Lee at this time would have had enormous power.[18] Perhaps acting on his old dislike of politics and prominence, he chose not to shape the momentous events before him. Instead he linked his fate to the volatile public will, stating that he must wait patiently, relying on God to order all things for the good.[19] When he was begged by statesmen and relatives to lead in brokering a peace, he remained resolutely out of the discussions.[20]

IN FACT LEE ALMOST GOT his wish that Virginia would remain with the Union. Pro-secession factions tried to force an early decision after South Carolina withdrew from the Union in December 1860, but through skillful diplomacy the choice was left to a statewide convention, which opened the following February. That the Old Dominion would secede was anything but a foregone conclusion. Thirty-one percent of its people were enslaved, the largest actual number of bondsmen of any state in the South. Yet in the 1850s Virginia had been heavily influenced by an influx of northern immigrants, the growth of railroads, and political reforms that were beginning to challenge the old seignorial class. With its diversified population and economy, it had more in common with Maryland, which remained with the Union, than it did with the Cotton States. Though there were some notably aggressive pro-secession personalities in the Old Dominion, overall there was no great leap to embrace the risky policies of South Carolina. Nowhere was this truer than in Lee's section of the state, where the economy was booming and the influence of slave culture waning. Union sentiment remained widespread in northern and western Virginia even as the final votes for secession were counted.[21]

During the early months of 1861 Virginia conducted an extraordinary public discussion of secession, unequaled elsewhere. This was not a debate about war: as Henry Adams would observe, few in America expected or wanted the horrors that rocked the land from 1861 to 1865.[22] Instead it was a sober attempt to resolve a conflict of incompatible regional differences, constitutional rights, and factional politicians. Secessionists tried to exploit the emotional aftershock of Lincoln's election, but in these early months they were overridden by those who still thought the Union offered the best guarantee of liberty and prosperity. Only one-third of the delegates to the state convention favored secession, and their arguments were not holding the day. Lee had legitimate grounds to hope that his home state and his country were at least feebly reconciled when he returned to Washington, at Scott's behest, on March 1, 1861.[23]

He found the atmosphere alive with tension. Washington was filled with edgy troops, called in for Lincoln's inauguration. Many, like Mary Lee, thought the lanky westerner should have resigned for the sake of the country rather than take the oath of office.[24] Though Lincoln tried to appear conciliatory, saying that he would not interfere with slavery where it existed, he also made clear that he recognized no independent states and intended to protect federal property. Lee's colleague Samuel Heintzelman attended the March 4 inauguration and thought the address a prescription for war. When he saw Lee at Scott's office the next day, Lee also expressed concern.[25] Lee's movements for the next month appear to have been low-key and cautious. In theory Scott had recalled him to sit on a board revising the army's regulations, and while the board was being formed, he remained at Arlington without official duties.[26] Lincoln was starting to put his administration together, making appointments and reassigning troops, and Lee's capabilities—and his allegiance—were under discussion. Lincoln had appointed Simon Cameron as secretary of war, and one aide recalled a meeting between Cameron and Scott that focused on Lee. "The Secretary asked the General if he had full confidence in Lee's loyalty, to which the General replied, 'Entire confidence, sir. He is true as steel, sir, true as steel!'"[27] In full dress uniform Lee attended a reception given at the White House on March 13 for seventy-eight military officers. It was probably the only time he met Lincoln.[28] A week later the new president promoted Lee to full colonel of the 1st Regiment of Cavalry—a coveted position that Lee was confident enough to accept immediately.[29]

But the tenuous chance for peaceful resolution was quickly shattered. In early April Lincoln made the difficult decision to resupply Fort Sumter, which was holding out against a rebel blockade in Charleston harbor. He apprised southern officials of his intention and essentially gave them an alternative: Would their response be peace or war? They chose war, firing at the fort on April 12. In the ensuing panic Lincoln made another fateful choice, this time calling for 75,000 soldiers to defend U.S. property. These two actions galvanized both sides, as the North feared wholesale revolution and Southerners believed Lincoln was preparing to invade their homes. Those who had so dexterously crafted a fragile peace in Virginia were caught in the fury, their months of compromise overturned. A woman who tried to defend the February decision against secession was told by Senator R. M. T. Hunter, "My dear lady you may place your little hand against Niagara with more certainty of staying the torrent than you can oppose this movement.[30] On April 17 the question was again put to the convention in Richmond. This time they chose secession.[31]

"EVENTS CROWD SO FAST I cannot write them in my diary," exclaimed the Lees' friend Elizabeth Lomax. "Virginia *has* seceded!! Heaven help us!"[32] The verdict was not yet finalized—that would depend on a popular referendum scheduled for May 23—but few doubted the outcome. At Arlington, Lee learned with dismay of the convention's impending vote—probably on April 16, when the rumors first reached Washington. According to one family story he dined that night with his brother Smith and cousin Phillips Lee, both U.S. naval officers. His two companions bantered awhile about how Cousin Phil, who intended to stay with the Union, would be bombarded by Smith Lee's Confederate forces, after which the two would discuss the contest over an amiable toast. During this levity Robert remained miserable and mute. Believing that his silence was born of indecision, Phillips Lee hastily told federal government officials that if they were to sway his cousin they must act quickly.[33] The next day a note was dispatched to Arlington, calling Lee to the offices of Francis Preston Blair, one of Lincoln's closest advisers, along with another message that requested his presence in General Scott's headquarters. At the meeting with Blair, Lee was told that Lincoln intended to offer him command of the forces being called up to defend the Union. The two talked for a long time, Blair "very wily and keen," playing on Lee's sense of responsibility and ambition. Lee declined on the spot. He saw nothing but "anarchy & ruin" in secession, he told Blair, yet he could not bring himself to raise his sword against his Virginia home and heritage.[34] From Blair's office Lee marched straight to see Scott, in such agitation that he dispensed with his usual courtesies and insisted on being admitted to the general's office. Lee and Scott, bound for so long in mutual admiration, talked candidly for several hours.[35] What can be pieced together from the available accounts is that Scott tried to persuade Lee that any forces amassed by the Union would be so vast they would stifle the South's will to rebel, making offensive action unnecessary. When Lee said he was convinced aggression was inevitable, and he could not lead an invasion of the South, Scott brusquely rejoined: "If you propose to resign it is proper that you should do so at once; your present attitude is equivocal." Now there was nothing left to say. A journalist was told the two men stood grasping each other's hands, "too full of feeling to find utterance for one word. . . ."[36]

The day had been cataclysmic for Lee, and he went to talk the matter over with Smith. Everything he had ever been, everything he had worked for, seemed to have culminated in that offer of command, and now he could not accept it. He did not want his state to secede, but had felt powerless to halt the course he believed would be so destructive. That night came reports that Virginia troops had seized the armory at Harper's Ferry, the same arsenal he had so recently defended against wild, prophetic John Brown, and he must have known that all chance of peaceful redress was over. He had wanted to hang on to his hopes, as well as his commission, until the May 23 referendum made secession irrevocable in Virginia. But Scott's pressure forced him to contemplate the loss of not only his job but his credibility within army circles.[37] Those who met him and his family in Alexandria noted the sharp contrast in their deep depression with the general exhilaration in the town. The people had "lost their senses:" Rooney remarked in dismay.[38] Agnes would write quietly to Mildred that nothing at Arlington was "talked or thought of except our troubles . . . our poor Father & brothers need all our prayers. . . ."[39]

For two terrible days Lee contemplated the matter. His wife, as torn as he was, told him that she would support whatever decision he made.[40] The slaves watched as their master "walked backwa'd and fo'ward on de po'ch steddyin'," noting that he "didn't cahr to go. No . . . he didn't cahr to go."[41] A little boy who was visiting the family also remembered seeing Lee pacing in the garden and hearing the floors creak as he knelt and prayed in his upstairs bedroom.[42] Arlington felt "as if there had been a death in it," said Agnes, "for the army was to him home and country."[43] At midnight the house was still ablaze with lights, as the family gathered with miserable anticipation in the parlor. Finally Lee bowed his head and wrote his resignation, as well as a short explanatory letter to General Scott. Then he slowly walked down the long staircase and handed the letters to his wife. "Mary," he said, "your husband is no longer an officer of the United States Army."[44]

LEE'S MOST RENOWNED BIOGRAPHER CALLED it the "answer he was born to make." Another writer stated that "it was not that the anguished man had any choice."[45] Yet everything we know indicates that the decision was, in his wife's words, "the severest struggle of his life."[46] This poignant moment, when a strong, steadfast man paced and prayed in despair, is a scene worthy of Shakespeare precisely because it so palpably exposes the contradiction in his heart. Why, if he believed all he said, did he come to this point? Lee's explanation was the spare, elegantly worded one he gave to his cousin Roger Jones and repeated nearly verbatim to each person who asked: "With all my devotion to the Union and the feeling of loyalty and duty of an American citizen, I have not been able to make up my mind to raise my hand against my relatives, my children, my home."[47] Yet even his formulaic language gives an impression quite the opposite from banal inevitability. In later years he confessed he held on to his resignation letter for a day before sending it, the moment was so painful.[48] Lee would later concoct elaborate constitutional theories to explain his decision, but they belied the words he spoke at the moment of crisis. His reticence speaks to his distress, and suggests he knew he must hold on to his conviction and avoid expressing its contradictions, lest he second-guess his own actions.

For in reality there were numerous options available to him, options that others in his situation did choose. Winfield Scott was a Virginian, and he knew that his path lay with the Union. When he was approached by state officials, he dismissed as an insult any suggestion that he would renege on his solemn oath of loyalty. So did George Thomas, with whom Lee had companionably ridden over the Texas desert. Both Thomas and Scott would suffer the social ostracism that Orton Williams prophesized in his resignation letter. " 'Fuss and Feathers' has distinguished himself," one prominent Virginian critically remarked. "You ought to hear how he is spoken of by his family and State."[49] Thomas's family never again communicated with him except to ask him to change his name.[50] A young Virginian, just out of West Point, acknowledged that by retaining his commission he had been shunned by all of his southern associates; yet still he derided those who would hold their obligations so lightly as to abandon the nation when it most needed them.[51] In all, about two-fifths of the officers from Virginia stayed in the U.S. Army after their state seceded, enduring varying degrees of censure for their stance.[52] Others opted not to fight on any side. West Point's Dennis Hart Mahan, another proud Virginian, chose not to uphold a cause he believed unworthy and sat out the war.[53] North Carolinian Alfred Mordecai resigned his commission, but rejected an offer to lead either the Confederate ordinance service or engineer department. He spent the war years teaching mathematics in Philadelphia.[54]

Lee had hoped to avoid pitting himself against his family, but that desire would also remain unfulfilled. In fact his decision was controversial in his innermost circles. "I feel no exalted respect for a man who takes part in a movement in which he can see nothing but 'anarchy & ruin' . . . and yet that very utterance scarce passed Robt Lees lips . . . when he starts off with delegates to treat with Traitors," was one response from his family. A young relative began a school fight when he was asked whether his father—a Unionist—was "the Rebel traitor Lee."[55] Roger Jones, whom Lee declined to advise, finally decided to fight for the Union. A bevy of relations in the army and navy followed suit. Phillips Lee never wavered from his Union loyalties, serving through the war with distinction. His younger brother John Fitzgerald Lee, an 1834 West Point graduate, retained his position as judge advocate of the Union army. Cousin John H. Upshur also resisted "tremendous pressure" in order to remain with the Union.[56] Orton Williams, of course, did resign; but his brother Laurence fought on the side of the North, serving at one point as an aide-de-camp to General McClellan.[57] Philip Fendall, whose family had done so much for Robert Lee's mother, never wavered from his Union loyalties.[58] Sister Anne was also not in agreement with Robert, and her son, Louis Marshall, fought with General John Pope against his uncle. No one in that family ever spoke to Lee again.[59] With great reluctance Smith Lee became a Confederate naval officer, where he served without enthusiasm, and as late as September 1863 still "pitched into" those responsible for "getting us into this snarl." Saying that both the Lees and his in-laws in the Mason family had pressured him with ideas that Virginia came first, he grumbled, "South Carolina be hanged. . . . How I did want to stay in the old navy!"[60] His wife tried to reverse their son Fitz Lee's pro-South decision and herself held "to the north end of the Long Bridge" until she was "dragged away from Washington . . . kicking."[61] In early 1861 Mary Lee was also conflicted, and her daughters teased her about her staunch Unionist talk. Though she sympathized with some of the South's complaints, she wrote, "for my part, I would rather endure the ills we know, than rush madly into greater evils & what could be greater than the Division of our glorious Republic into petty states, each seeking its private interests & unmindful of the whole."[62] Lee's sons joined the Confederate forces, but only after their father had declared his intentions. There is a strong chance that if Lee's decision had been different they would have followed his lead.[63] Had Robert Lee taken the part of the Union, he still would have faced confrontation within his border-state family, many of whom sided with the South. But his assertion that he was acting in simple solidarity with a like-minded group of relatives would never be borne out.

IN DESCRIBING HIS DECISION, LEE only twice uses the word *honor*. The first is in a letter to Markie in January 1861 in which he says there is no sacrifice he is unwilling to make for the Union "save that of honour." The second is the official "honor" he has of tendering his resignation from the army.[64] It is a weighty word, and its multiple meanings in Lee's situation may have made it too painful a choice for his pen. In southern society honor was bound up with family connections and local reputation and a desire to avoid public shame. For those who felt it keenly, the individual consideration of honor could take precedence over civic order or personal welfare—even culminating in violence—the cult of the duel being a notable illustration. Lee may have been influenced by this, though the split in his family makes the question of private loyalties a problematic one. There was no linear path to rectitude in Lee's case, and every avenue was strewn with irreconcilable principles. For example, one of the concerns that pressed Lee to resign quickly was the worry that he might be ordered by the army to undertake aggressive duty against the South; in military circles it was "dishonorable" to resign because of unwelcome orders. Lee acted on this definition of honor at the very time he was "dishonoring" vows of thirty years.[65] The concern that seems to have motivated him was the bullying of the North, which he had been complaining about since the 1830s.[66] It was not just his distaste for abolitionists or the fear of an increasingly powerful Northern majority so much as the horror of lost self-esteem, the rage of not being able to defend oneself in the face of mounting humiliations. Secession became the most "honorable" option to Southerners because it showed independence and a spirit of self-protection. Many of those who chose to fight for the South gave this as the reason for their fierce determination, and throughout the war the reaction against "subjugation" was a strong motivating force. It had nothing to do with the inherent principles in their cause; more accurately it could be called "pride" that second cousin of honor. In Lee's case this likely colored not only his decision to leave the U.S. Army, but his strongly aggressive performance on the battlefield.[67]

LEE SAT ON HIS DECISION for a day and then dispatched his letters to General Scott. Orton Williams, who had not yet left Scott's staff, reported that the resignation had been approved and that the whole army was "in a stir over it."[68] While Arlington's inhabitants were still in shock at the thought of having arrayed themselves against the flag of their country, Lee was contacted by Judge John Robertson, who Governor John Letcher had dispatched to assess his availability for service with Virginia. It must have been an agonizing afternoon, for Robertson was detained by a lengthy, unpleasant interview with Scott, and never arrived for Lee's appointment.[69] The next day, a Sunday, Lee was seen earnestly conferring with some strangers, probably Robertson and other representatives from Richmond, on the grounds of Christ Church. Several relatives stood with Agnes Lee and watched them, remembering that "the vibrations in the air were intense" and that Lee's face showed "a mortal struggle . . . much more terrible than any known to the din of battle." After a long conversation, Lee agreed to meet Judge Robertson the following morning on a train bound for Richmond. One family member thought he had gone to confer about peace; others believed that he was simply weighing his options.[70]

Much has been made about Lee's whirlwind transformation in those few April days, for outside the heightened moment it seems his transition from a loyal United States officer to a committed rebel was just a little too quick. Whether or not he was cagily playing both sides for the greatest advantage has been the subject of some debate.[71] Lee had indeed been approached by southern leaders as early as mid-March, but if he responded, the correspondence has yet to be found.[72] Certainly he was assessing every possibility, for it would have been unwise not to, given his beliefs and the precarious political climate. There is no indication, however, that he proffered his services, or ever sought information about receiving a commission in any southern army before his resignation. When he was finally offered the leadership of Virginia's forces, state officials took some trouble to avoid soliciting him before he had resigned his commission, feeling that it would be "dishonorable" to pressure anyone still under oath to defend the United States.[73] His cousins, always the sounding board of his soul, believed his preference was to outwait the crisis at Arlington, and Lee also mentioned that this was his intention.[74] Yet excitement and opportunity were in the air, and there was a good deal of discussion among resigning officers about who would pluck the limited number of plum positions with the southern forces. Lee may have succumbed, as did J. E. B. Stuart, to the urgency to act before "the southern army will all be drawn and you will have the place of the laggard."[75]

According to Judge Robertson, Lee did not know that he was to be offered any command until he boarded the train. He may have been interested in going to Richmond just to assess the situation; he later said, rather questionably, that he went to look at the Pamunkey estates. It seems unlikely that so cautious a man would have made the journey without a strong understanding of its purpose. Others had certainly caught wind of the state's intentions, and along the rail route Lee was excitedly cheered.[76] By the time he reached Richmond, the state convention had voted him commander in chief of all forces. Before he had much time to ruminate, he found himself being presented with George Washington's sword, and hailed a hero in a powerful tribute by the president of the convention. Was he caught unawares and forced to react too quickly, or was this really the very spot where he most longed to be? Was this finally the recognition Lee sought—the culmination of his skill and his self-discipline? It is hard to say, for Lee fell back on the accepted, courteous platitudes of his era, expressing surprise at the praise and protesting his inadequacy for the job. But it pleased him enough that a newspaper account of this triumph was found in his pocket diary at his death.[77]

The quick turnaround was probably entirely logical in Lee's heart, for he had said from the first that he would link his fate to Virginia's.

As can be imagined, however, few outside the South believed the decision reflected the noble principles he invoked to explain it. Honor was in the eye of the beholder in 1861, and from the beginning Lee's motives were criticized. Technically Lee had acted correctly by resigning when he felt that he could no longer uphold his vows to defend "the United States paramount to any and all allegiance . . . to any State" or "against all enemies or opposers."[78] The skeptics, however, believed that those who swore easy oaths in fine times, and then abandoned them, not only shamefully betrayed the country but had no honor. When she heard from Mary Lee that Robert had spent two prayerful days in decision, a cousin remarked acidly: "I wish he had read over his commission as well as his prayers."[79] At West Point someone drew a picture of Lee with his head attached to the body of an insect. Lincoln would use Lee's "deceitful" dealings as a justification for his suspension of habeas corpus.[80] The reaction of former army friends was just as sharp. "Robert Lee is commander in chief of the forces of the Commonwealth—'O Lucifer son of the morning star how art thou fallen,'" was the response of one colleague's family. The phrase echoed words that Light-Horse Harry's beloved Nathanael Greene had used to condemn Benedict Arnold.[81]

WHILE STILL IN FRONTIER TEXAS, Lee had recognized that his decision would be based on intangibles. "I know you think and feel very differently, but I can't help it," he had told esteemed northern colleagues. In the end it mattered not that Henry Lee believed "the good of the state is entwined with the good of the Union," or that his son's fortunes might prosper by following another course.[82] Solemn oaths and Unionist relatives ultimately could not override the pull of what Lee's cousin Anna Maria Fitzhugh called "a sweet binding to this spot of earth, this soil of Virginia that is irresistible."[83] Lee tried to disavow private interests in his statements, but in fact it was the intense personal quality of his struggle that made it emblematic of the nation's torment.[84] His decision came to represent more than a divided country, or divided regional fidelity; it went beyond a divisive vote on secession or a splintered family. It strikes a timeless chord because it evokes that lowest of all miseries: the nightmare of a divided soul.

That pensive, disciplined Robert E. Lee made an emotional decision affects each of us every day. One of the most trenchant "what-ifs" of the Civil War is the question of how Lee's stance shaped the course of the nation. We sense that history would have been altered if the options presented to Lee—resignation; leadership of the Union troops; acceptance of high command in Virginia—had been decided differently. We do not know exactly how this would have developed, but intuitively we know it to be true. Lee's dilemma was not simply a historic wrestling match between right and wrong, patriotism or treachery. It stands as a critical moment in our nation's pageant because it forces us to consider some very basic questions. What is patriotism? Who commands our first loyalty? Can loyalty be divided and still be true? And who defines truth anyway? It is the excruciating gray area that makes these questions universal. Lee tells us that the answer to each is highly subjective. By taking a stand and never turning back, Lee also teaches us that they must be faced by every individual at the moment they are summoned, no matter how unsure or unprepared, and that the grandest theories in the world fall away at the moment of heightened instinct. And then his decision tells us something more: that following the heart's truth may lead to censure, or agonizing defeat—and yet be honored in itself.[85]

Author's Note

Since the original publication of this essay, I have continued to probe Robert E. Lee's iconic decision to fight for the South. Several remarkable documents have recently come to light that amplify our understanding of this critical moment. These include the diary of a clergyman whom Lee consulted; revealing letters Lee wrote to female acquaintances; recollections by the messengers involved in bringing him to Richmond; and, most important, a letter drafted by his eldest daughter, Mary Custis Lee, which describes the scene at Arlington when her father determined his course. That letter is far more credible than the second-hand accounts which were previously our only sources. Not only was Mary Custis Lee an eyewitness to the scene, her letter was written only a few years after the war, whereas the traditional versions of the story did not appear until the 20th century.

This material gives us rich new detail about Lee's decision-making. It shows that despite his statements to the contrary, he was not opposed to secession in principle. He simply wanted to exhaust all peaceful means of redress first; remarking that then "we can with a clear conscience separate."[1] He was gravely distressed by the prospect of a prolonged and bloody war, warning about it repeatedly at a time when few anticipated a lengthy conflict.[2] Mary Custis Lee's letter also shows us that, unlike the conventional story of her father pacing and praying as he agonized over his future, he was quite calm, if "worn & harassed." He made his fateful choice alone in his office, without fanfare. Before breakfast on April 20, 1861 he entrusted his resignation letter to a slave, to be delivered at the War Department.[3]

The documents also offer striking new insights into Lee's motives during those chaotic days. Lee's explanation for his actions—that he could not raise his hand against his relatives and his state—is challenged by his daughter's account.[4] For in it she maintains that his decision was not taken under pressure from his family, but was actually made despite their opposition. Lee at first did not tell his immediate circle that he had resigned, and when he finally called them together, it was to apologize. "I suppose you will all think I have done very wrong," he lamented. Noting that the entire family, except herself, had been Unionist, and that her mother's allegiance to the federal government was particularly strong, Mary describes how the words left them stunned and speechless. Finally she alone spoke up, saying "Indeed Papa, I don't think you have done wrong at all." Lee then remarked that he did not believe Virginia had reason to secede—at least not yet. But he had refused the command of Union forces a few days earlier, and heard his mentor, General Winfield Scott, state that there was no place in the army for uncommitted men. Now, Lee acknowledged, "it had come to this & after my last interview with Gen. Scott I thought I ought to wait no longer."[5]

Indeed, Mary Custis Lee believed her father was actually unaware—or unconvinced—of Virginia's secession at the time he withdrew from the U.S. Army. Other documents show that this was not the case, though rumors and misinformation were rife at the time.[6] But her focus on military concerns compliments the justification Lee gave to his brother, Smith Lee, who was a naval officer. Lee told his brother that the conversation at the War Department had been pivotal. At that discussion Lee voiced his unwillingness to lead an invasion of the South—something Scott did not think would actually happen, but Lee believed inevitable. He also wanted to avoid receiving orders that would force him to take part in such an operation.[7]

The turmoil Lee's resignation caused at home was mirrored within the army. Mary Custis Lee describes how a cousin on Scott's staff rode over to Arlington, informing the family of the disarray her father had created at the War Department. Several other officers had quickly followed Lee's lead to quit the U.S. Army, and the old general had taken the news hard. "He laid on his sofa, refusing to see anyone & mourning, as if for the loss of a son. To some one . . . who rather lightly alluded to the fact, he said with great emotion, 'don't mention Robert Lee's name to me again, I cannot bear it.'"[8]

These are riveting details. But what is most striking about this depiction is the loneliness of Lee's decision. For the devastating message of Mary Custis Lee's account is that there was no pressure from kin or colleagues to give up the allegiances of a lifetime. Moreover, several of the Virginia counties where Lee was most closely connected would vote against the ordinance of secession. He knew that his sister, nephew, close cousins, and many Virginian army officers, including his revered General Scott, were choosing to remain with the Union. If even his wife and most of his children did not support his stand, he must personally have wanted very much to take this path. In this, our best information to date, Robert E. Lee made his decision, not in solidarity with his family, but in spite of their feelings. This was not an answer he was compelled to make for home and heritage. It was an actual *choice*, and it was his alone.

Elizabeth Brown Pryor
Richmond, Virginia
March 29, 2011

NOTES

Key to Abbreviations, Sources

AHA   Arlington House Archives, National Park Service

ANB   *American National Biography,* eds. John A. Garraty, Mark C. Carnes, 24 vols. (New York: Oxford University Press, 1999)

BLA   Kate Waller Barrett Library, Alexandria, Virginia

DE   DeButts-Ely Papers (all items in collection are photostats)

DSF   Douglas Southall Freeman Papers

DU   Special Collections, Duke University

EA-LC Ethel Armes Papers, Library of Congress

LC   Library of Congress

LFP   Lee Family Papers

LoV   Library of Virginia

MoC   Eleanor S. Brockenbrough Library, Museum of the Confederacy

NARA National Archives and Records Administration

SH   Jesse Ball duPont Library, Stratford Hall Plantation

TPA   Tudor Place Archives

USMA Special Collections, U.S. Military Academy

VHS   Virginia Historical Society

VMHB Virginia Magazine of History and Biography

WL   Special Collections, Leyburn Library, Washington and Lee University

Key to Abbreviations, People

CCL   Charles Carter Lee

EAL   Eleanor "Agnes" Lee

GWCL George Washington Custis Lee

MCL   Mary Custis Lee

MCW   Martha Custis Williams ("Markie")

MiCL   Mildred Childe Lee

REL   Robert E. Lee

1.   REL to [GWCL], Fort Mason, Texas, January 23, 1861, in William Jones, *Life and Letters of Robert Edward Lee, Soldier and Man* (repro, Harrisonville, Va.: Sprinkle, 1986), pp. 120–21. The letter as reproduced by Jones is actually an amalgam of two letters, the above and one written by REL to MCL, on the same day. A transcript of the latter is in DSF-LC.

2.   REL to "My dear Son" [GWCL], San Antonio, Texas, December 14, 1860,

REL-DU; and REL to EAL, Fort Mason, Texas, January 29, 1861, DE-LC.

3. REL to Annette Carter, Fort Mason, San Antonio P.O., January 16, 1861, Lennig Collection II, WL.

4. Charles Anderson, *Texas Before and on the Eve of the Rebellion* (Cincinnati: Peter G. Thompson, 1884), p. 32; and Darrow, "Recollections of the Twiggs Surrender," p. 36. Yet another acquaintance wrote that when he spoke of secession, "he showed more emotion than is recorded of him when he had won or lost a great battle later on." George B. Cosby quoted in Col. M. L. Crimmins, "What General Robert E. Lee's Generals Thought of Him," *West Texas Historical Association Yearbook* 12 (July 1936): 99.

5. REL to MCW, January 22, 1861, in Robert E. Lee, *"To Markie": The Letters of Robert E. Lee to Martha Custis Williams*, ed. Avery O. Craven (Cambridge, Mass.: Harvard University Press, 1933), p. 58.

6. R.W. Johnson, *A Soldier's Reminiscences in Peace and War* (Philadelphia: J.B. Lippincott, 1886), p. 133.

7. REL to "My dear Son," December 14, 1860, San Antonio, Texas, REL-DU.

8. Anderson, *Texas Before and on the Eve of the Rebellion*, pp. 30–33, quotation p. 31. For Lee's use of his father's model in determining his course. see Mary Boykin Chesnut, *Mary Chesnut's Civil War*, ed. C. Vann Woodward (New Haven: Yale University Press, 1981), p. 480; and REL to CCL, Lexington, March 14, 1867, MoC.

9. Fitzhugh Lee, *General Lee* (New York: D. Appleton, 1898), p. 11; and Charles Royster, *Light-Horse Harry Lee and the Legacy of the American Revolution* (New York, Alfred A. Knopf, 1981), p. 99.

10. REL to [GWCL], Fort Mason, Texas, January 23, 1861, in Jones, *Life and Letters*, pp. 120–21; and REL to "My dear Son," December 14, 1860, San Antonio, Texas, REL-DU.

11. For Lee's racial views, see chapter 9, "Humanity and the Law"; quotation REL to EAL, Fort Mason, Texas, January 29, 1861, DE-LC.

12. REL to EAL, January 29, 1861, Fort Mason, Texas, DE-LC. Lee's affinity with secessionist principles is discussed at some length in Alan T. Nolan, *Lee Considered* (Chapel Hill: University of North Carolina Press, 1991), pp. 46–49.

13. Lee speaks of this resentment in his letter to "My dear Son," December 14, 1860, San Antonio, Texas, REL-DU, but it was an old sore with him. See, for example, Lee's complaint that the "South has had to bear some hard kicks from all sides" on the issue of slavery, in REL to Capt. A. Talcott, Arlington, February 21, 1833, LFP-VHS.

14. One writer has gone so far as to say that Lee must have had a strong gift for self-delusion. Nolan, *Lee Considered*, pp. 50–52.

15. William Allan, "Memoranda of Conversations with General Robert E. Lee," in Gary W. Gallagher, ed., *Lee the Soldier* (Lincoln: University of Nebraska Press,1996), pp. 9–10, and Erasmus D. Keyes, *Fifty years' observation of men*

and events, civil and military (New York, C. Scribner's sons, 1884), pp. 205–6; REL to Reverdy Johnson, Lexington, Va., February 25, 1868, REL Letterbook #4, LFP-VHS; REL Telegram to Genl Philip St. George Cocke, April 23, 1861, in Executive Papers of Virginia, LoV; and Douglas Southall Freeman, *R. E. Lee* (New York: Charles Scribner's Sons, 1934-5), 1: 476-77.

16. REL to EAL, Fort Mason, Texas, January 29, 1861, DE-LC.

17. C[onstance] C[ary] Harrison, "A Virginia Girl in the First Year of the War," *Century Magazine* 3, no. 4 (August 1885), p. 606; Elizabeth Blair Lee to Phillips Lee, Silver Spring, July 3, 1861, in Elizabeth Blair Lee, *Wartime Washington: The Civil War Letters of Elizabeth Blair Lee,* ed. Virginia Jean Laas (Urbana: University of Illinois Press, 1991), pp. 55–56; quotation from Miss S. Lee, "War Time in Alexandria, Virginia" *South Atlantic Quarterly* 4, no. 3 (July 1905): 235.

18. Alexander Stephens quoted in William E. Brooks, *Lee of Virginia* (repr., Westport, Colo.: Greenwood Press, 1975), p. 99.

19. REL to MCL, Fort Mason, Texas, January 23, 1861, transcript, DSF-LC; and REL to MCW, January 22, 1861, in Lee, *"To Markie,"* pp. 58–59.

20. Cassius Lee to REL, Alex[a], April 23, 1861; James May to REL, Theological Seminary of Va, April 22, 1861; and REL to Cassius Lee, Richmond, April 25, 1861, all SH.

21. Daniel W. Crofts, "Late Antebellum Virginia Reconsidered," *VMHB* 107, no. 3 (Summer 1999): 253–286; William A. Link, *Roots of Secession: Slavery and Politics in Antebellum Virginia* (Chapel Hill: University of North Carolina Press, 2003), pp. 6–7; Henry T. Shanks, *The Secession Movement in Virginia,* 1847–61 (repr., New York: AMS Press, 1971), pp. 116, 206.

22. Henry Adams, *The Education of Henry Adams* (repr., New York: Oxford University Press, 1999), p. 86.

23. Link, *Roots of Secession,* pp. 8, 138–40, 171.

24. MCL to "My Dear Helen," Arlington, February 1, 1861, LFP-VHS.

25. William E. Gienapp, *Abraham Lincoln and Civil War America* (New York: Oxford University Press, 2002), pp. 50–52; Heintzelman Diary, March 4 and March 5, 1861, Heintzelman Papers, LC.

26. Allan, "Memoranda of Conversations," p. 9.

27. W.H. Cob, "Reminiscences of Washington in 1861," Simon Cameron Papers, LC.

28. "Reminiscences of John Caldwell Tidball," Washington, 1861, LC; Heintzelman Diary, March 13, 1861, Heintzelman Papers, LC.

29. The promotion was approved by Lincoln on March 20 and tendered to Lee on March 28, 1861. He accepted on March 30. Freeman, *R. E. Lee,* 1:433.

30. James M. McPherson, *Battle Cry of Freedom* (New York: Ballantine, 1988), pp. 272–75, quotation p. 274. Hunter is quoted in Pryor, *Reminiscences of Peace and War,* p. 124.

31. Shanks, *Secession Movement in Virginia,* p. 206.

32. Elizabeth Lindsay Lomax, *Leaves from an Old Washington Diary* (New York: E.P. Dutton, 1943), p. 149.

33. "Reminiscences of Cazenove G. Lee," BLA.

34. MCL to [Benson Lossing], May 1, 1861, typescript, AHA; "Statement of Francis Blair," in James Ford Rhodes, *History of the United States from the Compromise of 1850 to the McKinley-Bryan Campaign of 1896*, 8 vols. (reprint; Port Washington: Kennikat Press, 1967), 3:252n. Elizabeth Blair Lee to Samuel Phillips Lee, May 18, 1862, in Lee, *Wartime Washington*, p. 148. Elizabeth Blair Lee was the daughter of Francis Blair and heard the story through him. This is the closest to a contemporary account that we have of the Blair–R. E. Lee meeting. Both Secretary Simon Cameron and Lee later wrote descriptions of the encounter, which substantially agree. Sec REL to Reverdy Johnson, Lexington, Va., February 25, 1868, REL Letterbook #4, LFP-VHS; Allan, "Memoranda of Conversations," pp. 9–10; and "Statement of Simon Cameron" in Jones, *Life and Letters*, p. 130.

35. Allan, "Memoranda of Conversations," p. 10; Keyes, *Fifty Years Observation*, pp. 205–6.

36. Keyes, *Fifty Years Observation*, pp. 205–6; A. M. L. Washington to Fannie W. Reading, Washington, May 13, 1861, AHA; Robert E. L. deButts Jr., ed., "Mary Custis Lee's 'Reminiscences of the War,'" *VMHB* 109, no. 2 (Spring 2001): 314; Emily V. Mason, *Popular Life of General Robert E. Lee* (Baltimore: John Murphy, 1897); Freeman, *R. E. Lee*, 1:437; "General Lee and General Scott," *National Republican*, July 12, 1861.

37. REL to Smith Lee, Arlington, Va., April 20, 1861, in Lee, *General Lee*, pp. 88–89; and "Reminiscences of Cazenove G. Lee," BLA.

38. Murray H. Nelligan, "Old Arlington" (Ph.D. dissertation, Columbia University, 1954), p. 450.; quotation in Miss S. Lee, "War Time in Alexandria, Virginia," *South Atlantic Quarterly* 4, no. 3 (July 1905), pp. 235–36.

39. EAL to MiCL, Arlington, April 19, 1861, DE-LC.

40. Though she would later be accused of having influenced her husband, not until Yankee troops threatened Arlington did Mary Lee become an unswervingly loyal Confederate. For accusations against Mary Lee, see "Remarks of Mrs. P. R. Alger, Annapolis, Md." 1957, Montgomery C. Meigs Papers, LC; for the Lee daughters' remark that their mother was "such an awful Unionist," sec ACL to EAL, White House, May 2, [1861], REL-DU; for MCL's Unionist statements, see MCL to "My dear Helen" [Peter], Arlington, February 1, 1861, LFP-WL; MCL to Mrs. William Henry Stiles, Arlington, February 9, 1861, SH; MCL to MiCL, Arlington, February 24, [1861]; and MCL to "my dear child" [MiCL], Arlington, [April] 19, [1861], both DE-LC; and MCL to [Benson Lossing], May 1, 1861, typescript, AHA.

41. Jim Parks, "Colored Servant of Adopted Son of George Washington, *Christian Science Monitor*, September 24, 1924.

42. George Lyttleton Upshur, *As I Recall Them: Memories of Crowded Years* (New York: Wilson-Erickson, 1936), pp. 16–17. Upshur was a cousin of the Lees.

His book contains numerous errors, but his account of Lee pacing and praying corroborates other descriptions of the scene.

43. Agnes Lee quoted in Lee, "War Time in Alexandria," p. 235–36.

44. Allan, "Memoranda of Conversations," p. 10; Upshur, *As I Recall Them,* p. 17.

45. Freeman, *R. E. Lee,* 1:431; and Clifford Dowdey, *Lee* (Boston: Little, Brown, 1965), p. 134. Even the most contemporary writers follow this theme. "Lee had no choice in the matter," writes Bertram Wyatt-Brown as recently as 2005. "Robert E. Lee and the Concept of Honor," in Peter Wallenstein and Bertram Wyatt-Brown, eds., *Virginia's Civil War* (Charlottesville: University Press of Virginia, 2005), p. 37.

46. DeButts, "Mary Custis Lee's 'Reminiscences,'" p. 314.

47. This version is from Lee's letter to his sister Ann(e) Marshall. REL to Anne Lee Marshall, Arlington, Virginia, April 20, 1861, in Robert E. Lee Jr., *Recollections and Letters of General Robert E. Lee* (New York: Garden City Publishing Co., 1904), pp. 25–26.

48. Allan, "Memoranda of Conversations," p. 10.

49. Julia Tyler to mother, Sherwood Forest, Charles City Co., April 25, 1861, in Lyon G. Tyler, *The Letters and Times of the Tylers,* 2 vols. (repr., New York: Da Capo Press, 1970), 2:648.

50. John Robertson to Governor John Letcher, Richmond, April 23, 1861, Executive Papers of John Letcher, LoV; and Freeman Cleaves, *Rock of Chickamauga: The Life of George H. Thomas* (repr., Westport, Colo.: Greenwood Press, 1974), pp. 5, 67–69.

51. William Price Craighill to mother, West Point, August 20, 1861, USMA.

52. USMA Archives; George W. Cullum, *Biographical Registe of the Officers and Graduates of the U.S. Military Academy at West Point, N.Y.* (Boston, 1891), vols. 1 and 2; and William B. Skelton, *An American Profession of Arms* (Lawrence: University Press of Kansas, 1992), p. 358.

53. Peter L. Guth, "Dennis Hart Mahan," *ANB,* 14:338–39.

54. Skelton, *American Profession of Arms,* p. 355.

55. Elizabeth Blair Lee to Samuel Phillips Lee, Silver Spring, May 18, 1862, in Lee, *Wartime Washington,* p. 148; and Apolline Blair to Frances Preston Blair, Bethlehem, September 12, 1861, in Blair and Lee Family Papers, Special Collections, Princeton University.

56. Cullum, *Biographical Register,* 2:466–67. See letters of Elizabeth Blair Lee to Samuel Phillips Lee in Lee, *Wartime Washington,* pp. 15n, 302; Edmund Jennings Lee, *Lee of Virginia* (Baltimore, Genealogical Publishing, 1974), pp. 396–98; and Upshur, *As I Recall Them,* pp. 15–16.

57. Cullum, *Biographical Register,* 2:506; and George B. McClellan to MCW, May 24, 1862, copy in MCW's hand, Carter Papers, TPA.

58. Two of Fendall's sons also fought for the Union. Captain Philip R. Fendall served with the U.S. Marines, and Clarence Fendall, with the U.S. Coast

Guard, developed maps for the U.S. Navy. A third son, Lt. James Fendall, was an officer in the CSA marines. Introduction to Fendall Papers, DU.

59. MCL to ACL, "H. Hill," August 20, 1862; and REL to MCL, Near Richmond, July 28, 1862, both DE-LC.

60. Chesnut, *Diary*, p. 480.

61. Elizabeth Blair Lee to Samuel Phillips Lee, Philadelphia, June 4, 1861, in Lee, *Wartime Washington*, p. 43; and Chesnut, *Diary*, p. 131.

62. MCL to "My dear Helen" [Peter], Arlington, February 1, 1861, LFP-WL; MCL to Mrs. William Henry Stiles, Arlington, February 9, 1861, SH; MeL to MiCL, Arlington, February 24, [1861]; and MCL to "my dear child" [MCL], Arlington, [April] 19, [1861], both DE-LC.

63. Custis Lee was among those torn over the decision, reiterating his father's belief that "secession was nothing but revolution" and stating that if he had the power he would fortify Arlington Heights; he remained in the army more than a month after his father's resignation. For his and Rooney's dismay over Virginia's secession, see Lee, "War Time in Alexandria"; Bernice-Marie Yates, *The Perfect Gentleman: The Life and Letters of George Washington Custis Lee* (Longwood, Fla.: Xulon Press, 2003), 1:212–14, 223–26; and REL to MCL, May 13, 1861, in Lee, *General Lee*, p. 94. As he stated to Roger Jones and Orton Williams, Lee did not want to influence the decisions of others. "The present is a momentous question which every man must settle for himself and upon principle," he told his wife. Nonetheless, others did follow his lead. See Louise Humphrey Carter, "Reminiscences of War Days," Shirley, June 20, 1905, copy in DSF-LC; REL to "My Precious Life," Arlington, April 1, 1861, DE-LC; and Elizabeth Blair Lee to Samuel Phillips Lee, Silver Spring, July 3, 1861, in Lee, *Wartime Washington*, pp. 55–56.

64. REL to MCW, January 22, 1861, in Lee, *"To Markie,"* p. 58; and REL to Simon Cameron, Arlington, April 20, 1861, NARA.

65. REL to Smith Lee, Arlington, Virginia, April 20, 1860, in Lee, *General Lee*, pp. 88–89.

66. REL to Capt. A. Talcott, Arlington, February 21, 1833, LFP-VHS.

67. For more on the various notions of honor, and how they played into the debate on secession, see Bertram Wyatt-Brown, *Yankee Saints and Southern Sinners* (Baton Rouge: Louisiana State University Press, 1985).

68. Allan, "Memoranda of Conversations," pp. 8–10.

69. MCL to [Benson Lossing], May 1, 1861, typescript, AHA; John Robertson to Governor John Letcher, Richmond, April 23, 1861, Executive Papers of John Letcher, LoV.

70. John Robertson to Governor John Letcher, Richmond, April 23, 1861, Executive Papers of John Letcher, LoV; Lee, "War Time in Alexandria," p. 235; Harriotte Hopkins Lee Taliaferro, "Reminiscences of Robert E. Lee," typescript, BLA.

71. Alan Nolan has proposed that Lee's acceptance of a position in the Virginia forces could not have been made spontaneously in the thirty-six hours after he resigned from the U.S. Army, and has hypothesized that Lee had made prior contingency arrangements. Nolan, *Lee Considered,* pp. 44–50. However, Robertson's letter expresses great pride that no conflict of interest was in question; by the time Lee was given an official offer, he had resigned voluntarily, and "he was wholly unapprised of the generous intentions of the Convention . . . until we met [on April 22]." John Robertson to Governor John Letcher, Richmond, April 23, 1861, Executive Papers of John Letcher, LoV.

72. On March 15 Confederate Secretary of War L. P. Walker offered Lee a post as brigadier general in the army being formed—the highest rank then available in the Confederate service. Fellow Virginian George Thomas also received queries from the prosecessionist forces in Virginia around this time, and Lee may have been contacted as well. Cleaves, *Rock of Chickamauga,* pp. 5, 64–66.

73. John Robertson to Governor John Letcher, Richmond, April 23, 1861, Executive Papers of John Letcher, LoV.

74. "Reminiscences of Cazenove G. Lee," BLA; and Allan, "Memoranda of Conversations," p. 10.

75. John Esten Cooke to J. E. B. Stuart, Richmond, April 4, 1861, J. E. B. Stuart Papers, VHS.

76. One account has Lee confiding to Cassius Lee after the meetings in the churchyard that he had been tapped to lead Virginia's forces. "Reminiscences of Cazenove G. Lee," BLA. Also W. W. Scott, "Some Reminiscences of Famous Men," *Southern Magazine* 4 (July 1894): 628; and Allan, "Memoranda of Conversations," pp. 10–11.

77. Untitled newspaper clipping, Richmond, Virginia, April 23, 1861, in REL Memorandum Book, DE-LC. For a discussion of the quick turnabout from northern to southern forces, see Nolan, *Lee Considered,* pp. 41–45.

78. Oaths quoted in U.S. War Department, *General Regulations for the Army; or Military Institutes* (Washington, D.C.: Davis and Force, 1825), p. 410; and Nolan, *Lee Considered,* p. 39.

79. Elizabeth Blair Lee to Samuel Phillips Lee, Silver Spring, July 3, 1861, in Lee, *Wartime Washington,* p. 148.

80. The louse drawing is found in "Portraits and Views of Men and Events Connected with the Civil War," Box I, #8, USMA; *New York Daily Tribune,* May 9, 1861; for Lincoln's assertion that Lee was among those who should have been arrested on suspicion see Abraham Lincoln to Erastus Corning and Others, Executive Mansion; Washington, June 12, 1863, in Abraham Lincoln, *Speeches and Writing, 1859–1865,* ed. Don E. Fehrenbacher (New York: Library of America, 1989), pp. 454–63.

81. Greene's words were "Arnold the traitor must fall!—Oh Lucifer! How great will be thy fall." Nannie Rodgers Macomb to Montgomery C. Meigs, n.d. [1861], MCM-LC; and Greene quoted in 81. William Johnson, *Sketches of*

the *Life and Correspondence of Nathanael Greene*, 2 vols. (repr., New York: Da Capo Press, 1973), 2:40.

82. Hcnry Lee quoted in Royster, *Light-Horse Harry Lee*, p. 109.

83. Anna Maria Fitzhugh to CCL, November 12 [1830], Arlington, EA-LC.

84. Lee is reported as saying, "I cannot consult my own feelings in the matter." See *National Republican*, July 12, 1861.

85. This larger perspective was suggested to the author [Pryor] by David Halberstam's remarks in Thomas A. Bass, "The Spy Who Loved Us," *New Yorker* 81, no. 14 (May 23, 2005).

AUTHOR'S NOTE

1. RE Lee to Annette Carter, Fort Mason, San Antonio P.O., 16 Jan. 1861, typescript, Lennig Collection, Washington and Lee University.

2. *Ibid.*; Diary of Cornelius Walker, 26 March 1861 and 18 June 1861, Brockenbrough Library, Museum of the Confederacy; RE Lee to Mary Custis Lee, Richmond 30 April 1861, Lee Family Papers, Virginia Historical Society (hereafter VHS); RE Lee to "My dear Little H," Richmond 5 May 1861, James D. Barbor Papers, Library of Congress.

3. [Mary Custis Lee] to Dear Colonel [Charles Marshall], fragment, n.d. [Charles S. Marshall to Mary Custis Lee, Balt[imore], 14 Feb. 1871, indicates the letter was written in early February 1871], both Mary Custis Lee Papers, VHS.

4. Lee used this explanation in slightly varying forms many times. See, e.g., RE Lee to Cousin Roger [Jones], Arlington, 20 April 1861, US Military Academy; and Lee to "My dear Little H," Richmond, 5 May 1861, Barbor Papers, LC.

5. [Mary Custis Lee] to Dear Colonel [Charles Marshall], fragment, n.d. [Feb. 1871], Mary Custis Lee Papers, VHS.

6. RE Lee to Brother Smith [Lee], Arlington, 20 April 1861, in Robert E. Lee, Jr., *Recollections and Letters of General Robert E. Lee* (New York: Garden City Publishing Co., 1904), pp. 26-27; and Agnes Lee to Mildred Lee, Arlington, 19 April [1861], Lee Family Papers, VHS.

7. RE Lee to Brother Smith [Lee], Arlington, 20 April 1861, in Lee, Jr., *Recollections*, pp. 26-27; and RE Lee to Reverdy Johnson, Lexington, Virginia, 25 Feb. 1868, RE Lee Letterbook, Lee Family Papers, VHS.

8. [Mary Custis Lee] to Dear Colonel [Charles Marshall], fragment, n.d. [Feb. 1871], Mary Custis Lee Papers, VHS.

9

MARK TWAIN

"The Private History of
a Campaign That Failed"

1885

Mark Twain begins his most detailed account of his Civil War experiences by noting that his readers "have heard from a great many people who did something in the war." He does this because of the odd place in which his humorous reminiscences were first published—the *Century Magazine*'s "Battles and Leaders of the Civil War" series. Previous contributors had included Generals P. G. T. Beauregard, Lew Wallace, and Ulysses S. Grant. Perhaps fearing that his own experiences would pale too much in comparison, Twain concluded his allegedly autobiographical narrative with a shooting that never occurred. Twain's claim that he barely missed a battlefield encounter with U. S. Grant is also false, although he apparently believed it to be true.

This narrative appeared in the *Century Magazine* in December 1885.

YOU HAVE HEARD FROM A great many people who did something in the war; is it not fair and right that you listen a little moment to one who started out to do something in it, but didn't? Thousands entered the war, got just a taste of it, and then stepped out again, permanently. These, by their very numbers, are respectable, and are therefore entitled to a sort of voice,—not a loud one, but a modest one; not a boastful one, but an apologetic one. They ought not to be allowed much space among better people—people who did something—I grant that; but they ought at least to be allowed to state why they didn't do anything, and also to explain the process by which they didn't do anything. Surely this kind of light must have a sort of value.

I was visiting in the small town where my boyhood had been spent—Hannibal, Marion County. Several of us got together in a secret place by night and formed ourselves into a military company.

The first hour was all fun, all idle nonsense and laughter. But that could not be kept up. The steady trudging came to be like work; the play had somehow oozed out of it; the stillness of the woods and the somberness of the night began to throw a depressing influence over the spirits of the boys, and presently the talking died out and each person shut himself up in his own thoughts. During the last half of the second hour nobody said a word.

Now we approached a log farm-house where, according to report, there was a guard of five Union soldiers. Lyman called a halt; and there, in the deep gloom of the overhanging branches, he began to whisper a plan of assault upon that house, which made the gloom more depressing than it was before. It was a crucial moment; we realized, with a cold suddenness, that here was no jest—we were standing face to face with actual war. We were equal to the occasion. In our response there was no hesitation, no indecision: we said that if Lyman wanted to meddle with those soldiers, he could go ahead and do it; but if he waited for us to follow him, he would wait a long time.

Lyman urged, pleaded, tried to shame us, but it had no effect. Our course was plain, our minds were made up: we would flank the farm-house—go out around. And that is what we did.

We struck into the woods and entered upon a rough time, stumbling over roots, getting tangled in vines, and torn by briers. At last we reached an open place in a safe region, and sat down, blown and hot, to cool off and nurse our scratches and bruises. Lyman was annoyed, but the rest of us were cheerful; we had flanked the farm-house, we had made our first military movement, and it was a success; we had nothing to fret about, we were feeling just the other way. Horse-play and laughing began again; the expedition was become a holiday frolic once more.

Then we had two more hours of dull trudging and ultimate silence and depression; then, about dawn, we straggled into New London, soiled, heel-blistered, fagged with our little march, and all of us except Stevens in a sour and raspy humor and privately down on the war. We stacked our shabby old shot-guns in Colonel Ralls's barn, and then went in a body and breakfasted with that veteran of the Mexican war. Afterwards he took us to a distant meadow, and there in the shade of a tree we listened to an old-fashioned speech from him, full of gunpowder and glory, full of that adjective-piling, mixed metaphor, and windy declamation which were regarded as eloquence in that ancient time and that remote region; and then he swore us on the Bible to be faithful to the State of Missouri and drive all invaders from her soil, no matter whence they might come or under what flag they might march. This mixed us considerably, and we could not make out just what service we were embarked in; but Colonel Ralls, the practiced politician and phrase-juggler, was not similarly in doubt; he knew quite clearly that he had invested us in the cause of the Southern Confederacy. He closed the solemnities by belting around me the sword which his neighbor, Colonel Brown, had worn at Buena Vista and Molino del Rey; and he accompanied this act with another impressive blast.

Then we formed in line of battle and marched four miles to a shady and pleasant piece of woods on the border of the far-reaching expanses of a flowery prairie. It was an enchanting region for war—our kind of war.

Our scares were frequent. Every few days rumors would come that the enemy were approaching. In these cases we always fell back on some other camp of ours; we never staid where we were. But the rumors always turned out to be false; so at last even we began to grow indifferent to them. One night a negro was sent to our corn-crib with the same old warning: the enemy was hovering in our neighborhood. We all said let him hover. We resolved to stay still and be comfortable. It was a fine warlike resolution, and no doubt we all felt the stir of it in our veins—for a moment. We had been having a very jolly time, that was full of horse-play and school-boy hilarity; but that cooled down now, and presently the fast-waning fire of forced jokes and forced laughs died out altogether, and the company became silent. Silent and nervous. And soon uneasy—worried—apprehensive. We had said we would stay, and we were committed. We could have been persuaded to go, but there was nobody brave enough to suggest it. An almost noiseless movement presently began in the dark, by a general but unvoiced impulse. When the movement was completed, each man knew that he was not the only person who had crept to the front wall and had his eye at a crack between the logs. No, we were all there; all there with our hearts in our throats, and staring out toward the sugar-troughs where the forest foot-path came through. It was late, and there was a deep woodsy stillness everywhere. There was a veiled moonlight, which was only just strong enough to enable us to mark the general shape of objects. Presently a muffled sound caught our ears, and we recognized it as the hoof-beats of a horse or horses. And right away a figure appeared in the forest path; it could have been made of smoke, its mass had so little sharpness of outline. It was a man on horseback; and it seemed to me that there were others behind him. I got hold of a gun in the dark, and pushed it through a crack between the logs, hardly knowing what I was doing, I was so dazed with fright. Somebody said "Fire!" I pulled the trigger. I seemed to see a hundred flashes and hear a hundred reports, then I saw the man fall down out of the saddle. My first feeling was of surprised gratification; my first impulse was an apprentice-sportsman's impulse to run and pick up his game. Somebody said, hardly audibly, "Good—we've got him!—wait for the rest." But the rest did not come. We waited—listened—still no more came. There was not a sound, not the whisper of a leaf; just perfect stillness; an uncanny kind of stillness, which was all the more uncanny on account of the damp, earthy, late-night smells now rising and pervading it. Then, wondering, we crept stealthily out, and approached the man. When we got to him the moon revealed him distinctly. He was lying on his back, with his arms abroad; his mouth was open and his chest heaving with long gasps, and his white shirt-front was all splashed with blood. The thought shot through me that I was a murderer; that I had killed a man—a man who had never done me any harm. That was the coldest sensation that ever went through my marrow. I was down by him in a moment, helplessly stroking his forehead; and I would have given anything then—my own life freely—to make him again what he had been five minutes before. And all the boys seemed to be feeling in the same way; they hung over him, full of pitying interest, and tried all they could to help him, and said all sorts of regretful things. They had forgotten all about the enemy; they thought only of this one forlorn unit of the foe. Once my imagination persuaded me that the dying man gave me a reproachful look out of his shadowy eyes, and it seemed to me that I could rather he had stabbed me than done that. He muttered and mumbled like a dreamer in his sleep, about his wife and his child; and I thought with a new despair, "This thing that I have done does not end with him; it falls upon *them* too, and they never did me any harm, any more than he."

In a little while the man was dead. He was killed in war; killed in fair and legitimate war; killed in battle, as you may say; and yet he was as sincerely mourned by the opposing force as if he had been their brother. The boys stood there a half hour sorrowing over him, and recalling the details of the tragedy, and wondering who he might be, and if he were a spy, and saying that if it were to do over again they would not hurt him unless he attacked them first. It soon came out that mine was not the only shot fired; there were five others,—a division of the guilt which was a grateful relief to me, since it in some degree lightened and diminished the burden I was carrying. There were six shots fired at once; but I was not in my right mind at the time, and my heated imagination had magnified my one shot into a volley.

The man was not in uniform, and was not armed. He was a stranger in the country; that was all we ever found out about him. The thought of him got to preying upon me every night; I could not get rid of it. I could not drive it away, the taking of that unoffending life seemed such a wanton thing. And it seemed an epitome of war; that all war must be just that—the killing of strangers against whom you feel no personal animosity; strangers whom, in other circumstances, you would help if you found them in trouble, and who would help you if you needed it. My campaign was spoiled. It seemed to me that I was not rightly equipped for this awful business; that war was intended for men, and I for a child's nurse. I resolved to retire from this avocation of sham soldiership while I could save some remnant of my self-respect. These morbid thoughts clung to me against reason; for at bottom I did not believe I had touched that man. The law of probabilities decreed me guiltless of his blood; for in all my small experience with guns I had never hit anything I had tried to hit, and I knew I had done my best to hit him. Yet there was no solace in the thought. Against a diseased imagination, demonstration goes for nothing.

The rest of my war experience was of a piece with what I have already told of it. We kept monotonously falling back upon one camp or another, and eating up the country. I marvel now at the patience of the farmers and their families. They ought to have shot us; on the contrary, they were as hospitably kind and courteous to us as if we had deserved it. In one of these camps we found Ab Grimes, an Upper Mississippi pilot, who afterwards became famous as a dare-devil rebel spy, whose career bristled with desperate adventures. The look and style of his comrades suggested that they had not come into the war to play, and their deeds made good the conjecture later. They were fine horsemen and good revolver-shots; but their favorite arm was the lasso. Each had one at his pommel, and could snatch a man out of the saddle with it every time, on a full gallop, at any reasonable distance.

In another camp the chief was a fierce and profane old black-smith of sixty, and he had furnished his twenty recruits with gigantic home-made bowie-knives, to be swung with the two hands, like the *machetes* of the Isthmus. It was a grisly spectacle to see that earnest band practicing their murderous cuts and slashes under the eye of that remorseless old fanatic.

The last camp which we fell back upon was in a hollow near the village of Florida, where I was born—in Monroe County. Here we were warned, one day, that a Union colonel was sweeping down on us with a whole regiment at his heels. This looked decidedly serious. Our boys went apart and consulted; then we went back and told the other companies present that the war was a disappointment to us and we were going to disband. They were getting ready, themselves, to fall back on some place or other, and were only waiting for General Tom Harris, who was expected to arrive at any moment; so they tried to persuade us to wait a little while, but the majority of us said no, we were accustomed to falling back, and didn't need any of Tom Harris's help; we could get along perfectly well without him— and save time too. So about half of our fifteen, including myself, mounted and left on the instant; the others yielded to persuasion and staid—staid through the war.

An hour later we met General Harris on the road, with two or three people in his company—his staff, probably, but we could not tell; none of them were in uniform; uniforms had not come into vogue among us yet. Harris ordered us back; but we told him there was a Union colonel coming with a whole regiment in his wake, and it looked as if there was going to be a disturbance; so we had concluded to go home. He raged a little, but it was of no use; our minds were made up. We had done our share; had killed one man, exterminated one army, such as it was; let him go and kill the rest, and that would end the war. I did not see that brisk young general again until last year; then he was wearing white hair and whiskers.

In time I came to know that Union colonel whose coming frightened me out of the war and crippled the Southern cause to that extent—General Grant. I came within a few hours of seeing him when he was as unknown as I was myself; at a time when anybody could have said, "Grant?—Ulysses S. Grant? I do not remember hearing the name before." It seems difficult to realize that there was once a time when such a remark could be rationally made; but there was, and I was within a few miles of the place and the occasion too, though proceeding in the other direction.

The thoughtful will not throw this war-paper of mine lightly aside as being valueless. It has this value: it is a not unfair picture of what went on in many and many a militia camp in the first months of the rebellion, when the green recruits were without discipline, without the steadying and heartening influence of trained leaders; when all their circumstances were new and strange, and charged with exaggerated terrors, and before the invaluable experience of actual collision in the field had turned them from rabbits into soldiers. If this side of the picture of that early day has not before been put into history, then history has been to that degree incomplete, for it had and has its rightful place there. There was more Bull Run material scattered through the early camps of this country than exhibited itself at Bull Run. And yet it learned its trade presently, and helped to fight the great battles later. I could have become a soldier myself, if I had waited. I had got part of it learned; I knew more about retreating than the man that invented retreating.

10

SARAH MORGAN

Excerpts from *Sarah Morgan: The Civil War Diary of a Southern Woman*

May 9 and May 17, 1862

May 9th

Our lawful (?) owners have at last arrived. About sunset day before yesterday, the Iroquois anchored here, and a graceful young Federal stepped ashore, carrying a Yankee flag over his shoulder, and asked the way to the Mayor's office.[1] I like the style! If we girls of B.R. had been at the landing instead of the men, that Yankee should never have insulted us by flying his flag in our faces! *We* would have opposed his landing except under a flag of truce; but the men let him alone, and he even found a poor Dutchman willing to show him the road! He did not accomplish much; said a formal demand would be made next day, and asked if it was safe for the men to come ashore and buy a few necessaries, when he was assured the air of B.R. was very unhealthy for Federal soldiers at night. He promised very magnanimously not [to] shell us out, if we did not molest him; but I notice none of them dare set their feet on terra-firma, except the officer who has now called three times on the Mayor,[2] and who is said to tremble visibly as he walks the streets.

Last evening came the demand: the town must [be] surrendered immediately; the federal flag Must be raised, they would grant us the same terms they granted to New Orleans. Jolly terms those were! The answer was worthy of a Southerner. It was "the town was defenseless, if we had cannon, there were not men enough to resist; but if forty vessels lay at the landing,—it was intimated that we were in their power, and more ships coming up—we would not surrender; if they wanted, they might come Take us; if they wished the Federal flag hoisted over the Arsenal, they might put it up for themselves, the town had no control over Government property." Glorious! What a pity they did not shell the town! But they are taking us at our word, and this morning they are landing at the Garrison, and presently the Bloody banner will be floating over our heads. "Better days are coming, we'll all go right."

"All devices, signs, and flags of the confederacy shall be suppressed." So says Picayune Butler.[3] Good. I devote all my red, white, and blue silk to the manufacture of Confederate flags. As soon as one is confiscated, I make another, until my ribbon is exhausted, when I will sport a duster emblazoned in high colors, "Hurra! for the Bonny blue flag!" Henceforth, I wear one pinned to my bosom—not a duster, but a little flag—the man who says take it off, will have to pull it off for himself; the man who dares attempt it—well! a pistol in my pocket will fill up the gap. I am capable, too.

This is a dreadful war to make even the hearts of women so bitter! I hardly know myself these last few weeks. I, who have such a horror of bloodshed, consider even killing in self defense murder, who cannot wish them the slightest evil, whose only prayer is to have them sent back in peace to their own country, *I* talk of killing them! for what else do I wear a pistol and carving knife? I am afraid I *will* try them on the first one who says an insolent word to me. Yes, and repent for ever after in sack cloth and ashes! O if I was only a man! Then I could don the breeches, and slay them with a will! If some few Southern women were in the ranks, they could set the men an example they would not blush to follow. Pshaw! there are *no* women here! We are *all* men!

May 17th

One of these days, when we are at peace, and all quietly settled in some corner of this wide world without anything particularly exciting to alarm us every few moments, and with the knowledge of what is the Future to us now, and will be the Past to us then, seeing it has all come right in the end, and has been for the best, we will wonder how we could ever have been foolish enough to await each day and hour with such anxiety, and if it were really possible that half the time as we lay down to sleep, we did not know but that we might be homeless and beggars in the morning. It will look unreal then; we will say it was imagination; but it is bitterly true now.

The Yankees left us some four days ago, to attack Vicksburg, leaving their flag flying in the Garrison, without a man to protect it, with the understanding that the town would be held responsible for it. It was meant for a trap, and the bait took, for night before last it was pulled down, and torn to pieces. Now, unless Will will have the kindness to sink a dozen of their ships up there—I hear he has command of the lower batteries—they will be back in a few days, and will execute their threat of shelling the town. If they do, what will become of us? All we expect, in the way of earthly property, is as yet mere paper; which will be so much trash if the South is ruined, as it consists of debts due father by many planters for professional services rendered, who, of course, will be ruined too, so all money is gone.

That is nothing; we will not be ashamed to earn our bread, so let it go. But this house, is really something to us, a shelter from the weather at least, if all associations and pecuniary values were put aside, and our servants too, we are loath to part with. Here the Yankees are on the side of the river, longing for an opportunity of "giving us a lesson," and a band of guerillas now organizing just back of us who will soon number over two thousand, are generally eager to have a "brush" with the enemy. With fire front and rear what chance is there for poor Baton Rouge? We will be burnt up in a few hours, with these people fighting over our heads, as it were.

The men say all women and children must be removed. Where to? Charlie suggests Greenwell for us. If we go, even if the town is spared the ordeal of fire, our house will be broken open by the soldiers and pillaged, for Butler has decreed that no unoccupied house will be respected. If we stay and witness the fight, if *they* are victorious, we are subject to hourly insult, for I understand that the officers who were here said "if the people did not treat them decently, they would know what it was, when Billy Wilson's crew got here. *They* would give them a lesson!" That select crowd is now in the city. Heaven help us when they will reach here! It is these small cities which suffer the greatest outrages. What are we to do?

A new proclamation from Butler has just come. It seems that the ladies have an ugly way of gathering their skirts when the Federals pass, to prevent contact, and some even turn up their noses—unladylike to say the least, but which may be owing to the odor they have, which is said to be unbearable even at this early season of year. Butler says, whereas the so called *ladies* of New Orleans insult his men and officers, he gives one and all, permission to insult *any* or all who so treat them, then and there, with the assurance that the women will not receive the slightest protection from the government, and the men will all be justified.[4] I did not have time to read it, but repeat it as it was told me by mother who is in perfect despair at the brutality of the thing.

These are our brothers? None for me! Let us hope for the honor of this nation that Butler is not counted among the *gentlemen* of the land. And so, if any man takes a fancy to kiss me, or put his arm around me, he will be upheld in the outrage if he only says I pulled my dress from under his feet? That will justify them! And if we decline receiving their visits, it is another excuse to insult us, on the plea of prior insult to them!

O my brothers, George, Gibbes and Jimmy, never did we more need protection! where are you? If Charlie must go, we are defenseless. Come to my bosom O my discarded carving knife, laid aside under the impression (fate it seems) that these were *gentlemen* sent to conquer us. Come, I say, and though sheathless now, I will find you a sheath in the body of the first man who attempts to Butlerize—or brutalize—(the terms are synonymous) me! I didn't kiss *my* sweetheart even! shall I let some northern beggar take the first? With the blessing of Heaven, no! It is a hard case to kiss someone's [sic] else, if you cant kiss your own sweetheart. If I was only a man! I dont know a woman here who does not groan over her misfortune in being clothed in petticoats; why cant we fight as well as the men?

Still not a word from the boys; we hear Norfolk has been evacu-
ated but no particulars, and George was there. Gibbes is where ever
Johnston[5] is, supposed to be on the Rappahannock, but we have not
heard from either for more than six weeks, and all communication is
now cut off. And Jimmy—I groan in spirit every time I think of him.
Suppose he is lying sick, or perhaps dying, on the road? I wont think
of it. I shut my eyes tightly and say please God take care of him. O
if He will only send back the boys in safety how thankful we shall
be! I know our fate though; the men of our family who are worth
something, will die off in their prime; while we worthless women, of
no value or importance to ourselves or the rest of the world, will live
on, useless trash in creation. Pleasant, is it not?

O for Peace! If it were not for the idea that it must dawn on us
before many months were over, I would lie down and die at once.
Hope alone sustains me. Yet I do not say give up; let us all die first.
But Peace—! what a blessing it would be! No one who has not passed
through such times can appreciate it. Think of meeting your brothers and friends again—such as are spared! Think of the blessing of
lying down in quiet at night, and waking in safety in the morning,
with no thought of bomb shells breaking the silence of the night,
or of thieving lawless soldiers searching for plunder. Think of settling quietly into the life Heaven has appointed for you, whether in
comfort or poverty, content because He sends it, and because either
will be rest, and quiet at last!

NOTES

1. The officer had been sent by Captain James S. Palmer, commanding the *Iroquois*.

2. The mayor was Benjamin F. Bryan.

3. One of the nicknames given General Benjamin F. Butler, from a minstrel song
    of that name. The picayune was a small coin and Butler was a small man, or
    at least a short one. He was better known as Beast Butler for his iron-fisted
    military rule in New Orleans.

4. Butler's infamous General Orders No. 28, issued May 15, 1862, stated that
    "hereafter when any female shall by word, gesture, or movement insult or show
    contempt for any officer or soldier of the United States she shall be regarded
    and held liable to be treated as a woman of the town plying her avocation."
    *The War of the Rebellion: A Compilation of the Official Records of the Union and
    Confederate Armies* (Washington, 1880-1901), ser. I, 15:426.

5. General Joseph E. Johnston, then in command of the Army of Northern Virginia, was on the Peninsula, pulling his army back toward Richmond.

PART 3

Making Sense of Shiloh

Battle of Pittsburgh Landing, Shiloh, Tennessee:
Centre, Sunday Morning (detail), April 6, 1862, by Henri Lovie

The horrifying battle of Shiloh in April 1862 changed Americans' understanding of the Civil War. Coming almost exactly a year after Fort Sumter and the secession of Virginia, the battle near the border of Tennessee and Mississippi not only redefined the borders of the military conflict but also the boundaries of the imaginable. Thousands of men with little training and no experience in war were thrown against one another in days of inexpressible suffering and waste. A desperate and defiant effort by the Confederacy to stop the progress of the United States Army and Navy in the lower Mississippi Valley and to push the Union Army all the way back to the Ohio River, the Battle of Shiloh shattered any fantasies people had that the war would be won easily by either side. While the United States prevented the Confederacy from seizing the great victory it had imagined, the Union general—Ulysses S. Grant—was widely attacked for incompetence, and worse.

The third conversation in this series uses the battle at Shiloh to confront the experience of war. Ambrose Bierce, perhaps the best writer to emerge from the American Civil War, offers an unflinching report of what he saw in that battle. Although written in 1881, when formulaic and self-congratulatory memoirs of the war dominated, Bierce wrote in a self-mocking, disillusioned tone. Four years later, Ulysses S. Grant, the great hero of the war and former president of the United States, dying of cancer, told his own version of Shiloh. In what is often considered one of the finest pieces of writing to come out of the war, Grant's *Personal Memoirs* views the battle from the perspective of the general responsible for coordinating the movements of tens of thousands of men, many of whom will be killed or shattered for life as a result.

Shelby Foote, later famous for his three-volume history of the war, juxtaposes the perspectives of Northerners and Southerners, enlisted men and officers, in his 1952 novel named after the battle at Shiloh. Foote, like Bierce, depicts battle as barely ordered chaos. In this selection, Foote adopts the perspective of a young Mississippi man, a boy really, who sees war for the first time. His innocence strips away the bombast of speeches he can barely hear.

In a very different kind of imagining, written thirty years after Foote's, Bobbie Ann Mason uses Shiloh as a window on life in our own times. The gory battlefield has become a picnic spot, a manicured park where a husband hopes that broken lives can be put back together. The final selection for this conversation is only a single page long and out of chronological order: a letter from Confederate General Braxton Bragg to his troops a few weeks after Shiloh. In his words, we see the fierce dreams that would keep the Confederacy alive for three more years, unbowed by the horror at Shiloh.

This discussion adds a new dimension to the five sessions: conversation across time as well as genre, focused on a single battle. As you read the various accounts, notice what we can learn and not learn from each witness. Is Grant's perspective truer than Bierce's or Bragg's? What gives an account veracity? What responsibility do writers of fiction have to historical accuracy? Does Mason's story trivialize the memory of Shiloh or honestly connect us to the emotions many people today would feel?

To learn more about Shiloh, you may want to read Larry J. Daniel, *Shiloh: The Battle that Changed the Civil War* (1997) and Stephen D. Engle, *Struggle for the Heartland: The Campaigns from Fort Henry to Corinth* (2001), which places Shiloh within the larger context of the western campaign in early 1862.

11

AMBROSE BIERCE

"What I Saw of Shiloh"

1881

I

This is a simple story of a battle; such a tale as may be told by a soldier who is no writer to a reader who is no soldier.

The morning of Sunday, the sixth day of April, 1862, was bright and warm. Reveille had been sounded rather late, for the troops, wearied with long marching, were to have a day of rest. The men were idling about the embers of their bivouac fires; some preparing breakfast, others looking carelessly to the condition of their arms and accoutrements, against the inevitable inspection; still others were chatting with indolent dogmatism on that never-failing theme, the end and object of the campaign. Sentinels paced up and down the confused front with a lounging freedom of mien and stride that would not have been tolerated at another time. A few of them limped unsoldierly in deference to blistered feet. At a little distance in rear of the stacked arms were a few tents out of which frowsyheaded officers occasionally peered, languidly calling to their servants to fetch a basin of water, dust a coat or polish a scabbard. Trim young mounted orderlies, bearing dispatches obviously unimportant, urged their lazy nags by devious ways amongst the men, enduring with unconcern their good-humored raillery, the penalty of superior station. Little negroes of not very clearly defined status and function lolled on their stomachs, kicking their long, bare heels[1] in the sunshine, or slumbered peacefully, unaware of the practical waggery prepared by white hands for their undoing.

Presently the flag hanging limp and lifeless at headquarters was seen to lift itself spiritedly from the staff. At the same instant was heard a dull, distant sound like the heavy breathing of some great animal below the horizon. The flag had lifted its head to listen. There was a momentary lull in the hum of the human swarm; then, as the flag drooped the hush passed away. But there were some hundreds more men on their feet than before; some thousands of hearts beating with a quicker pulse.

Again the flag made a warning sign, and again the breeze bore to our ears the long, deep sighing of iron lungs. The division, as if it had received the sharp word of command, sprang to its feet, and stood in groups at "attention." Even the little blacks got up. I have since seen similar effects produced by earthquakes; I am not sure but the ground was trembling then. The mess-cooks, wise in their generation, lifted the steaming camp-kettles off the fire and stood by to cast out. The mounted orderlies had somehow disappeared. Officers came ducking from beneath their tents and gathered in groups. Headquarters had become a swarming hive.

The sound of the great guns now came in regular throbbings—the strong, full pulse of the fever of battle. The flag flapped excitedly, shaking out its blazonry of stars and stripes with a sort of fierce delight. Toward the knot of officers in its shadow dashed from somewhere—he seemed to have burst out of the ground in a cloud of dust—a mounted aide-de-camp, and on the instant rose the sharp, clear notes of a bugle, caught up and repeated, and passed on by other bugles, until the level reaches of brown fields, the line of woods trending away to far hills, and the unseen valleys beyond were "telling of the sound," the farther, fainter strains half drowned in ringing cheers as the men ran to range themselves behind the stacks of arms. For this call was not the wearisome "general" before which the tents go down; it was the exhilarating "assembly," which goes to the heart as wine and stirs the blood like the kisses of a beautiful woman. Who that has heard it calling to him above the grumble of great guns can forget the wild intoxication of its music?

II

The Confederate forces in Kentucky and Tennessee had suffered a series of reverses, culminating in the loss of Nashville.[2] The blow was severe: immense quantities of war material had fallen to the victor, together with all the important strategic points. General Johnston[3] withdrew Beauregard's[4] army to Corinth, in northern Mississippi, where he hoped so to recruit and equip it as to enable it to assume the offensive and retake the lost territory.

The town of Corinth was a wretched place—the capital of a swamp. It is a two days' march west of the Tennessee River, which here and for a hundred and fifty miles farther, to where it falls into the Ohio at Paducah, runs nearly north. It is navigable to this point—that is to say, to Pittsburg Landing, where Corinth got to it by a road worn through a thickly wooded country seamed with ravines and bayous, rising nobody knows where and running into the river under sylvan arches heavily draped with Spanish moss. In some places they were obstructed by fallen trees. The Corinth road was at certain seasons a branch of the Tennessee River. Its mouth was Pittsburg Landing. Here in 1862 were some fields and a house or two; now there are a national cemetery and other improvements.

It was at Pittsburg Landing that Grant established his army, with a river in his rear and two toy steamboats as a means of communication with the east side, whither General Buell with thirty thousand men was moving from Nashville to join him. The question has been asked, Why did General Grant occupy the enemy's side of the river in the face of a superior force before the arrival of Buell? Buell had a long way to come; perhaps Grant was weary of waiting.[5] Certainly Johnston was, for in the gray of the morning of April 6th, when Buell's leading division was *en bivouac* near the little town of Savannah, eight or ten miles below, the Confederate forces, having moved out of Corinth two days before, fell upon Grant's advance brigades and destroyed them. Grant was at Savannah, but hastened to the Landing in time to find his camps in the hands of the enemy and the remnants of his beaten army cooped up with an impassable river at their backs for moral support. I have related how the news of this affair came to us at Savannah. It came on the wind—a messenger that does not bear copious details.

III

On the side of the Tennessee River, over against Pittsburg Landing, are some low bare hills, partly inclosed by a forest. In the dusk of the evening of April 6 this open space, as seen from the other side of the stream—whence, indeed, it was anxiously watched by thousands of eyes, to many of which it grew dark long before the sun went down—would have appeared to have been ruled in long, dark lines, with new lines being constantly drawn across. These lines were the regiments of Buell's leading division, which having moved up from Savannah through a country presenting nothing but interminable swamps and pathless "bottom lands," with rank overgrowths of jungle, was arriving at the scene of action breathless, footsore and faint with hunger. It had been a terrible race; some regiments had lost a third of their number from fatigue, the men dropping from the ranks as if shot, and left to recover or die at their leisure. Nor was the scene to which they had been invited likely to inspire the moral confidence that medicines physical fatigue. True, the air was full of thunder and the earth was trembling beneath their feet; and if there is truth in the theory of the conversion of force, these men were storing up energy from every shock that burst its waves upon their bodies. Perhaps this theory may better than another explain the tremendous endurance of men in battle. But the eyes reported only matter for despair.

Before us ran the turbulent river, vexed with plunging shells and obscured in spots by blue sheets of low-lying smoke. The two little steamers were doing their duty well. They came over to us empty and went back crowded, sitting very low in the water, apparently on the point of capsizing. The farther edge of the water could not be seen; the boats came out of the obscurity, took on

their passengers and vanished in the darkness. But on the heights
above, the battle was burning brightly enough; a thousand lights
kindled and expired in every second of time. There were broad
flushings in the sky, against which the branches of the trees
showed black. Sudden flames burst out here and there, singly and
in dozens. Fleeting streaks of fire crossed over to us by way of
welcome. These expired in blinding flashes and fierce little rolls of
smoke, attended with the peculiar metallic ring of bursting shells,
and followed by the musical humming of the fragments as they
struck into the ground on every side, making us wince, but doing
little harm. The air was full of noises. To the right and the left the
musketry rattled smartly and petulantly; directly in front it sighed
and growled. To the experienced ear this meant that the death-
line was an arc of which the river was the chord. There were deep,
shaking explosions and smart shocks; the whisper of stray bullets
and the hurtle of conical shells; the rush of round shot. There were
faint, desultory cheers, such as announce a momentary or partial
triumph. Occasionally, against the glare behind the trees, could
be seen moving black figures, singularly distinct but apparently
no longer than a thumb. They seemed to me ludicrously like the
figures of demons in old allegorical prints of hell. To destroy these
and all their belongings the enemy needed but another hour of
daylight; the steamers in that case would have been doing him fine
service by bringing more fish to his net. Those of us who had the
good fortune to arrive late could then have eaten our teeth in im-
potent rage. Nay, to make his victory sure it did not need that the
sun should pause in the heavens; one of the many random shots
falling into the river would have done the business had chance directed it into the engine-room of a steamer. You can perhaps fancy
the anxiety with which we watched them leaping down.

But we had two other allies besides the night. Just where the
enemy had pushed his right flank to the river was the mouth of
a wide bayou, and here two gunboats had taken station. They too
were of the toy sort, plated perhaps with railway metals, perhaps
with boiler-iron. They staggered under a heavy gun or two each. The
bayou made an opening in the high bank of the river. The bank was

a parapet, behind which the gunboats crouched, firing up the bayou as through an embrasure. The enemy was at this disadvantage: he could not get at the gunboats, and he could advance only by exposing his flank to their ponderous missiles, one of which would have broken a half-mile of his bones and made nothing of it. Very annoying this must have been—these twenty gunners beating back an army because a sluggish creek had been pleased to fall into a river at one point rather than another. Such is the part that accident may play in the game of war.

As a spectacle this was rather fine. We could just discern the black bodies of these boats, looking very much like turtles. But when they let off their big guns there was a conflagration. The river shuddered in its banks, and hurried on, bloody, wounded, terrified! Objects a mile away sprang toward our eyes as a snake strikes at the face of its victim. The report stung us to the brain, but we blessed it audibly. Then we could hear the great shell tearing away through the air until the sound died out in the distance; then, a surprisingly long time afterward, a dull, distant explosion and a sudden silence of small-arms told their own tale.

IV

There was, I remember, no elephant on the boat that passed us across that evening, nor, I think, any hippopotamus. These would have been out of place. We had, however, a woman. Whether the baby was somewhere on board I did not learn. She was a fine creature, this woman; somebody's wife. Her mission, as she understood it, was to inspire the failing heart with courage; and when she selected mine I felt less flattered by her preference than astonished by her penetration. How did she learn? She stood on the upper deck with the red blaze of battle bathing her beautiful face, the twinkle of a thousand rifles mirrored in her eyes; and displaying a small ivory-handled pistol, she told me in a sentence punctuated by the thunder of great guns that if it came to the worst she would do her duty like a man! I am proud to remember that I took off my hat to this little fool.

V

Along the sheltered strip of beach between the river bank and the water was a confused mass of humanity—several thousands of men. They were mostly unarmed; many were wounded; some dead. All the camp-following tribes were there; all the cowards; a few officers. Not one of them knew where his regiment was, nor if he had a regiment. Many had not. These men were defeated, beaten, cowed. They were deaf to duty and dead to shame. A more demented crew never drifted to the rear of broken battalions. They would have stood in their tracks and been shot down to a man by a provost-marshal's guard, but they could not have been urged up that bank. An army's bravest men are its cowards. The death which they would not meet at the hands of the enemy they will meet at the hands of their officers, with never a flinching.

Whenever a steamboat would land, this abominable mob had to be kept off her with bayonets; when she pulled away, they sprang on her and were pushed by scores into the water, where they were suffered to drown one another in their own way. The men disembarking insulted them, shoved them, struck them. In return they expressed their unholy delight in the certainty of our destruction by the enemy.

By the time my regiment had reached the plateau night had put an end to the struggle. A sputter of rifles would break out now and then, followed perhaps by a spiritless hurrah. Occasionally a shell from a faraway battery would come pitching down somewhere near, with a whir crescendo, or flit above our heads with a whisper like that made by the wings of a night bird, to smother itself in the river. But there was no more fighting. The gunboats, however, blazed away at set intervals all night long, just to make the enemy uncomfortable and break him of his rest.

For us there was no rest. Foot by foot we moved through the dusky fields, we knew not whither. There were men all about us, but no campfires; to have made a blaze would have been madness. The men were of strange regiments; they mentioned the names of unknown generals. They gathered in groups by the wayside, asking eagerly our numbers. They recounted the depressing incidents of the day. A thoughtful officer shut their mouths with a sharp word as he passed; a wise one coming after encouraged them to repeat their doleful tale all along the line.

Hidden in hollows and behind clumps of rank brambles were large tents, dimly lighted with candles, but looking comfortable. The kind of comfort they supplied was indicated by pairs of men entering and reappearing, bearing litters; by low moans from within and by long rows of dead with covered faces outside. These tents were constantly receiving the wounded, yet were never full; they were continually ejecting the dead, yet were never empty. It was as if the helpless had been carried in and murdered, that they might not hamper those whose business it was to fall to-morrow.

The night was now black-dark; as is usual after a battle, it had begun to rain. Still we moved; we were being put into position by somebody. Inch by inch we crept along, treading on one another's heels by way of keeping together. Commands were passed along the line in whispers; more commonly none were given. When the men had pressed so closely together that they could advance no farther they stood stock-still, sheltering the locks of their rifles with their ponchos. In this position many fell asleep. When those in front suddenly stepped away those in the rear, roused by the tramping, hastened after with such zeal that the line was soon choked again. Evidently the head of the division was being piloted at a snail's pace by some one who did not feel sure of his ground. Very often we struck our feet against the dead; more frequently against those who still had spirit enough to resent it with a moan. These were lifted carefully to one side and abandoned. Some had sense enough to ask in their weak way for water. Absurd! Their clothes were soaken, their hair dank; their white faces, dimly discernible, were clammy and cold. Besides, none of us had any water. There was plenty coming, though, for before midnight a thunderstorm broke upon us with great violence. The rain, which had for hours been a dull drizzle, fell with a copiousness that stifled us; we moved in running water up to our ankles. Happily, we were in a forest of great trees heavily "decorated" with Spanish moss, or with an enemy standing to his guns the disclosures of the lightning might have been inconvenient. As it was, the incessant blaze enabled us to consult our watches and encouraged us by displaying our numbers; our black, sinuous line, creeping like a giant serpent beneath the trees, was apparently interminable. I am almost ashamed to say how sweet I found the companionship of those coarse men.

So the long night wore away, and as the glimmer of morning crept in through the forest we found ourselves in a more open country. But where? Not a sign of battle was here. The trees were neither splintered nor scarred, the underbrush was unmown, the ground had no footprints but our own. It was as if we had broken into glades sacred to eternal silence. I should not have been surprised to see sleek leopards come fawning about our feet, and milk-white deer confront us with human eyes.

A few inaudible commands from an invisible leader had placed us in order of battle. But where was the enemy? Where, too, were the riddled regiments that we had come to save? Had our other divisions arrived during the night and passed the river to assist us? or were we to oppose our paltry five thousand breasts to an army flushed with victory? What protected our right? Who lay upon our left? Was there really anything in our front?

There came, borne to us on the raw morning air, the long, weird note of a bugle. It was directly before us. It rose with a low, clear, deliberate warble, and seemed to float in the gray sky like the note of a lark. The bugle calls of the Federal and the Confederate armies were the same: it was the "assembly"! As it died away I observed that the atmosphere had suffered a change; despite the equilibrium established by the storm, it was electric. Wings were growing on blistered feet. Bruised muscles and jolted bones, shoulders pounded by the cruel knapsack, eyelids leaden from lack of sleep—all were pervaded by the subtle fluid, all were unconscious of their clay. The men thrust forward their heads, expanded their eyes and clenched their teeth. They breathed hard, as if throttled by tugging at the leash. If you had laid your hand in the beard or hair of one of these men it would have crackled and shot sparks.

VI

I suppose the country lying between Corinth and Pittsburg Landing could boast a few inhabitants other than alligators. What manner of people they were it is impossible to say, inasmuch as the fighting dispersed, or possibly exterminated them; perhaps in merely classing them as non-saurian I shall describe them with sufficient particularity and at the same time avert from myself the natural suspicion attaching to a writer who points out to persons who do not know him the peculiarities of persons whom he does not know. One thing, however, I hope I may without offense affirm of these swamp-dwellers—they were pious. To what deity their veneration was given—whether, like the Egyptians, they worshiped the crocodile, or, like other Americans, adored themselves, I do not presume to guess. But whoever, or whatever, may have been the divinity whose ends they shaped, unto Him, or It, they had builded a temple. This humble edifice, centrally situated in the heart of a solitude, and conveniently accessible to the supersylvan crow, had been christened Shiloh Chapel, whence the name of the battle. The fact of a Christian church—assuming it to have been a Christian church—giving name to a wholesale cutting of Christian throats by Christian hands need not be dwelt on here; the frequency of its recurrence in the history of our species has somewhat abated the moral interest that would otherwise attach to it.

VII

Owing to the darkness, the storm and the absence of a road, it had been impossible to move the artillery from the open ground about the Landing. The privation was much greater in a moral than in a material sense. The infantry soldier feels a confidence in this cumbrous arm quite unwarranted by its actual achievements in thinning out the opposition. There is something that inspires confidence in the way a gun dashes up to the front, shoving fifty or a hundred men to one side as if it said, "Permit *me!*" Then it squares its shoulders, calmly dislocates a joint in its back, sends away its twenty-four legs and settles down with a quiet rattle which says as plainly as possible, "I've come to stay." There is a superb scorn in its grimly defiant attitude, with its nose in the air; it appears not so much to threaten the enemy as deride him.

Our batteries were probably toiling after us somewhere; we could only hope the enemy might delay his attack until they should arrive. "He may delay his defense if he like," said a sententious young officer to whom I had imparted this natural wish. He had read the signs aright; the words were hardly spoken when a group of staff officers about the brigade commander shot away in divergent lines as if scattered by a whirlwind, and galloping each to the commander of a regiment gave the word. There was a momentary confusion of tongues, a thin line of skirmishers detached itself from the compact front and pushed forward, followed by its diminutive reserves of half a company each—one of which platoons it was my fortune to command. When the straggling line of skirmishers had swept four or five hundred yards ahead, "See," said one of my comrades, "she moves!" She did indeed, and in fine style, her front as straight as a string, her reserve regiments in columns doubled on the center, following in true subordination; no braying of brass to apprise the enemy, no fifing and drumming to amuse him; no ostentation of gaudy flags; no nonsense. This was a matter of business.

In a few moments we had passed out of the singular oasis that had so marvelously escaped the desolation of battle, and now the evidences of the previous day's struggle were present in profusion. The ground was tolerably level here, the forest less dense, mostly clear of undergrowth, and occasionally opening out into small natural meadows. Here and there were small pools—mere discs of rainwater with a tinge of blood. Riven and torn with cannonshot, the trunks of the trees protruded bunches of splinters like hands, the fingers above the wound interlacing with those below. Large branches had been lopped, and hung their green heads to the ground, or swung critically in their netting of vines, as in a hammock. Many had been cut clean off and their masses of foliage seriously impeded the progress of the troops. The bark of these trees, from the root upward to a height of ten or twenty feet, was so thickly pierced with bullets and grape that one could not have laid a hand on it without covering several punctures. None had escaped. How the human body survives a storm like this must be explained by the fact that it is exposed to it but a few moments at a time, whereas these grand old trees had had no one to take their places, from the rising to the going down of the sun. Angular bits of iron, concavo-convex, sticking in the sides of muddy depressions, showed where shells had exploded in their furrows. Knapsacks, canteens, haversacks distended with soaken and swollen biscuits, gaping to disgorge, blankets beaten into the soil by the rain, rifles with bent barrels or splintered stocks, waist-belts, hats and the omnipresent sardine-box—all the wretched débris of the battle still littered the spongy earth as far as one could see, in every direction. Dead horses were everywhere; a few disabled caissons, or limbers, reclining on one elbow, as it were; ammunition wagons standing disconsolate behind four or six sprawling mules. Men? There were men enough; all dead, apparently, except one, who lay near where I had halted my platoon to await the slower movement of the line—a Federal sergeant, variously hurt, who had been a fine giant in his time. He lay face upward, taking in his breath in convulsive, rattling snorts, and blowing it out in sputters of froth which crawled creamily down his cheeks, piling itself alongside his neck and ears. A bullet had clipped a groove in his skull, above the temple; from this the brain protruded in bosses, dropping off in flakes and strings. I had not previously known one could get on, even in this unsatisfactory fashion, with so little brain. One of my men, whom I knew for a womanish fellow, asked if he should put his bayonet through him. Inexpressibly shocked by the cold-blooded proposal, I told him I thought not; it was unusual, and too many were looking.

VIII

It was plain that the enemy had retreated to Corinth. The arrival of our fresh troops and their successful passage of the river had disheartened him. Three or four of his gray cavalry videttes moving amongst the trees on the crest of a hill in our front, and galloping out of sight at the crack of our skirmishers' rifles, confirmed us

in the belief; an army face to face with its enemy does not employ
cavalry to watch its front. True, they might be a general and his
staff. Crowning this rise we found a level field, a quarter of a mile
in width; beyond it a gentle acclivity, covered with an undergrowth
of young oaks, impervious to sight. We pushed on into the open,
but the division halted at the edge. Having orders to conform to
its movements, we halted too; but that did not suit; we received an
intimation to proceed. I had performed this sort of service before,
and in the exercise of my discretion deployed my platoon, pushing it
forward at a run, with trailed arms, to strengthen the skirmish line,
which I overtook some thirty or forty yards from the wood. Then—
I can't describe it—the forest seemed all at once to flame up and
disappear with a crash like that of a great wave upon the beach—a
crash that expired in hot hissings, and the sickening "spat" of lead
against flesh. A dozen of my brave fellows tumbled over like tenpins.
Some struggled to their feet, only to go down again, and yet again.
Those who stood fired into the smoking brush and doggedly retired.
We had expected to find, at most, a line of skirmishers similar to
our own; it was with a view to overcoming them by a sudden *coup* at
the moment of collision that I had thrown forward my little reserve.
What we had found was a line of battle, coolly holding its fire till it
could count our teeth. There was no more to be done but get back
across the open ground, every superficial yard of which was throw-
ing up its little jet of mud provoked by an impinging bullet. We got
back, most of us, and I shall never forget the ludicrous incident of a
young officer who had taken part in the affair walking up to his colonel, who had been a calm and apparently impartial spectator, and
gravely reporting: "The enemy is in force just beyond this field, sir."

IX

In subordination to the design of this narrative, as defined by its
title, the incidents related necessarily group themselves about my
own personality as a center; and, as this center, during the few terrible hours of the engagement, maintained a variably constant relation to the open field already mentioned, it is important that the

reader should bear in mind the topographical and tactical features of the local situation. The hither side of the field was occupied by the front of my brigade—a length of two regiments in line, with proper intervals for field batteries. During the entire fight the enemy held the slight wooded acclivity beyond. The debatable ground to the right and left of the open was broken and thickly wooded for miles, in some places quite inaccessible to artillery and at very few points offering opportunities for its successful employment. As a consequence of this the two sides of the field were soon studded thickly with confronting guns, which flamed away at one another with amazing zeal and rather startling effect. Of course, an infantry attack delivered from either side was not to be thought of when the covered flanks offered inducements so unquestionably superior; and I believe the riddled bodies of my poor skirmishers were the only ones left on this "neutral ground" that day. But there was a very pretty line of dead continually growing in our rear, and doubtless the enemy had at his back a similar encouragement.

The configuration of the ground offered us no protection. By lying flat on our faces between the guns we were screened from view by a straggling row of brambles, which marked the course of an obsolete fence; but the enemy's grape was sharper than his eyes, and it was poor consolation to know that his gunners could not see what they were doing, so long as they did it. The shock of our own pieces nearly deafened us, but in the brief intervals we could hear the battle roaring and stammering in the dark reaches of the forest to the right and left, where our other divisions were dashing themselves again and again into the smoking jungle. What would we not have given to join them in their brave, hopeless task! But to lie inglorious beneath showers of shrapnel darting divergent from the unassailable sky—meekly to be blown out of life by level gusts of grape—to clench our teeth and shrink helpless before big shot pushing noisily through the consenting air—this was horrible! "Lie down, there!" a captain would shout, and then get up himself to see that his order was obeyed. "Captain, take cover, sir!" the lieutenant-colonel would shriek, pacing up and down in the most exposed position that he could find.

O those cursed guns!—not the enemy's, but our own. Had it not been for them, we might have died like men. They must be supported, forsooth, the feeble, boasting bullies! It was impossible to conceive that these pieces were doing the enemy as excellent a mischief as his were doing us; they seemed to raise their "cloud by day" solely to direct aright the streaming procession of Confederate missiles. They no longer inspired confidence, but begot apprehension; and it was with grim satisfaction that I saw the carriage of one and another smashed into matchwood by a whooping shot and bundled out of the line.

X

The dense forests wholly or partly in which were fought so many battles of the Civil War, lay upon the earth in each autumn a thick deposit of dead leaves and stems, the decay of which forms a soil of surprising depth and richness. In dry weather the upper stratum is as inflammable as tinder. A fire once kindled in it will spread with a slow, persistent advance as far as local conditions permit, leaving a bed of light ashes beneath which the less combustible accretions of previous years will smolder until extinguished by rains. In many of the engagements of the war the fallen leaves took fire and roasted the fallen men. At Shiloh, during the first day's fighting, wide tracts of woodland were burned over in this way and scores of wounded who might have recovered perished in slow torture. I remember a deep ravine a little to the left and rear of the field I have described, in which, by some mad freak of heroic incompetence, a part of an Illinois regiment had been surrounded, and refusing to surrender was destroyed, as it very well deserved. My regiment having at last been relieved at the guns and moved over to the heights above this ravine for no obvious purpose, I obtained leave to go down into the valley of death and gratify a reprehensible curiosity.

Forbidding enough it was in every way. The fire had swept every superficial foot of it, and at every step I sank into ashes to the ankle. It had contained a thick undergrowth of young saplings, every one of which had been severed by a bullet, the foliage of the prostrate tops being afterward burnt and the stumps charred. Death had put his sickle into this thicket and fire had gleaned the field. Along a line which was not that of extreme depression, but was at every point significantly equidistant from the heights on either hand, lay the bodies, half buried in ashes; some in the unlovely looseness of attitude denoting sudden death by the bullet, but by far the greater number in postures of agony that told of the tormenting flame. Their clothing was half burnt away—their hair and beard entirely; the rain had come too late to save their nails. Some were swollen to double girth; others shriveled to manikins. According to degree of exposure, their faces were bloated and black or yellow and shrunken. The contraction of muscles which had given them claws for hands had cursed each countenance with a hideous grin. Faugh! I cannot catalogue the charms of these gallant gentlemen who had got what they enlisted for.

XI

It was now three o'clock in the afternoon, and raining. For fifteen hours we had been wet to the skin. Chilled, sleepy, hungry and disappointed—profoundly disgusted with the inglorious part to which they had been condemned—the men of my regiment did everything doggedly. The spirit had gone quite out of them. Blue sheets of powder smoke, drifting amongst the trees, settling against the hillsides and beaten into nothingness by the falling rain, filled the air with their peculiar pungent odor, but it no longer stimulated. For miles on either hand could be heard the hoarse murmur of the battle, breaking out near by with frightful distinctness, or sinking to a murmur in the distance; and the one sound aroused no more attention than the other.

We had been placed again in rear of those guns, but even they and their iron antagonists seemed to have tired of their feud, pounding away at one another with amiable infrequency. The right of the regiment extended a little beyond the field. On the prolongation of the line in that direction were some regiments of another division, with one in reserve. A third of a mile back lay the remnant of somebody's brigade looking to its wounds. The line of forest bounding this end of the field stretched as straight as a wall from the right of my regiment to Heaven knows what regiment of the enemy. There suddenly appeared, marching down along this wall, not more than two hundred yards in our front, a dozen files of gray-clad men with rifles on the right shoulder. At an interval of fifty yards they were followed by perhaps half as many more; and in fair supporting distance of these stalked with confident mien a single man! There seemed to me something indescribably ludicrous in the advance of this handful of men upon an army, albeit with their left flank protected by a forest. It does not so impress me now. They were the exposed flanks of three lines of infantry, each half a mile in length. In a moment our gunners had grappled with the nearest pieces, swung them half round, and were pouring streams of canister into the invaded wood. The infantry rose in masses, springing into line. Our threatened regiments stood like a wall, their loaded rifles at "ready," their bayonets hanging quietly in the scabbards. The right wing of my own regiment was thrown slightly backward to threaten the flank of the assault. The battered brigade away to the rear pulled itself together.

Then the storm burst. A great gray cloud seemed to spring out of the forest into the faces of the waiting battalions. It was received with a crash that made the very trees turn up their leaves. For one instant the assailants paused above their dead, then struggled forward, their bayonets glittering in the eyes that shone behind the smoke. One moment, and those unmoved men in blue would be impaled. What were they about? Why did they not fix bayonets? Were they stunned by their own volley? Their inaction was maddening! Another tremendous crash!—the rear rank had fired! Humanity, thank Heaven! is not made for this, and the shattered gray mass drew back a score of paces, opening a feeble fire. Lead had scored its old-time victory over steel; the heroic had broken its great heart against the commonplace. There are those who say that it is sometimes otherwise.

All this had taken but a minute of time, and now the second Confederate line swept down and poured in its fire. The line of blue staggered and gave way; in those two terrific volleys it seemed to have quite poured out its spirit. To this deadly work our reserve regiment now came up with a run. It was surprising to see it spitting fire with never a sound, for such was the infernal din that the ear could take in no more. This fearful scene was enacted within fifty paces of our toes, but we were rooted to the ground as if we had grown there. But now our commanding officer rode from behind us to the front, waved his hand with the courteous gesture that says *après vous,* and with a barely audible cheer we sprang into the fight. Again the smoking front of gray receded, and again, as the enemy's third line emerged from its leafy covert, it pushed forward across the piles of dead and wounded to threaten with protruded steel. Never was seen so striking a proof of the paramount importance of numbers. Within an area of three hundred yards by fifty there struggled for front places no fewer than six regiments; and the accession of each, after the first collision, had it not been immediately counterpoised, would have turned the scale.

As matters stood, we were now very evenly matched, and how long we might have held out God only knows. But all at once something appeared to have gone wrong with the enemy's left; our men had somewhere pierced his line. A moment later his whole front gave way, and springing forward with fixed bayonets we pushed him in utter confusion back to his original line. Here, among the tents from which Grant's people had been expelled the day before, our broken and disordered regiments inextricably intermingled, and drunken with the wine of triumph, dashed confidently against a pair of trim battalions, provoking a tempest of hissing lead that made us stagger under its very weight. The sharp onset of another against our flank sent us whirling back with fire at our heels and fresh foes in merciless pursuit—who in their turn were broken upon the front of the invalided brigade previously mentioned, which had moved up from the rear to assist in this lively work.

As we rallied to reform behind our beloved guns and noted the ridiculous brevity of our line—as we sank from sheer fatigue, and tried to moderate the terrific thumping of our hearts—as we caught our breath to ask who had seen such-and-such a comrade, and laughed hysterically at the reply—there swept past us and over us into the open field a long regiment with fixed bayonets and rifles on the right shoulder. Another followed, and another; two—three— four! Heavens! where do all these men come from, and why did they not come before? How grandly and confidently they go sweeping on like long blue waves of ocean chasing one another to the cruel rocks! Involuntarily we draw in our weary feet beneath us as we sit, ready to spring up and interpose our breasts when these gallant lines shall come back to us across the terrible field, and sift brokenly through among the trees with spouting fires at their backs. We still our breathing to catch the full grandeur of the volleys that are to tear them to shreds. Minute after minute passes and the sound does not come. Then for the first time we note that the silence of the whole region is not comparative, but absolute. Have we become stone deaf? See; here comes a stretcher-bearer, and there a surgeon! Good heavens! a chaplain!

The battle was indeed at an end.

XII

And this was, O so long ago! How they come back to me—dimly and brokenly, but with what a magic spell—those years of youth when I was soldiering! Again I hear the far warble of blown bugles. Again I see the tall, blue smoke of camp-fires ascending from the dim valleys of Wonderland. There steals upon my sense the ghost of an odor from pines that canopy the ambuscade. I feel upon my cheek the morn- ing mist that shrouds the hostile camp unaware of its doom, and my blood stirs at the ringing rifle-shot of the solitary sentinel. Unfamiliar landscapes, glittering with sunshine or sullen with rain, come to me demanding recognition, pass, vanish and give place to others. Here in the night stretches a wide and blasted field studded with half-extinct fires burning redly with I know not what presage of evil. Again I shud- der as I note its desolation and its awful silence. Where was it? To what monstrous inharmony of death was it the visible prelude?

O days when all the world was beautiful and strange; when un- familiar constellations burned in the Southern midnights, and the mockingbird poured out his heart in the moon-gilded magnolia; when there was something new under a new sun; will your fine, far memories ever cease to lay contrasting pictures athwart the harsher features of this later world, accentuating the ugliness of the longer and tamer life? Is it not strange that the phantoms of a blood-stained period have so airy a grace and look with so tender eyes?—that I recall with difficulty the danger and death and horrors of the time, and without effort all that was gracious and picturesque? Ah, Youth, there is no such wizard as thou! Give me but one touch of thine artist hand upon the dull canvas of the Present; gild for but one moment the drear and somber scenes of to-day, and I will willingly surrender another life than the one that I should have thrown away at Shiloh.

NOTES

1. Long heels: The United States Army assisted in the scientific racism of the day by doing anthropometric measurements of black soldiers. One of its findings illustrated that African American soldiers have longer heels than white soldiers, a finding not notable itself except to racists who could claim that difference meant inferiority.

2. Nashville was occupied by federal forces under General Carlos Buell on February 25, 1862. E. B. Long, *The Civil War Day by Day: An Almanac, 1861–1865* (Garden City, N.Y.: Doubleday, 1971).

3. Albert Sidney Johnston (1803–1862), the second-highest ranking officer in the Confederacy, commanded the western theater, and was the mastermind of the attack on Grant at Shiloh, where he was killed. Bierce mistakenly puts Johnston under Beauregard when it was the other way around. Stewart Sifakis, *The Compendium of the Confederate Armies* (New York: Facts of File, 1992).

4. Pierre Gustave Toutant Beauregard (1811–1893) commanded the South Carolina troops who had fired upon Fort Sumter to start the Civil War. He took command after the death of Albert Sidney Johnston. Sifakis.

5. Major-General Ulysses S. Grant's tactics at Shiloh have been debated for seven score years since the battle. Much of the debate has to do with finger pointing between Grant and Buell. Grant has often been portrayed as drunk and Buell as slow or disloyal. For Grant's side of the story, see his *Personal Memoirs of U.S. Grant* (New York: Webster, 1885), 171–87, and "The Battle of Shiloh," *Battles and Leaders of the Civil War*, edited by Robert Underwood Johnson and Clarence Clough Buel (New York: Century, 1887-88), 1:465–86.

12

ULYSSES GRANT

Excerpt from *Personal Memoirs* *of U.S. Grant*

1885

DURING THE WHOLE OF SUNDAY I was continuously engaged in passing from one part of the field to another, giving directions to division commanders. In thus moving along the line, however, I never deemed it important to stay long with Sherman. Although his troops were then under fire for the first time, their commander, by his constant presence with them, inspired a confidence in officers and men that enabled them to render services on that bloody battle-field worthy of the best of veterans. McClernand was next to Sher-man, and the hardest fighting was in front of these two divisions. McClernand told me on that day, the 6th, that he profited much by having so able a commander supporting him. A casualty to Sherman that would have taken him from the field that day would have been a sad one for the troops engaged at Shiloh. And how near we came to this! On the 6th Sherman was shot twice, once in the hand, once in the shoulder, the ball cutting his coat and making a slight wound, and a third ball passed through his hat. In addition to this he had several horses shot during the day.

The nature of this battle was such that cavalry could not be used in front; I therefore formed ours into line in rear, to stop strag-glers—of whom there were many. When there would be enough of them to make a show, and after they had recovered from their fright, they would be sent to reinforce some part of the line which needed support, without regard to their companies, regiments or brigades.

On one occasion during the day I rode back as far as the river and met General Buell, who had just arrived; I do not remember the hour, but at that time there probably were as many as four or five thousand stragglers lying under cover of the river bluff, panic-stricken, most of whom would have been shot where they lay, without resistance, before they would have taken muskets and marched to the front to protect themselves. This meeting between General Buell and myself was on the dispatch-boat used to run between the landing and Savannah. It was brief, and related specially to his getting his troops over the river. As we left the boat together, Buell's attention was attracted by the men lying under cover of the river bank. I saw him berating them and trying to shame them into joining their regiments. He even threatened them with shells from the gunboats near by. But it was all to no effect. Most of these men afterward proved themselves as gallant as any of those who saved the battle from which they had deserted. I have no doubt that this sight impressed General Buell with the idea that a line of retreat would be a good thing just then. If he had come in by the front instead of through the stragglers in the rear, he would have thought and felt differently. Could he have come through the Confederate rear, he would have witnessed there a scene similar to that at our own. The distant rear of an army engaged in battle is not the best place from which to judge correctly what is going on in front. Later in the war, while occupying the country between the Tennessee and the Mississippi, I learned that the panic in the Confederate lines had not differed much from that within our own. Some of the country people estimated the stragglers from Johnston's army as high as 20,000. Of course this was an exaggeration.

[...]

So confident was I before firing had ceased on the 6th that the next day would bring victory to our arms if we could only take the initiative, that I visited each division commander in person before any reinforcements had reached the field. I directed them to throw out heavy lines of skirmishers in the morning as soon as they could see, and push them forward until they found the enemy, following with their entire divisions in supporting distance, and to engage the enemy as soon as found. To Sherman I told the story of the assault at Fort Donelson, and said that the same tactics would win at Shiloh. Victory was assured when Wallace arrived, even if there had been no other support. I was glad, however, to see the reinforcements of Buell and credit them with doing all there was for them to do.

During the night of the 6th the remainder of Nelson's division, Buell's army crossed the river and were ready to advance in the morning, forming the left wing. Two other divisions, Crittenden's and McCook's, came up the river from Savannah in the transports and were on the west bank early on the 7th. Buell commanded them in person. My command was thus nearly doubled in numbers and efficiency.

During the night rain fell in torrents and our troops were exposed to the storm without shelter. I made my headquarters under a tree a few hundred yards back from the river bank. My ankle was so much swollen from the fall of my horse the Friday night preceding, and the bruise was so painful, that I could get no rest.

The drenching rain would have precluded the possibility of sleep without this additional cause. Some time after midnight, growing restive under the storm and the continuous pain, I moved back to the log-house under the bank. This had been taken as a hospital, and all night wounded men were being brought in, their wounds dressed, a leg or an arm amputated as the case might require, and everything being done to save life or alleviate suffering. The sight was more unendurable than encountering the enemy's fire, and I returned to my tree in the rain.

The advance on the morning of the 7th developed the enemy in the camps occupied by our troops before the battle began, more than a mile back from the most advanced position of the Confederates on the day before. It is known now that they had not yet learned of the arrival of Buell's command. Possibly they fell back so far to get the shelter of our tents during the rain, and also to get away from the shells that were dropped upon them by the gunboats every fifteen minutes during the night.

The position of the Union troops on the morning of the 7th was as follows: General Lew. Wallace on the right; Sherman on his left; then McClernand and then Hurlbut. Nelson, of Buell's army, was on our extreme left, next to the river.

Crittenden was next in line after Nelson and on his right, Mc-Cook followed and formed the extreme right of Buell's command. My old command thus formed the right wing, while the troops directly under Buell constituted the left wing of the army. These relative positions were retained during the entire day, or until the enemy was driven from the field.

In a very short time the battle became general all along the line. This day everything was favorable to the Union side. We had now become the attacking party. The enemy was driven back all day, as we had been the day before, until finally he beat a precipitate retreat. The last point held by him was near the road leading from the landing to Corinth, on the left of Sherman and right of McClernand. About three o'clock, being near that point and seeing that the enemy was giving way everywhere else, I gathered up a couple of regiments, or parts of regiments, from troops near by, formed them in line of battle and marched them forward, going in front myself to prevent premature or long-range firing. At this point there was a clearing between us and the enemy favorable for charging, although exposed. I knew the enemy were ready to break and only wanted a little encouragement from us to go quickly and join their friends who had started earlier. After marching to within musket-range I stopped and let the troops pass. The command, CHARGE, was given, and was executed with loud cheers and with a run; when the last of the enemy broke.

DURING THIS SECOND DAY OF the battle I had been moving from right to left and back, to see for myself the progress made. In the early part of the afternoon, while riding with Colonel McPherson and Major Hawkins, then my chief commissary, we got beyond the left of our troops. We were moving along the northern edge of a clearing, very leisurely, toward the river above the landing. There did not appear to be an enemy to our right, until suddenly a battery with musketry opened upon us from the edge of the woods on the other side of the clearing. The shells and balls whistled about our ears very fast for about a minute. I do not think it took us longer than that to get out of range and out of sight. In the sudden start we made, Major Hawkins lost his hat. He did not stop to pick it up. When we arrived at a perfectly safe position we halted to take an account of damages. McPherson's horse was panting as if ready to drop. On examination it was found that a ball had struck him forward of the flank just back of the saddle, and had gone entirely through. In a few minutes the poor beast dropped dead; he had given no sign of injury until we came to a stop. A ball had struck the metal scabbard of my sword, just below the hilt, and broken it nearly off; before the battle was over it had broken off entirely. There were three of us: one had lost a horse, killed; one a hat and one a sword-scabbard. All were thankful that it was no worse.

After the rain of the night before and the frequent and heavy rains for some days previous, the roads were almost impassable. The enemy carrying his artillery and supply trains over them in his retreat, made them still worse for troops following. I wanted to pursue, but had not the heart to order the men who had fought desperately for two days, lying in the mud and rain whenever not fighting, and I did not feel disposed to positively order Buell, or any part of his command, to pursue. Although the senior in rank at the time I had been so only a few weeks. Buell was, and had been for some time past, a department commander, while I commanded only a district. I did not meet Buell in person until too late to get troops ready and pursue with effect; but had I seen him at the moment of the last charge I should have at least requested him to follow.

I rode forward several miles the day after the battle, and found that the enemy had dropped much, if not all, of their provisions, some ammunition and the extra wheels of their caissons, lightening their loads to enable them to get off their guns. About five miles out we found their field hospital abandoned. An immediate pursuit must have resulted in the capture of a considerable number of prisoners and probably some guns.

Shiloh was the severest battle fought at the West during the war, and but few in the East equalled it for hard, determined fighting. I saw an open field, in our possession on the second day, over which the Confederates had made repeated charges the day before, so covered with dead that it would have been possible to walk across the clearing, in any direction, stepping on dead bodies, without a foot touching the ground. On our side National and Confederate troops were mingled together in about equal proportions; but on the remainder of the field nearly all were Confederates. On one part, which had evidently not been ploughed for several years, probably because the land was poor, bushes had grown up, some to the height of eight or ten feet. There was not one of these left standing unpierced by bullets. The smaller ones were all cut down.

Contrary to all my experience up to that time, and to the experience of the army I was then commanding, we were on the defensive. We were without intrenchments or defensive advantages of any sort, and more than half the army engaged the first day was without experience or even drill as soldiers. The officers with them, except the division commanders and possibly two or three of the brigade commanders, were equally inexperienced in war. The result was a Union victory that gave the men who achieved it great confidence in themselves ever after.

The enemy fought bravely, but they had started out to defeat and destroy an army and capture a position. They failed in both, with very heavy loss in killed and wounded, and must have gone back discouraged and convinced that the "Yankee" was not an enemy to be despised.

[...]

Up to the battle of Shiloh I, as well as well as thousands of other citizens, believed that the rebellion against the Government would collapse suddenly and soon, if a decisive victory could be gained over any of its armies. Donelson and Henry were such victories. An army of more than 21,000 men was captured or destroyed. Bowling Green, Columbus and Hickman, Kentucky, fell in consequence, and Clarksville and Nashville, Tennessee, the last two with an immense amount of stores, also fell into our hands. The Tennessee and Cumberland rivers, from their mouths to the head of navigation, were secured. But when Confederate armies were collected which not only attempted to hold a line farther south, from Memphis to Chattanooga, Knoxville and on to the Atlantic, but assumed the offensive and made such a gallant effort to regain what had been lost, then, indeed, I gave up all idea of saving the Union except by complete conquest. Up to that time it had been the policy of our army, certainly of that portion commanded by me, to protect the property of the citizens whose territory was invaded, without regard to their sentiments, whether Union or Secession. After this, however, I regarded it as humane to both sides to protect the persons of those found at their homes, but to consume everything that could be used to support or supply armies. Protection was still continued over such supplies as were within lines held by us and which we expected to continue to hold; but such supplies within the reach of Confederate armies I regarded as much contraband as arms or ordnance stores. Their destruction was accomplished without bloodshed and tended to the same result as the destruction of armies. I continued this policy to the close of the war. Promiscuous pillaging, however, was discouraged and punished. Instructions were always given to take provisions and forage under the direction of commissioned officers who should give receipts to owners, if at home, and turn the property over to officers of the quartermaster or commissary departments to be issued as if furnished from our Northern depots. But much was destroyed without receipts to owners, when it could not be brought within our lines and would otherwise have gone to the support of secession and rebellion.

This policy I believe exercised a material influence in hastening the end.

The battle of Shiloh, or Pittsburg landing, has been perhaps less understood, or, to state the case more accurately, more persistently misunderstood, than any other engagement between National and Confederate troops during the entire rebellion. Correct reports of the battle have been published, notably by Sherman, Badeau and, in a speech before a meeting of veterans, by General Prentiss; but all of these appeared long subsequent to the close of the rebellion and after public opinion had been most erroneously formed.

I myself made no report to General Halleck, further than was contained in a letter, written immediately after the battle informing him that an engagement had been fought and announcing the result. A few days afterwards General Halleck moved his headquarters to Pittsburg landing and assumed command of the troops in the field. Although next to him in rank, and nominally in command of my old district and army, I was ignored as much as if I had been at the most distant point of territory within my jurisdiction; and although I was in command of all the troops engaged at Shiloh I was not permitted to see one of the reports of General Buell or his subordinates in that battle, until they were published by the War Department long after the event. For this reason I never made a full official report of this engagement.

13

SHELBY FOOTE

Excerpt from *Shiloh: A Novel*

1952

WHEN I WENT TO SLEEP the stars were out and there was even a
moon, thin like a sickle and clear against the night, but when I woke
up there was only the blackness and the wind sighing high in the
treetops. That was what roused me I believe, because for a minute
I disremembered where I was. I thought I was back home, woke up
early and laying in bed waiting for pa to come with the lantern to
turn me out to milk (that was the best thing about the army: no
cows) and ma was in the kitchen humming a hymn while she shook
up the stove. But then I realized part of the sound was the breathing and snoring of the men all around me, with maybe a whimper or
a moan every now and again when the bad dreams came, and I remembered. We had laid down to sleep in what they call Line of Battle
and now the night was nearly over. And when I remembered I wished
I'd stayed asleep: because that was the worst part, to lie there alone,
feeling lonely, and no one to tell you he was feeling the same.

But it was warm under the blanket and my clothes had dried and
I could feel my new rifle through the cloth where I had laid it to be
safe from the dew when I wrapped the covers round me. Then it was
the same as if theyd all gone away, or *I* had; I was back home with my
brothers and sisters again, myself the oldest by over a year, and they
were gathered around to tell me goodbye the way they did a month

ago when I left to join up in Corinth after General Beauregard sent word that all true men were needed to save the country. That was the way he said it. I was just going to tell them I would be back with a Yankee sword for the fireplace, like pa did with the Mexican one, when I heard somebody talking in a hard clear voice not like any of *my* folks, and when I looked up it was Sergeant Tyree.

"Roll out there," he said. "Roll out to fight."

I had gone to sleep and dreamed of home, but here I was, away up in Tennessee, further from Ithaca and Jordan County than I'd ever been in all my life before. It was Sunday already and we were fixing to hit them where they had their backs to the river, the way it was explained while we were waiting for our marching orders three days ago. I sat up.

From then on everything moved fast with a sort of mixed-up jerkiness, like Punch and Judy. Every face had a kind of drawn look, the way it would be if a man was picking up on something heavy. Late ones like myself were pulling on their shoes or rolling their blankets. Others were already fixed. They squatted with their rifles across their thighs, sitting there in the darkness munching biscuits, those that had saved any, and not doing much talking. They nodded their heads with quick flicky motions, like birds, and nursed their rifles, keeping them out of the dirt. I had gotten to know them all in a month and a few of them were even from the same end of the county I was, but now it was like I was seeing them for the first time, different. All the put-on had gone out of their faces—they were left with what God gave them at the beginning.

We lined up. And while Sergeant Tyree passed among us, checking us one by one to make sure everything was where it was supposed to be, dawn begun to come through, faint and high. While we were answering roll-call the sun rose big and red through the trees and all up and down the company front they begun to get excited and jabber at one another: "The sun of oyster itch," whatever that meant. I was glad to see the sun again, no matter what they called it.

One minute we were standing there, shifting from leg to leg, not saying much and more or less avoiding each other's eyes: then we were going forward. It happened that sudden. There was no bugle or drum or anything like that. The men on our right started moving and we moved too, lurching forward through the underbrush and trying to keep the line straight the way we had been warned to do, but we couldnt. Captain Plummer was cussing. "Dwess it up," he kept saying, cussing a blue streak; "Dwess it up, dod dam it, dwess it up," all the way through the woods. So after a while, when the trees thinned, we stopped to straighten the line.

There was someone on a tall claybank horse out front, a fine-looking man in a new uniform with chicken guts on the sleeves all the way to his elbows, spruce and spang as a gamecock. He had on a stiff red cap, round and flat on top like a sawed-off dice box, and he was making a speech. "Soldiers of the South!" he shouted in a fine proud voice, a little husky, and everybody cheered. All I could hear was the cheering and yipping all around me, but I could see his eyes light up and his mouth moving the way it will do when a man is using big words. I thought I heard something about defenders and liberty and even something about the women back home but I couldnt be sure; there was so much racket. When he was through he stood in the stirrups, raising his cap to us as we went by, and I recognized him. It was General Beauregard, the man I'd come to fight for, and I hadnt hardly heard a word he said.

We stayed lined up better now because we were through the worst of the briers and vines, but just as we got going good there was a terrible clatter off to the right, the sound of firecrackers mixed with a roaring and yapping like a barn full of folks at a Fourth of July dogfight or a gouging match. The line begun to crook and weave because some of the men had stopped to listen, and Captain Plummer was cussing them, tongue-tied. Joe Marsh was next to me—he was nearly thirty, middle-aged, and had seen some battle up near Bowling Green. "There you are," he said, slow and calm and proud of himself. "Some outfit has met the elephant." That was what the ones who had been in action always called it: the elephant.

They had told us how it would be. They said we would march two days and on the third day we would hit them where they were camped between two creeks with their backs to the Tennessee River. We would drive them, the colonel told us, and when they were pushed against the river we would kill or capture the whole she-bang. I didnt understand it much because what the colonel said was full of tactics talk. Later the captain explained it, and that was bet-ter but not much. So then Sergeant Tyree showed it to us by drawing lines on the ground with a stick. That way it was clear as could be.

It sounded fine, the way he told it; it sounded simple and easy. Maybe it was too simple, or something. Anyhow things didnt turn out so good when it came to doing them. On the third day we were still marching, all day, and here it was the fourth day and we were still just marching, stop and go but mostly stop—the only real dif-ference was that the column was moving sideways now, through the woods instead of on the road. From all that racket over on the right I thought maybe the other outfits would have the Yankees pushed back and captured before we even got to see it. The noise had died down for a minute, but as we went forward it swelled up again, roll-ing toward the left where we were, rifles popping and popping and the soldiers yelling crazy in the distance. It didnt sound like any elephant to me.

We came clear of the woods where they ended on a ridge over-looking a valley with a little creek running through it. The ground was open all across the valley, except where the creek bottom was overgrown, and mounted to another ridge on the other side where the woods began again. There were white spots in the fringe of trees—these were tents, I made out. We were the left brigade of the whole army. The 15th Arkansas, big men mostly, with bowie knives and rolled-up sleeves, was spread across the front for skirmishers, advanced a little way in the open. There was a Tennessee regiment on our right and two more on our left and still another at the left rear with flankers out. Then we were all in the open, lined up with our flags riffling in the breeze. Colonel Thornton was out front, be-tween us and the skirmishers. His saber flashed in the sun. Looking down the line I saw the other regimental commanders, and all their sabers were flashing sunlight too. It was like a parade just before it begins.

This is going to be what they promised us, I said to myself. This is going to be the charge.

That was when General Johnston rode up. He came right past where I was standing, a fine big man on a bay stallion. He had on a broad-brim hat and a cape and thigh boots with gold spurs that twinkled like sparks of fire. I watched him ride by, his mustache flaring out from his mouth and his eyes set deep under his forehead. He was certainly the handsomest man I ever saw, bar none; he made the other officers on his staff look small. There was a little blond-headed lieutenant bringing up the rear, the one who would go all red in the face when the men guyed him back on the march. He looked about my age, but that was the only thing about us that was alike. He had on a natty uniform: bobtail jacket, red silk neckerchief, fire-gilt buttons, and all. I said to myself, I bet his ma would have a fit if she could see him now.

General Johnston rode between our regiment and the Tennessee boys on our right, going forward to where the skirmish line was waiting. When the colonel in charge had reported, General Johnston spoke to the skirmishers: "Men of Arkansas, they say you boast of your prowess with the bowie knife. Today you wield a nobler weapon: the bayonet. Employ it well." They stood there holding their rifles and looking up at him, shifting their feet a little and looking sort of embarrassed. He was the only man I ever saw who wasnt a preacher and yet could make that high-flown way of talking sound right. Then he turned his horse and rode back through our line, and as he passed he leaned sideways in the saddle and spoke to us: "Look along your guns, and fire low." It made us ready and anxious for what was coming.

Captain Plummer walked up and down the company front. He was short, inclined to fat, and walked with a limp from the blisters he developed on the march. "Stay dwessed on me, wherever I go," he said. "And shoot low. Aim for their knees." All up and down the line the flags were flapping and other officers were speaking to their men.

I was watching toward the front, where we would go, but all I could see was that empty valley with the little creek running through it and the rising ground beyond with the trees on top. While I was looking, trying hard to see was anybody up there, all of a sudden there was a Boom! Boom! Boom! directly in the rear and it scared me so bad

I almost broke for cover. But when I looked around I saw they had brought up the artillery and it was shooting over our heads towards the left in a shallow swale. I felt real sheepish from having jumped but when I looked around I saw that the others had jumped as much as I had, and now they were joking at one another about who had been the most scared, carrying it off all brave-like but looking kind of hang-dog about it too. I was still trying to see whatever it was out front that the artillery was shooting at, but all I could see was that valley with the creek in it and the dark trees on the flanks.

I was still mixed up, wondering what it all meant, when we begun to go forward, carrying our rifles at right shoulder shift the way we had been taught to do on parade. Colonel Thornton was still out front, flashing his saber and calling back over his shoulder: "Close up, men. Close up. Guiiide centerrrrr!" The skirmishers went out of sight in the swale, the same as if they had marched into the ground. When we got to where they had gone down, we saw them again, but closer now, kneeling and popping little white puffs of smoke from their rifles. The rattle of firing rolled across the line and back again, and then it broke into just general firing. I still couldnt see what they were shooting at, specially not now that the smoke was banking up and drifting back against us with a stink like burning feathers.

Then, for the first time since we left Corinth, bugles begun to blare and it passed to the double. The line wavered like a shaken rope, gaining in places and lagging in others and all around me they were yelling those wild crazy yells. General Cleburne was on his mare to our left, between us and the 5th Tennessee. He was waving his sword and the mare was plunging and tossing her mane. I could hear him hollering the same as he would when we did wrong on the drill field—he had that thick, Irish way of speaking that came on him when he got mad. We were trotting by then.

As we went forward we caught up with the skirmishers. They had given around a place where the ground was flat and dark green and there was water in the grass, sparkling like silver. It was a bog. We gave to the right to stay on hard ground and the 5th Tennessee gave to the left; the point of swampland was between us, growing wider as we went. General Cleburne rode straight ahead, waving his sword and bawling at us to close the gap, close the gap, and before he knew what had separated us, the mare was pastern-deep in it, floundering and bucking to get rid of the general's weight. He was waving his sword with one hand and shaking his fist at us with the other, so that when the mare gave an extra hard buck General Cleburne went flying off her nigh side and landed on his hands and knees in the mud. We could hear him cussing across two hundred yards of bog. The last I saw of him he was walking out, still waving the sword, picking his knees high and sinking almost to his boot-tops every step. His face was red as fire.

The brigade was split, two regiments on the right and four on the left, with a swamp between us; we would have to charge the high ground from two sides. By this time we had passed around where the other slope came out to a point leading down to the bog and we couldnt even see the other regiments. When we hit the rise we begun to run. I could hear Colonel Thornton puffing like a switch engine and I thought to myself, He's too old for this. Nobody was shooting yet because we didnt see anything to shoot at; we were so busy trying to keep up, we didnt have a chance to see anything at all. The line was crooked as a ram's horn. Some men were pushing out front and others were beginning to breathe hard and lag behind. My heart was hammering at my throat—it seemed like every breath would bust my lungs. I passed a fat fellow holding his side and groaning. At first I thought he was shot, but then I realized he just had a stitch. It was Burt Tapley, the one everybody jibed about how much he ate; he was a great one for the sutlers. Now all that fine food, canned peaches and suchlike, was staring him in the face.

When we were halfway up the rise I begun to see black shapes against the rim where it sloped off sharp. At first I thought they were scarecrows—they looked like scarecrows. That didnt make sense, except they looked so black and stick-like. Then I saw they were moving, wiggling, and the rim broke out with smoke, some of it going straight up and some jetting toward our line, rolling and jumping with spits of fire mixed in and a humming like wasps past my ears. I thought: *Lord to God, theyre shooting; theyre shooting at me!* And it surprised me so, I stopped to look. The smoke kept rolling up and out, rolling and rolling, still with the stabs of fire mixed in, and some of the men passed me, bent forward like they were running into a high wind, rifles held crossways so that the bayonets glinted and snapped in the sunlight, and their faces were all out of shape from the yelling.

When I stopped I begun to hear all sorts of things I hadnt heard while I was running. It was like being born again, coming into a new world. There was a great crash and clatter of firing, and over all this I could hear them all around me, screaming and yelping like on a foxhunt except there was something crazy mixed up in it too, like horses trapped in a burning barn. I thought theyd all gone crazy—they looked it, for a fact. Their faces were split wide open with screaming, mouths twisted every which way, and this wild lunatic yelping coming out. It wasnt like they were yelling with their mouths: it was more like the yelling was something pent up inside them and they were opening their mouths to let it out. That was the first time I really knew how scared I was.

If I'd stood there another minute, hearing all this, I would have gone back. I thought: Luther, you got no business mixed up in all this ruckus. This is all crazy, I thought. But a big fellow I never saw before ran into me full tilt, knocking me forward so hard I nearly went sprawling. He looked at me sort of desperate, like I was a post or something that got in the way, and went by, yelling. By the time I got my balance I was stumbling forward, so I just kept going. And that was better. I found that as long as I was moving I was all right, because then I didnt hear so much or even see so much. Moving, it was more like I was off to myself, with just my own particular worries.

I kept passing men lying on the ground, and at first I thought they were winded, like the fat one—that was the way they looked to me. But directly I saw a corporal with the front of his head mostly gone, what had been under his skull spilling over his face, and I knew they were down because they were hurt. Every now and then there would be one just sitting there holding an arm or leg and groaning. Some of them would reach out at us and even call us by name, but we stayed clear. For some reason we didnt like them, not even the sight of them. I saw Lonny Parker that I grew up with; he was holding his stomach, bawling like a baby, his face all twisted and big tears on his cheeks. But it wasnt any different with Lonny—I stayed clear of him too, just like I'd never known him, much less grown up with him back in Jordan County. It wasnt a question of luck, the way some folks will tell you; they will tell you it's bad luck to be near the wounded. It was just that we didnt want to be close to them any longer than it took to run past, the way you wouldnt want to be near someone who had something catching, like smallpox.

We were almost to the rim by then and I saw clear enough that they werent scarecrows—that was a foolish thing to think anyhow. They were men, with faces and thick blue uniforms. It was only a glimpse, though, because then we gave them a volley and smoke rolled out between us. When we came through the smoke they were gone except the ones who were on the ground. They lay in every position, like a man I saw once that had been drug out on bank after he was run over by a steamboat and the paddles hit him. We were running and yelling, charging across the flat ground where white canvas tents stretched out in an even row. The racket was louder now, and then I knew why. It was because I was yelling too, crazy and blood-curdled as the rest of them.

I passed one end of the row of tents. That must have been where their officers stayed, for breakfast was laid on a table there with a white cloth nice as a church picnic. When I saw the white-flour biscuits and the coffee I understood why people called them the Feds and us the Corn-feds. I got two of the biscuits (I had to grab quick; everybody was snatching at them) and while I was stuffing one in my mouth and the other in my pocket, I saw Burt Tapley. He'd caught up when we stopped to give them that volley, I reckon, and he was holding the coffee pot like a loving-cup, drinking scalding coffee in big gulps. It ran from both corners of his mouth, down onto the breast of his uniform.

Officers were running around waving their swords and hollering. "Form!" they yelled at us. "Form for attack!" But nobody paid them much mind—we were too busy rummaging the tents. So they begun to lay about with the flats of their swords, driving us away from the plunder. It didnt take long. When we were formed in line again, reloading our guns, squads and companies mixed every which way, they led us through the row of tents at a run. All around me, men were tripping on the ropes and cussing and barking their shins on the stakes. Then we got through and I saw why the officers had been yelling for us to form.

There was a gang of Federal soldiers standing shoulder to shoulder in the field beyond the tents. I thought it was the whole Yankee army, lined up waiting for us. Those in front were kneeling under the guns of the men in the second line, a great bank of blue uniforms and rifle barrels and white faces like rows of eggs, one above another. When they fired, the smoke came at us in a solid wall. Things plucked at my clothes and twitched my hat, and when I looked around I saw men all over the ground, in the same ugly positions as the men back on the slope, moaning and whimpering, clawing at the grass. Some were gut-shot, making high yelping sounds like a turpentined dog.

Smoke was still thick when the second volley came. For a minute I thought I was the only one left alive. Then I saw the others through the smoke, making for the rear, and I ran too, back toward the tents and the slope where we'd come up. They gave us another volley as we ran but it was high; I could hear the balls screech over my head. I cleared the ridge on the run, and when I came over I saw them stopping. I pulled up within twenty yards or so and lay flat on the ground, panting.

No bullets were falling here but everybody laid low because they were crackling and snapping in the air over our heads on a line with the rim where our men were still coming over. They would come over prepared to run another mile, and then they would see us lying there and they would try to stop, stumbling and sliding downhill.

I saw one man come over, running sort of straddle-legged, and just as he cleared the rim I saw the front of his coat jump where the shots came through. He was running down the slope, stone dead already, the way a deer will do when it's shot after picking up speed. This man kept going for nearly fifty yards downhill before his legs stopped pumping and he crashed into the ground on his stomach. I could see his face as he ran, and there was no doubt about it, no doubt at all: he was dead and I could see it in his face.

That scared me worse than anything up to then. It wasnt really all that bad, looking back on it: it was just that he'd been running when they shot him and his drive kept him going down the slope. But it seemed so wrong, so scandalous, somehow so un*religious* for a dead man to have to keep on fighting—or running, anyhow—that it made me sick at my stomach. I didnt want to have any more to do with the war if this was the way it was going to be.

They had told us we would push them back to the river. Push, they said; that was the word they used. I really thought we were going to push them—with bullets and bayonets of course, and of course I knew there were going to be men killed: I even thought I might get killed myself; it crossed my mind a number of times. But it wasnt the way they said. It wasnt that way at all. Because even the dead and dying didnt have any decency about them—first the Yankees back on the slope, crumpled and muddy where their own men had overrun them, then the men in the field beyond the tents, yelping like gut- shot dogs while they died, and now this one, this big fellow running straddle-legged and stone cold dead in the face, that wouldnt stop running even after he'd been killed.

I was what you might call unnerved, for they may warn you there's going to be bleeding in battle but you dont believe it till you see the blood. What happened from then on was all mixed up in the smoke. We formed again and went back through the tents. But the same thing happened: they were there, just as before, and when they threw that wall of smoke and humming bullets at us, we came running back down the slope. Three times we went through and it was the same every time. Finally a fresh brigade came up from the reserve and we went through together.

This trip was different—we could tell it even before we got started. We went through the smoke and the bullets, and that was the first time we used bayonets. For a minute it was jab and slash, everyone yelling enough to curdle your blood just with the shrill-ness. I was running, bent low with the rifle held out front, the way they taught me, and all of a sudden I saw I was going to have it with a big Yank wearing his coat unbuttoned halfway, showing a red flannel undershirt. I was running and he was waiting, braced, and it occurred to me, the words shooting through my mind: What kind of a man is this, would wear a red wool undershirt in April?

I saw his face from below, but he had bent down and his eyebrows were drawn in a straight line like a black bar over his eyes. He was full-grown, with a wide brown mustache; I could see the individual hairs on each side of the shaved line down the middle. I'd have had to say Sir to him back home. Then something hit my arm a jar—I stumbled against him, lifting my rifle and falling sideways. Ee! I'm killed! I thought. He turned with me and we were falling, first a slow fall the way it is in dreams, then sudden, and the ground came up and hit me: ho! We were two feet apart, looking at each other. He seemed even bigger now, up close, and there was something wrong with the way he looked. Then I saw why.

My bayonet had gone in under his jaw, the hand-guard tight against the bottom of his chin, and the point must have stuck in his head bone because he appeared to be trying to open his mouth but couldnt. It was like he had a mouthful of something bitter and couldnt spit—his eyes were screwed up, staring at me and blinking a bit from the strain. All I could do was look at him; I couldnt look away, no matter how I tried. A man will look at something that is making him sick but he cant stop looking until he begins to vomit—something holds him. That was the way it was with me. Then, while I was watching him, this fellow reached up and touched the handle of the bayonet under his chin. He touched it easy, using the tips of his fingers, tender-like. I could see he wanted to grab and pull it out but he was worried about how much it would hurt and he didnt dare.

I let go of the rifle and rolled away. There were bluecoats running across the field and through the woods beyond. All around me men were kneeling and shooting at them like rabbits as they ran. Captain Plummer and two lieutenants were the only officers left on their feet. Two men were bent over Colonel Thornton where they had propped him against a tree with one of his legs laid crooked. Captain Plummer wasnt limping now—he'd forgotten his blisters, I reckon. He wasnt even hurt, so far as I could see, but the skirt of his coat was ripped where somebody had taken a swipe at him with a bayonet or a saber.

He went out into the open with a man carrying the colors, and then begun to wave his sword and call in a high voice: "6th Mississippi, wally here! 6th Mississippi, wally here!"

Men begun straggling over, collecting round the flag, so I got up and went over with them. We were a sorry lot. My feet were so heavy I could barely lift them, and I had to carry my left arm with my right, the way a baby would cradle a doll. The captain kept calling, "Wally here! 6th Mississippi, wally here!" but after a while he saw there werent any more to rally so he gave it up. There were a little over a hundred of us, all that were left out of the four hundred and twenty-five that went in an hour before.

Our faces were gray, the color of ashes. Some had powder burns red on their cheeks and foreheads and running back into singed patches in their hair. Mouths were rimmed with grime from biting cartridges, mostly a long smear down one corner, and hands were blackened with burnt powder off the ramrods. We'd aged a lifetime since the sun came up. Captain Plummer was calling us to rally, rally here, but there wasnt much rally left in us. There wasnt much left in me, anyhow. I felt so tired it was all I could do to make it to where the flag was. I was worried, too, about not having my rifle. I remembered what Sergeant Tyree was always saying: "Your rifle is your best friend. Take care of it." But if that meant pulling it out of the man with the mustache, it would just have to stay there. Then I looked down and be durn if there wasnt one just like it at my feet. I picked it up, stooping and nursing my bad arm, and stood there with it.

Joe Marsh was next to me. At first I didnt know him. He didnt seem bad hurt, but he had a terrible look around the eyes and there was a knot on his forehead the size of a walnut where some Yank had bopped him with a rifle butt. I thought to ask him how the Tennessee breed of elephant compared with the Kentucky breed, but I didnt. He looked at me, first in the face till he finally recognized me, then down at my arm.

"You better get that tended to."

"It dont hurt much," I said.

"All right. Have it your way."

He didnt pay me any mind after that. He had lorded it over

me for a month about being a greenhorn, yet here I was, just gone through meeting as big an elephant as any he had met, and he was still trying the same high-and-mightiness. He was mad now because he wasnt the only one who had seen some battle. He'd had his big secret to throw up to us, but not any more. We all had it now.

We were milling around like ants when their hill is upset, trying to fall-in the usual way, by platoons and squads, but some were all the way gone and others had only a couple of men. So we gave that up and just fell-in in three ranks, not even making a good-sized company. Captain Plummer went down the line, looking to see who was worst hurt. He looked at the way I was holding my arm.

"Bayonet?"

"Yes sir."

"Cut you bad?"

"It dont hurt much, captain. I just cant lift it no higher than this."

He looked me in the face, and I was afraid he thought I was lying to keep from fighting any more. "All wight," he said. "Fall out and join the others under that twee."

There were about two dozen of us under it when he got through, including some that hadnt been able to get in ranks in the first place. They were hacked up all kinds of ways. One had lost an ear and he was the worst worried man of the lot; "Does it look bad?" he kept asking, wanting to know how it would seem to the folks back home. We sat under the tree and watched Captain Plummer march what was left of the regiment away. They were a straggly lot. We were supposed to wait there under the tree till the doctor came.

We waited, hearing rifles clattering and cannons booming and men yelling further and further in the woods, and the sun climbed up and it got burning hot. I could look back over the valley where we had charged. It wasnt as wide as it had been before. There were men left all along the way, lying like bundles of dirty clothes. I had a warm, lazy feeling, like on a summer Sunday in the scuppernong arbor back home; next thing I knew I was sound asleep. Now that was strange. I was never one for sleeping in the daytime, not even in that quiet hour after dinner when all the others were taking their naps.

When I woke up the sun was past the overhead and only a dozen or so of the wounded were still there. The fellow next to me (he was hurt in the leg) said they had drifted off to find a doctor. "Aint no doctor coming here," he said. "They aint studying us now we're no more good to them." He had a flushed look, like a man in a fever, and he was mad at the whole army, from General Johnston down to me.

My arm was stiff and the blood had dried on my sleeve. There was just a slit where the bayonet blade went in. It felt itchy, tingling in all directions from the cut, like the spokes of a wheel, but I still hadnt looked at it and I wasnt going to. All except two of the men under the tree were leg wounds, not counting myself, and those two were shot up bad around the head. One was singing a song about the bells of Tennessee but it didnt make much sense.

"Which way did they go?"

"Ever which way," one said.

"Yonder ways, mostly," another said, and pointed over to the right. The shooting was a long way off now, loudest toward the right front. It seemed reasonable that the doctors would be near the loudest shooting.

I thought I would be dizzy when I stood up but I felt fine, light on my feet and tingly from not having moved for so long. I walked away nursing my arm. When I reached the edge of the field I looked back. They were spread around the tree trunk, sprawled out favoring their wounds. I could hear that crazy one singing the Tennessee song.

I walked on, getting more and more light-headed, till finally it felt like I was walking about six inches off the ground. I thought I was still asleep, dreaming, except for the ache in my arm. And I saw things no man would want to see twice. There were dead men all around, Confederate and Union, some lying where they fell and others up under bushes where theyd crawled to keep from getting trampled. There were wounded men too, lots of them, wandering around like myself, their faces dazed and pale from losing blood and being scared.

I told myself: You better lay down before you fall down. Then I said: No, youre not bad hurt; keep going. It was like an argument, two voices inside my head and neither one of them mine:

You better lay down.

—No: you feel fine.

Youll fall and theyll never find you.

—Thats not true. Youre just a little light-headed. Youll be all right.

No you wont. Youre hurt. Youre hurt worse than you think. Lay down.

They went on like that, arguing, and I followed the road, heading south by the sun until I came to a log cabin with a cross on its ridge-pole and a little wooden signboard, hand-lettered: Shiloh Meeting House. It must have been some kind of headquarters now because there were officers inside, bending over maps, and messengers kept galloping up with papers.

I took a left where the road forked, and just beyond the fork there was a sergeant standing with the reins of two horses going back over his shoulder. When I came up he looked at me without saying anything.

"Where is a doctor?" I asked him. My voice sounded strange from not having used it for so long.

"I dont know, bud," he said. But he jerked his thumb down the road toward the sound of the guns. "Should be some of them up there, back of where the fighting is." He was a Texan, by the sound of his voice; it came partly through his nose.

So I went on down the road. It had been a line of battle that morning, the dead scattered thick on both sides. I was in a fever by then, thinking crazy, and it seemed to me that all the dead men got there this way:

God was making men and every now and then He would do a bad job on one, and He would look at it and say, "This one wont do," and He would toss it in a tub He kept there, maybe not even finished with it. And finally, 6 April 1862, the tub got full and God emptied it right out of heaven and they landed here, along this road, tumbled down in all positions, some without arms and legs, some with their heads and bodies split open where they hit the ground so hard.

I was in a fever bad, to think a thing like that. So there's no telling how long I walked or how far, but I know I came near covering that battlefield from flank to flank. It must have been a couple of hours and maybe three miles, but far as I was concerned it could have been a year and a thousand miles. At first all I wanted was a doctor. Finally I didnt even want that. All I wanted was to keep moving. I had an idea if I stopped I wouldnt be able to start again. That kept me going.

I didnt notice much along the way, but once I passed an open space with a ten-acre peach orchard in bloom at the far end and cannons puffing smoke up through the blossoms. Great crowds of men were trying to reach the orchard—they would march up in long lines and melt away; there would be a pause and then other lines would march up and melt away. Then, I was past all this, in the woods again, and I came to a little gully where things were still and peaceful, like in another world almost; the guns seemed far away. That was the place for me to stop, if any place was. I sat down, leaning back against a stump, and all the weariness came down on me at once. I knew I wouldnt get up then, not even if I could, but I didnt mind.

I didnt mind anything. It was like I was somewhere outside myself, looking back. I had reached the stage where a voice can tell you it is over, youre going to die, and that is all right too. Dying is as good as living, maybe better. The main thing is to be left alone, and if it takes dying to be let alone, a man thinks: All right, let me die. He thinks: Let me die, then.

This gully was narrow and deep, really a little valley, less than a hundred yards from ridge to ridge. The trees were thick but I could see up to the crest in each direction. There were some dead men and some wounded scattered along the stream that ran through, but I think they must have crawled in after water—there hadnt been any fighting here and there werent any bullets in the trees. I leaned back against the stump, holding my arm across my lap and facing the forward ridge. Then I saw two horsemen come over, side by side, riding close together, one leaning against the other. The second had his arm around the first, holding him in the saddle.

The second man was in civilian clothes, a boxback coat and a wide black hat. It was Governor Harris; I used to see him when he visited our brigade to talk to the Tennessee boys—electioneering, he called it; he was the Governor of Tennessee. The first man had his head down, reeling in the saddle, but I could see the braid on his sleeves and the wreath of stars on his collar. Then he lolled the other way, head rolling, and I saw him full in the face. It was General Johnston.

His horse was shot up, wounded in three legs, and his uniform had little rips in the cape and trouser-legs where minie balls had nicked him. One bootsole flapped loose, cut crossways almost through. In his right hand he held a tin cup, one of his fingers still hooked through the handle. I heard about the cup afterwards—he got it earlier in the day. He was riding through a captured camp and one of his lieutenants came out of a Yank colonel's tent and showed him a fine brier pipe he'd found there. General Johnston said "None of that, Sir. We are not here for plunder." Then he must have seen he'd hurt the lieutenant's feelings, for he leaned down from his horse and picked up this tin cup off a table and said, "Let this be my share of the spoils today," and used it instead of a sword to direct the battle.

They came down the ridge and stopped under a big oak at the bottom, near where I was, and Governor Harris got off between the horses and eased the general down to the ground. He began to ask questions, trying to make him answer, but he wouldnt—couldnt. He undid the general's collar and unfastened his clothes, trying to find where he was shot, but he couldnt find it. He took out a bottle and tried to make him drink (it was brandy; I could smell it) but he wouldnt swallow, and when Governor Harris turned his head the brandy ran out of his mouth.

Then a tall man, wearing the three stars of a colonel, came hurrying down the slope, making straight for where General Johnston was laid out on the ground. He knelt down by his side, leaning forward so that their faces were close together, eye to eye, and begun to nudge him on the shoulder and speak to him in a shaky voice: "Johnston, do you know me? Johnston, do you know me?"

But the general didnt know him; the general was dead. He still looked handsome, lying there with his eyes glazing over.

14

BOBBIE ANN MASON

"Shiloh"

1982

LEROY MOFFITT'S WIFE, NORMA JEAN, is working on her pectorals. She lifts three-pound dumbbells to warm up, then progresses to a twenty-pound barbell. Standing with her legs apart, she reminds Leroy of Wonder Woman.

"I'd give anything if I could just get these muscles to where they're real hard," says Norma Jean. "Feel this arm. It's not as hard as the other one."

"That's 'cause you're right-handed," says Leroy, dodging as she swings the barbell in an arc.

"Do you think so?"

"Sure."

Leroy is a truckdriver. He injured his leg in a highway accident four months ago, and his physical therapy, which involves weights and a pulley, prompted Norma Jean to try building herself up. Now she is attending a body-building class. Leroy has been collecting temporary disability since his tractor-trailer jackknifed in Missouri, badly twisting his left leg in its socket. He has a steel pin in his hip. He will probably not be able to drive his rig again. It sits in the backyard, like a gigantic bird that has flown home to roost. Leroy has been home in Kentucky for three months, and his leg is almost healed, but the accident frightened him and he does not want to drive any more long hauls. He is not sure what to do next. In the meantime, he makes things from craft kits. He started by building a miniature log cabin from notched Popsicle sticks. He varnished it and placed it on the TV set, where it remains. It reminds him of a rustic Nativity scene. Then he tried string art (sailing ships on black velvet), a macrame owl kit, a snap-together B-17 Flying Fortress, and a lamp made out of a model truck, with a light fixture screwed in the top of the cab. At first the kits were diversions, something to kill time, but now he is thinking about building a full-scale log house from a kit. It would be considerably cheaper than building a regular house, and besides, Leroy has grown to appreciate how things are put together. He has begun to realize that in all the years he was on the road he never took time to examine anything. He was always flying past scenery.

"They won't let you build a log cabin in any of the new subdivisions," Norma Jean tells him.

"They will if I tell them it's for you," he says, teasing her. Ever since they were married, he has promised Norma Jean he would build her a new home one day. They have always rented, and the house they live in is small and nondescript. It does not even feel like a home, Leroy realizes now.

Norma Jean works at the Rexall drugstore, and she has acquired an amazing amount of information about cosmetics. When she explains to Leroy the three stages of complexion care, involving creams, toners, and moisturizers, he thinks happily of other petroleum products—axle grease, diesel fuel. This is a connection between him and Norma Jean. Since he has been home, he has felt unusually tender about his wife and guilty over his long absences. But he can't tell what she feels about him. Norma Jean has never complained about his traveling; she has never made hurt remarks, like calling his truck a "widow-maker." He is reasonably certain she has been faithful to him, but he wishes she would celebrate his permanent homecoming more happily. Norma Jean is often startled to find Leroy at home, and he thinks she seems a little disappointed about it. Perhaps he reminds her too much of the early days of their marriage, before he went on the road. They had a child who died as an infant, years ago. They never speak about their memories of Randy, which have almost faded, but now that Leroy is home all the time, they sometimes feel awkward around each other, and Leroy wonders if one of them should mention the child. He has the feeling that they are waking up out of a dream together—that they must create a new marriage, start afresh. They are lucky they are still married. Leroy has read that for most people losing a child destroys the marriage—or else he heard this on *Donahue*. He can't always remember where he learns things anymore.

At Christmas, Leroy bought an electric organ for Norma Jean. She used to play the piano when she was in high school. "It don't leave you," she told him once. "It's like riding a bicycle."

The new instrument had so many keys and buttons that she was bewildered by it at first. She touched the keys tentatively, pushed some buttons, then pecked out "Chopsticks." It came out in an amplified fox-trot rhythm, with marimba sounds.

"It's an orchestra!" she cried.

The organ had a pecan-look finish and eighteen preset chords, with optional flute, violin, trumpet, clarinet, and banjo accompaniments. Norma Jean mastered the organ almost immediately. At first she played Christmas songs. Then she bought *The Sixties Songbook* and learned every tune in it, adding variations to each with the rows of brightly colored buttons.

"I didn't like these old songs back then," she said. "But I have this crazy feeling I missed something."

"You didn't miss a thing," said Leroy.

Leroy likes to lie on the couch and smoke a joint and listen to Norma Jean play "Can't Take My Eyes Off You" and "I'll Be Back." He is back again. After fifteen years on the road, he is finally settling down with the woman he loves. She is still pretty. Her skin is flawless. Her frosted curls resemble pencil trimmings.

NOW THAT LEROY HAS COME home to stay, he notices how much the town has changed. Subdivisions are spreading across western Kentucky like an oil slick. The sign at the edge of town says "Pop: 11,500"—only seven hundred more than it said twenty years before.

Leroy can't figure out who is living in all the new houses. The farmers who used to gather around the courthouse square on Saturday afternoons to play checkers and spit tobacco juice have gone. It has been years since Leroy has thought about the farmers, and they have disappeared without his noticing.

Leroy meets a kid named Stevie Hamilton in the parking lot at the new shopping center. While they pretend to be strangers meeting over a stalled car, Stevie tosses an ounce of marijuana under the front seat of Leroy's car. Stevie is wearing orange jogging shoes and a T-shirt that says CHATTAHOOCHEE SUPER-RAT. His father is a prominent doctor who lives in one of the expensive subdivisions in a new white-columned brick house that looks like a funeral parlor. In the phone book under his name there is a separate number, with the listing "Teenagers."

"Where do you get this stuff?" asks Leroy. "From your pappy?"

"That's for me to know and you to find out," Stevie says. He is slit-eyed and skinny.

"What else you got?"

"What you interested in?"

"Nothing special. Just wondered."

Leroy used to take speed on the road. Now he has to go slowly. He needs to be mellow. He leans back against the car and says, "I'm aiming to build me a log house, soon as I get time. My wife, though, I don't think she likes the idea."

"Well, let me know when you want me again," Stevie says. He has a cigarette in his cupped palm, as though sheltering it from the wind. He takes a long drag, then stomps it on the asphalt and slouches away.

Stevie's father was two years ahead of Leroy in high school. Leroy is thirty-four. He married Norma Jean when they were both eighteen, and their child Randy was born a few months later, but he died at the age of four months and three days. He would be about Stevie's age now. Norma Jean and Leroy were at the drive-in, watching a double feature (*Dr. Strangelove* and *Lover Come Back*), and the baby was sleeping in the back seat. When the first movie ended, the baby was dead. It was the sudden infant death syndrome. Leroy remembers handing Randy to a nurse at the emergency room, as though he were offering her a large doll as a present. A dead baby feels like a sack of flour. "It just happens sometimes," said the doctor, in what Leroy always recalls as a nonchalant tone. Leroy can hardly remember the child anymore, but he still sees vividly a scene from *Dr. Strangelove* in which the President of the United States was talking in a folksy voice on the hot line to the Soviet premier about the bomber accidentally headed toward Russia. He was in the War Room, and the world map was lit up. Leroy remembers Norma Jean standing catatonically beside him in the hospital and himself thinking: Who is this strange girl? He had forgotten who she was. Now scientists are saying that crib death is caused by a virus. Nobody knows anything, Leroy thinks. The answers are always changing.

When Leroy gets home from the shopping center, Norma Jean's mother, Mabel Beasley, is there. Until this year, Leroy has not realized how much time she spends with Norma Jean. When she visits, she inspects the closets and then the plants, informing Norma Jean when a plant is droopy or yellow. Mabel calls the plants "flowers," although there are never any blooms. She always notices if Norma Jean's laundry is piling up. Mabel is a short, overweight woman whose tight, brown-dyed curls look more like a wig than the actual wig she sometimes wears. Today she has brought Norma Jean an off-white dust ruffle she made for the bed; Mabel works in a custom-upholstery shop.

"This is the tenth one I made this year," Mabel says. "I got started and couldn't stop."

"It's real pretty," says Norma Jean.

"Now we can hide things under the bed," says Leroy, who gets along with his mother-in-law primarily by joking with her. Mabel has never really forgiven him for disgracing her by getting Norma Jean pregnant. When the baby died, she said that fate was mocking her.

"What's that thing?" Mabel says to Leroy in a loud voice, pointing to a tangle of yarn on a piece of canvas.

Leroy holds it up for Mabel to see. "It's my needlepoint," he explains. "This is a *Star Trek* pillow cover."

"That's what a woman would do," says Mabel. "Great day in the morning!"

"All the big football players on TV do it," he says.

"Why, Leroy, you're always trying to fool me. I don't believe you for one minute. You don't know what to do with yourself—that's the whole trouble. Sewing!"

"I'm aiming to build us a log house," says Leroy. "Soon as my plans come."

"Like *heck* you are," says Norma Jean. She takes Leroy's needlepoint and shoves it into a drawer. "You have to find a job first. Nobody can afford to build now anyway."

Mabel straightens her girdle and says, "I still think before you get tied down y'all ought to take a little run to Shiloh."

"One of these days, Mama," Norma Jean says impatiently.

Mabel is talking about Shiloh, Tennessee. For the past few years, she has been urging Leroy and Norma Jean to visit the Civil War battleground there. Mabel went there on her honeymoon—the only real trip she ever took. Her husband died of a perforated ulcer when Norma Jean was ten, but Mabel, who was accepted into the United Daughters of the Confederacy in 1975, is still preoccupied with going back to Shiloh.

"I've been to kingdom come and back in that truck out yonder," Leroy says to Mabel, "but we never yet set foot in that battleground. Ain't that something? How did I miss it?"

"It's not even that far," Mabel says.

After Mabel leaves, Norma Jean reads to Leroy from a list she has made. "Things you could do," she announces. "You could get a job as a guard at Union Carbide, where they'd let you set on a stool. You could get on at the lumberyard. You could do a little carpenter work, if you want to build so bad. You could—"

"I can't do something where I'd have to stand up all day."

"You ought to try standing up all day behind a cosmetics counter. It's amazing that I have strong feet, coming from two parents that never had strong feet at all." At the moment Norma Jean is holding on to the kitchen counter, raising her knees one at a time as she talks. She is wearing two-pound ankle weights.

"Don't worry," says Leroy. "I'll do something."

"You could truck calves to slaughter for somebody. You wouldn't have to drive any big old truck for that."

"I'm going to build you this house," says Leroy. "I want to make you a real home."

"I don't want to live in any log cabin."

"It's not a cabin. It's a house."

"I don't care. It looks like a cabin."

"You and me together could lift those logs. It's just like lifting weights."

Norma Jean doesn't answer. Under her breath, she is counting. Now she is marching through the kitchen. She is doing goose steps.

BEFORE HIS ACCIDENT, WHEN LEROY came home he used to stay in the house with Norma Jean, watching TV in bed and playing cards. She would cook fried chicken, picnic ham, chocolate pie—all his favorites. Now he is home alone much of the time. In the mornings, Norma Jean disappears, leaving a cooling place in the bed. She eats a cereal called Body Buddies, and she leaves the bowl on the table, with the soggy tan balls floating in a milk puddle. He sees things about Norma Jean that he never realized before. When she chops onions, she stares off into a corner, as if she can't bear to look. She puts on her house slippers almost precisely at nine o'clock every evening and nudges her jogging shoes under the couch. She saves bread heels for the birds. Leroy watches the birds at the feeder. He notices the peculiar way goldfinches fly past the window. They close their wings, then fall, then spread their wings to catch and lift themselves. He wonders if they close their eyes when they fall. Norma Jean closes her eyes when they are in bed. She wants the lights turned out. Even then, he is sure she closes her eyes.

He goes for long drives around town. He tends to drive a car rather carelessly. Power steering and an automatic shift make a car feel so small and inconsequential that his body is hardly involved in the driving process. His injured leg stretches out comfortably. Once or twice he has almost hit something, but even the prospect of an accident seems minor in a car. He cruises the new subdivisions, feeling like a criminal rehearsing for a robbery. Norma Jean is probably right about a log house being inappropriate here in the new subdivisions. All the houses look grand and complicated. They depress him.

One day when Leroy comes home from a drive he finds Norma Jean in tears. She is in the kitchen making a potato and mushroom-soup casserole, with grated-cheese topping. She is crying because her mother caught her smoking.

"I didn't hear her coming. I was standing here puffing away pretty as you please," Norma Jean says, wiping her eyes.

"I knew it would happen sooner or later," says Leroy, putting his arm around her.

"She don't know the meaning of the word 'knock,'" says Norma Jean. "It's a wonder she hadn't caught me years ago."

"Think of it this way," Leroy says. "What if she caught me with a joint?"

"You better not let her!" Norma Jean shrieks. "I'm warning you, Leroy Moffitt!"

"I'm just kidding. Here, play me a tune. That'll help you relax."

Norma Jean puts the casserole in the oven and sets the timer. Then she plays a ragtime tune, with horns and banjo, as Leroy lights up a joint and lies on the couch, laughing to himself about Mabel's catching him at it. He thinks of Stevie Hamilton—a doctor's son pushing grass. Everything is funny. The whole town seems crazy and small. He is reminded of Virgil Mathis, a boastful policeman Leroy used to shoot pool with. Virgil recently led a drug bust in a back room at a bowling alley, where he seized ten thousand dollars' worth of marijuana. The newspaper had a picture of him holding up the bags of grass and grinning widely. Right now, Leroy can imagine Virgil breaking down the door and arresting him with a lungful of smoke. Virgil would probably have been alerted to the scene because of all the racket Norma Jean is making. Now she sounds like a hard-rock band. Norma Jean is terrific. When she switches to a Latin-rhythm version of "Sunshine Superman," Leroy hums along. Norma Jean's foot goes up and down, up and down.

"Well, what do you think?" Leroy says, when Norma Jean pauses to search through her music.

"What do I think about what?"

His mind has gone blank. Then he says, "I'll sell my rig and build us a house." That wasn't what he wanted to say. He wanted to know what she thought—what she really thought—about them.

"Don't start in on that again," says Norma Jean. She begins playing "Who'll Be the Next in Line?"

Leroy used to tell hitchhikers his whole life story—about his travels, his hometown, the baby. He would end with a question: "Well, what do you think?" It was just a rhetorical question. In time, he had the feeling that he'd been telling the same story over and over to the same hitchhikers. He quit talking to hitchhikers when he realized how his voice sounded—whining and self-pitying, like some teenage-tragedy song. Now Leroy has the sudden impulse to tell Norma Jean about himself, as if he had just met her. They have known each other so long they have forgotten a lot about each other. They could become reacquainted. But when the oven timer goes off and she runs to the kitchen, he forgets why he wants to do this.

THE NEXT DAY, MABEL DROPS by. It is Saturday and Norma Jean is cleaning. Leroy is studying the plans of his log house, which have finally come in the mail. He has them spread out on the table—big sheets of stiff blue paper, with diagrams and numbers printed in white. While Norma Jean runs the vacuum, Mabel drinks coffee. She sets her coffee cup on a blueprint.

"I'm just waiting for time to pass," she says to Leroy, drumming her fingers on the table.

As soon as Norma Jean switches off the vacuum, Mabel says in a loud voice, "Did you hear about the datsun dog that killed the baby?"

Norma Jean says, "The word is 'dachshund.'"

"They put the dog on trial. It chewed the baby's legs off. The mother was in the next room all the time." She raises her voice. "They thought it was neglect."

Norma Jean is holding her ears. Leroy manages to open the refrigerator and get some Diet Pepsi to offer Mabel. Mabel still has some coffee and she waves away the Pepsi.

"Datsuns are like that," Mabel says. "They're jealous dogs. They'll tear a place to pieces if you don't keep an eye on them."

"You better watch out what you're saying, Mabel," says Leroy.

"Well, facts is facts."

Leroy looks out the window at his rig. It is like a huge piece of furniture gathering dust in the backyard. Pretty soon it will be an antique. He hears the vacuum cleaner. Norma Jean seems to be cleaning the living room rug again.

Later, she says to Leroy, "She just said that about the baby because she caught me smoking. She's trying to pay me back."

"What are you talking about?" Leroy says, nervously shuffling blueprints.

"You know good and well," Norma Jean says. She is sitting in a kitchen chair with her feet up and her arms wrapped around her knees. She looks small and helpless. She says, "The very idea, her bringing up a subject like that! Saying it was neglect."

"She didn't mean that," Leroy says.

"She might not have *thought* she meant it. She always says things like that. You don't know how she goes on."

"But she didn't really mean it. She was just talking."

Leroy opens a king-sized bottle of beer and pours it into two glasses, dividing it carefully. He hands a glass to Norma Jean and she takes it from him mechanically. For a long time, they sit by the kitchen window watching the birds at the feeder.

Something is happening. Norma Jean is going to night school. She has graduated from her six-week body-building course and now she is taking an adult-education course in composition at Paducah Community College. She spends her evenings outlining paragraphs.

"First you have a topic sentence," she explains to Leroy. "Then you divide it up. Your secondary topic has to be connected to your primary topic."

To Leroy, this sounds intimidating. "I never was any good in English," he says.

"It makes a lot of sense."

"What are you doing this for, anyhow?"

She shrugs. "It's something to do." She stands up and lifts her dumbbells a few times.

"Driving a rig, nobody cared about my English."

"I'm not criticizing your English."

Norma Jean used to say, "If I lose ten minutes' sleep, I just drag all day." Now she stays up late, writing compositions. She got a B on her first paper—a how-to theme on soup-based casseroles. Recently Norma Jean has been cooking unusual foods—tacos, lasagna, Bombay chicken. She doesn't play the organ anymore, though her second paper was called "Why Music Is Important to Me." She sits at the kitchen table, concentrating on her outlines, while Leroy plays with his log house plans, practicing with a set of Lincoln Logs. The thought of getting a truckload of notched, numbered logs scares him, and he wants to be prepared. As he and Norma Jean work together at the kitchen table, Leroy has the hopeful thought that they are sharing something, but he knows he is a fool to think this. Norma Jean is miles away. He knows he is going to lose her. Like Mabel, he is just waiting for time to pass.

One day, Mabel is there before Norma Jean gets home from work, and Leroy finds himself confiding in her. Mabel, he realizes, must know Norma Jean better than he does.

"I don't know what's got into that girl," Mabel says. "She used to go to bed with the chickens. Now you say she's up all hours. Plus her a-smoking. I like to died."

"I want to make her this beautiful home," Leroy says, indicating the Lincoln Logs. "I don't think she even wants it. Maybe she was happier with me gone."

"She don't know what to make of you, coming home like this."

"Is that it?"

Mabel takes the roof off his Lincoln Log cabin. "You couldn't get *me* in a log cabin," she says. "I was raised in one. It's no picnic, let me tell you."

"They're different now," says Leroy.

"I tell you what," Mabel says, smiling oddly at Leroy.

"What?"

"Take her on down to Shiloh. Y'all need to get out together, stir a little. Her brain's all balled up over them books."

Leroy can see traces of Norma Jean's features in her mother's face. Mabel's worn face has the texture of crinkled cotton, but suddenly she looks pretty. It occurs to Leroy that Mabel has been hinting all along that she wants them to take her with them to Shiloh.

"Let's all go to Shiloh," he says. "You and me and her. Come Sunday."

Mabel throws up her hands in protest. "Oh, no, not me. Young folks want to be by theirselves."

When Norma Jean comes in with groceries, Leroy says excitedly, "Your mama here's been dying to go to Shiloh for thirty-five years. It's about time we went, don't you think?"

"I'm not going to butt in on anybody's second honeymoon," Mabel says.

"Who's going on a honeymoon, for Christ's sake?" Norma Jean says loudly.

"I never raised no daughter of mine to talk that-a-way," Mabel says.

"You ain't seen nothing yet," says Norma Jean. She starts putting away boxes and cans, slamming cabinet doors. "There's a log cabin at Shiloh," Mabel says. "It was there during the battle. There's bullet holes in it."

"When are you going to *shut up* about Shiloh, Mama?" asks Norma Jean.

"I always thought Shiloh was the prettiest place, so full of history," Mabel goes on. "I just hoped y'all could see it once before I die, so you could tell me about it." Later, she whispers to Leroy, "You do what I said. A little change is what she needs."

"YOUR NAME MEANS 'THE KING,'" Norma Jean says to Leroy that evening. He is trying to get her to go to Shiloh, and she is reading a book about another century.

"Well, I reckon I ought to be right proud."

"I guess so."

"Am I still king around here?"

Norma Jean flexes her biceps and feels them for hardness. "I'm not fooling around with anybody, if that's what you mean," she says.

"Would you tell me if you were?"

"I don't know."

"What does *your* name mean?"

It was Marilyn Monroe's real name."

"No kidding!"

"Norma comes from the Normans. They were invaders," she says. She closes her book and looks hard at Leroy. "I'll go to Shiloh with you if you'll stop staring at me."

ON SUNDAY, NORMA JEAN PACKS a picnic and they go to Shiloh. To Leroy's relief, Mabel says she does not want to come with them. Norma Jean drives, and Leroy, sitting beside her, feels like some boring hitchhiker she has picked up. He tries some conversation, but she answers him in monosyllables. At Shiloh, she drives aimlessly through the park, past bluffs and trails and steep ravines. Shiloh is an immense place, and Leroy cannot see it as a battleground. It is not what he expected. He thought it would look like a golf course. Monuments are everywhere, showing through the thick clusters of trees. Norma Jean passes the log cabin Mabel mentioned. It is surrounded by tourists looking for bullet holes.

"That's not the kind of log house I've got in mind," says Leroy apologetically.

"I know *that*."

"This is a pretty place. Your mama was right."

"It's O.K.," says Norma Jean. "Well, we've seen it. I hope she's satisfied."

They burst out laughing together.

At the park museum, a movie on Shiloh is shown every half hour, but they decide that they don't want to see it. They buy a souvenir Confederate flag for Mabel, and then they find a picnic spot near the cemetery. Norma Jean has brought a picnic cooler, with pimiento sandwiches, soft drinks, and Yodels. Leroy eats a sandwich and then smokes a joint, hiding it behind the picnic cooler. Norma

Jean has quit smoking altogether. She is picking cake crumbs from the cellophane wrapper, like a fussy bird.

Leroy says, "So the boys in gray ended up in Corinth. The Union soldiers zapped 'em finally. April 7, 1862."

They both know that he doesn't know any history. He is just talking about some of the historical plaques they have read. He feels awkward, like a boy on a date with an older girl. They are still just making conversation.

"Corinth is where Mama eloped to," says Norma Jean.

They sit in silence and stare at the cemetery for the Union dead and, beyond, at a tall cluster of trees. Campers are parked nearby, bumper to bumper, and small children in bright clothing are cavorting and squealing. Norma Jean wads up the cake wrapper and squeezes it tightly in her hand. Without looking at Leroy, she says, "I want to leave you."

Leroy takes a bottle of Coke out of the cooler and flips off the cap. He holds the bottle poised near his mouth but cannot remember to take a drink. Finally he says, "No, you don't."

"Yes, I do."

"I won't let you."

"You can't stop me."

"Don't do me that way."

Leroy knows Norma Jean will have her own way. "Didn't I promise to be home from now on?" he says.

"In some ways, a woman prefers a man who wanders," says Norma Jean. "That sounds crazy, I know."

"You're not crazy."

Leroy remembers to drink from his Coke. Then he says, "Yes, you *are* crazy. You and me could start all over again. Right back at the beginning."

"We *have* started all over again," says Norma Jean. "And this is how it turned out."

"What did I do wrong?"

"Nothing."

"Is this one of those women's lib things?" Leroy asks.

"Don't be funny."

The cemetery, a green slope dotted with white markers, looks like a subdivision site. Leroy is trying to comprehend that his marriage is breaking up, but for some reason he is wondering about white slabs in a graveyard.

"Everything was fine till Mama caught me smoking," says Norma Jean, standing up. "That set something off."

"What are you talking about?"

"She won't leave me alone—*you* won't leave me alone." Norma Jean seems to be crying, but she is looking away from him. "I feel eighteen again. I can't face that all over again." She starts walking away. "No, it *wasn't* fine. I don't know what I'm saying. Forget it."

Leroy takes a lungful of smoke and closes his eyes as Norma Jean's words sink in. He tries to focus on the fact that thirty-five hundred soldiers died on the grounds around him. He can only think of that war as a board game with plastic soldiers. Leroy almost smiles, as he compares the Confederates' daring attack on the Union camps and Virgil Mathis's raid on the bowling alley. General Grant, drunk and furious, shoved the Southerners back to Corinth, where Mabel and Jet Beasley were married years later, when Mabel was still thin and good-looking. The next day, Mabel and Jet visited the battleground, and then Norma Jean was born, and then she married Leroy and they had a baby, which they lost, and now Leroy and Norma Jean are here at the same battleground. Leroy knows he is leaving out a lot. He is leaving out the insides of history. History was always just names and dates to him. It occurs to him that building a house out of logs is similarly empty—too simple. And the real inner workings of a marriage, like most of history, have escaped him. Now he sees that building a log house is the dumbest idea he could have had. It was clumsy of him to think Norma Jean would want a log house. It was a crazy idea. He'll have to think of something else, quickly. He will wad the blueprints into tight balls and fling them into the lake. Then he'll get moving again. He opens his eyes. Norma Jean has moved away and is walking through the cemetery, following a serpentine brick path.

Leroy gets up to follow his wife, but his good leg is asleep and his bad leg still hurts him. Norma Jean is far away, walking rapidly toward the bluff by the river, and he tries to hobble toward her. Some children run past him, screaming noisily. Norma Jean has reached the bluff, and she is looking out over the Tennessee River. Now she turns toward Leroy and waves her arms. Is she beckoning to him? She seems to be doing an exercise for her chest muscles. The sky is unusually pale—the color of the dust ruffle Mabel made for their bed.

15

GENERAL BRAXTON BRAGG

Speech to the Army of the Mississippi

May 3, 1862

HDQRS. SECOND CORPS, ARMY OF THE MISSISSIPPI
Corinth, Miss., May 3, 1862.

SOLDIERS: You are again to encounter the mercenary invader who pollutes the sacred soil of our beloved country. Severely punished by you and driven from his chosen positions with a loss of his artillery and his honor at Shiloh when double your numbers, he now approaches cautiously and timidly, unwilling to advance, unable to retreat.

Could his rank and file enjoy a freeman's right not one would remain within our limits, but they are goaded on under a tyrant's lash by desperate leaders, whose only safety lies in success.

Such a foe ought never to conquer freemen battling upon their own soil.

You will encounter him in your chosen position, strong by nature and improved by art, away from his main support and reliance—gunboats and heavy batteries—and for the first time in this war with nearly equal numbers. The slight reverses we have met on the seaboard have worked us good as well as evil. The brave troops so long retained there have hastened to swell your numbers, while the gallant Van Dorn and invincible Price, with the ever-successful

"Army of the West," are now in your midst with numbers almost equaling the "Army of Shiloh." We have, then, but to strike and destroy, and, as the enemy's whole resources are concentrated here, we shall not only redeem Tennessee, Kentucky, and Missouri at one blow, but open the portals of the whole Northwest.

BRAXTON BRAGG
General, Commanding Second Corps

PART 4

The Shape of War

Citizen volunteers assisting wounded in the field of battle,
September 17, 1862, by Alfred R. Waud

The fourth conversation in this series begins with the companion work *Crossroads of Freedom: Antietam* by James McPherson. McPherson is the most widely respected Civil War historian of the last quarter-century, known especially for his Pulitzer Prize-winning survey, *Battle Cry of Freedom* (1988). In *Crossroads of Freedom*, he works on a smaller canvas, placing the story of a single battle in larger context. The historian does what novelists and writers of memoirs are not obligated to do: tell the story in as objective a way as possible, with documentation.

In McPherson's understanding, Antietam, fought in Sharpsburg, Maryland, in September 1862—months after Shiloh, but in a different theater of the war, with different leaders and armies—was the pivotal point in the war. As at Shiloh, neither the Union nor the Confederacy could claim a glorious victory at Antietam, but the Union turned back another Confederate offensive that could have altered the course of the war.

For McPherson, the crucial victories at Antietam lay beyond the battlefield, in the diplomatic, political, and racial realms. England and France rejected the idea of supporting the Confederacy; Lincoln's Republican party, under relentless attack from the Democrats, gained credibility; and the United States announced emancipation as a war aim. After those three events, McPherson believes, the stage was set for ultimate Union victory.

Other historians, of course, differ in their interpretations, pointing out that the Confederacy fought effectively for two more long years, that the European powers never came to the side of the United States, that Lincoln was barely renominated by his own party in 1864, and that slavery proved remarkably resilient in places where the Union Army could not reach. The selection here from Gary Gallagher emphasizes the strength of the Confederate Army and the nation it embodied across four years of all-consuming warfare, suggesting that Antietam may not have been as decisive a crossroads as McPherson argues. The Confederate Army fought many more battles after the summer of 1862, after all, and believed that the crucial test would come in the Northern election of 1864.

A different kind of perspective on the war appears in Drew Gilpin Faust's prize-winning *This Republic of Suffering*, published in 2008. Faust shifts our focus from the course of battle and politics to the suffering of families and communities. She wants us to understand the many meanings of death and the ways death was confronted. Faust would not deny the importance of understanding the issues that McPherson and Gallagher wrestle with, but she would ask that we broaden our vision.

History is written to foster such discussions. Did the Civil War have a clear turning point? What were the possible futures of slavery? What stakes did the world have in America's war? How did Americans deal with the terrible personal costs of battles such as Shiloh, Antietam, and the many that followed?

16

DREW GILPIN FAUST

Excerpt from *This Republic of Suffering: Death and the American Civil War**

2008

The Work of Death

Mortality defines the human condition. "We all have our dead—we all have our Graves," a Confederate Episcopal bishop observed in an 1862 sermon. Every era, he explained, must confront "like miseries"; every age must search for "like consolation." Yet death has its discontinuities as well. Men and women approach death in ways shaped by history, by culture, by conditions that vary over time and across space. Even though "we all have our dead," and even though we all die, we do so differently from generation to generation and from place to place.[1]

In the middle of the nineteenth century, the United States embarked on a new relationship with death, entering into a civil war that proved bloodier than any other conflict in American history, a war that would presage the slaughter of World War I's Western Front and the global carnage of the twentieth century. The number of soldiers who died between 1861 and 1865, an estimated 620,000, is approximately equal to the total American fatalities in the

---

Revolution, the War of 1812, the Mexican War, the Spanish-American War, World War I, World War II, and the Korean War combined. The Civil War's rate of death, its incidence in comparison with the size of the American population, was six times that of World War II. A similar rate, about 2 percent, in the United States today would mean six million fatalities. As the new southern nation struggled for survival against a wealthier and more populous enemy, its death toll reflected the disproportionate strains on its human capital. Confederate men died at a rate three times that of their Yankee counterparts; one in five white southern men of military age did not survive the Civil War.[2]

But these military statistics tell only a part of the story. The war killed civilians as well, as battles raged across farm and field, as encampments of troops spread epidemic disease, as guerrillas ensnared women and even children in violence and reprisals, as draft rioters targeted innocent citizens, as shortages of food in parts of the South brought starvation. No one sought to document these deaths systematically, and no one has devised a method of undertaking a retrospective count. The distinguished Civil War historian James McPherson has estimated that there were fifty thousand civilian deaths during the war, and he has concluded that the overall mortality rate for the South exceeded that of any country in World War I and that of all but the region between the Rhine and the Volga in World War II. The American Civil War produced carnage that has often been thought reserved for the combination of technological proficiency and inhumanity characteristic of a later time.[3]

The impact and meaning of the war's death toll went beyond the sheer numbers who died. Death's significance for the Civil War generation arose as well from its violation of prevailing assumptions about life's proper end—about who should die, when and where, and under what circumstances. Death was hardly unfamiliar to mid-nineteenth-century Americans. By the beginning of the 1860s the rate of death in the United States had begun to decline, although dramatic improvements in longevity would not appear until late in the century. Americans of the immediate prewar era continued to be more closely acquainted with death than are their twenty-first-century counterparts. But the patterns to which they were accustomed were in significant ways different from those the war would introduce. The Civil War represented a dramatic shift in both incidence and experience. Mid-nineteenth-century Americans endured a high rate of infant mortality but expected that most individuals who reached young adulthood would survive at least into middle age. The war took young, healthy men and rapidly, often instantly, destroyed them with disease or injury. This marked a sharp and alarming departure from existing preconceptions about who should die. As Francis W. Palfrey wrote in an 1864 memorial for Union soldier Henry L. Abbott, "the blow seems heaviest when it strikes down those who are in the morning of life." A soldier was five times more likely to die than he would have been if he had not entered the army. As a chaplain explained to his Connecticut regiment in the middle of the war, "neither he nor they had ever lived and faced death in such a time, with its peculiar conditions and necessities." Civil War soldiers and civilians alike distinguished what many referred to as "ordinary death," as it had occurred in prewar years, from the manner and frequency of death in Civil War battlefields, hospitals, and camps, and from the war's interruptions of civilian lives.[4]

In the Civil War the United States, North and South, reaped what many participants described as a "harvest of death." By the midpoint of the conflict, it seemed that in the South, "nearly every household mourns some loved one lost." Loss became commonplace; death was no longer encountered individually; death's threat, its proximity, and its actuality became the most widely shared of the war's experiences. As a Confederate soldier observed, death "reigned with universal sway," ruling homes and lives, demanding attention and response. The Civil War matters to us today because it ended slavery and helped to define the meanings of freedom, citizenship, and equality. It established a newly centralized nation-state and launched it on a trajectory of economic expansion and world influence. But for those Americans who lived in and through the Civil War, the texture of the experience, its warp and woof, was the presence of death. At war's end this shared suffering would override persisting differences about the meanings of race, citizenship, and nationhood to establish sacrifice and its memorialization as the ground on which North and South would ultimately reunite. Even in our own time this fundamentally elegiac understanding of the Civil War retains a powerful hold.[5]

Death transformed the American nation as well as the hundreds of thousands of individuals directly affected by loss. The war created a veritable "republic of suffering," in the words that Frederick Law Olmsted chose to describe the wounded and dying arriving at Union hospital ships on the Virginia Peninsula. Sacrifice and the state became inextricably intertwined. Citizen soldiers snatched from the midst of life generated obligations for a nation defining its purposes and polity through military struggle. A war about union, citizenship, freedom, and human dignity required that the government attend to the needs of those who had died in its service. Execution of these newly recognized responsibilities would prove an important vehicle for the expansion of federal power that characterized the transformed postwar nation. The establishment of national cemeteries and the emergence of the Civil War pension system to care for both the dead and their survivors yielded programs of a scale and reach unimaginable before the war. Death created the modern American union—not just by ensuring national survival, but by shaping enduring national structures and commitments.[6]

Civil War Americans often wrote about what they called "the work of death," meaning the duties of soldiers to fight, kill, and die, but at the same time invoking battle's consequences: its slaughter, suffering, and devastation. "Work" in this usage incorporated both effort and impact—and the important connection between the two. Death in war does not simply happen; it requires action and agents. It must, first of all, be inflicted; and several million soldiers of the 1860s dedicated themselves to that purpose. But death also usually requires participation and response; it must be experienced and handled. It is work to die, to know how to approach and endure life's last moments. Of all living things, only humans consciously anticipate death; the consequent need to choose how to behave in its face—to worry about how to die—distinguishes us from other animals. The need to manage death is the particular lot of humanity.[7]

It is work to deal with the dead as well, to remove them in the literal sense of disposing of their bodies, and it is also work to remove them in a more figurative sense. The bereaved struggle to separate themselves from the dead through ritual and mourning. Families and communities must repair the rent in the domestic and social fabric, and societies, nations, and cultures must work to understand and explain unfathomable loss.

[*This Republic of Suffering*] is a book about the work of death in the American Civil War. It seeks to describe how between 1861 and 1865—and into the decades that followed—Americans undertook a kind of work that history has not adequately understood or recognized. Human beings are rarely simply passive victims of death. They are actors even if they are the diers; they prepare for death, imagine it, risk it, endure it, seek to understand it. And if they are survivors, they must assume new identities established by their persistence in face of others' annihilation. The presence and fear of death touched Civil War Americans' most fundamental sense of who they were, for in its threat of termination and transformation, death inevitably inspired self-scrutiny and self-definition. Beginning with individuals' confrontation with dying and killing, the book explores how those experiences transformed society, culture, and politics in what became a broader republic of shared suffering. Some of the changes death brought were social, as wives turned into widows, children into orphans; some were political, as African American soldiers hoped to win citizenship and equality through their willingness both to die and to kill; some were philosophical and spiritual, as the carnage compelled Americans to seek meaning and explanation for war's destruction.

Every death involved "the great change" captured in the language and discourse of nineteenth-century Christianity, the shift from this life to whatever might come next. A subject of age-old concern for believers and nonbelievers alike, the existence and nature of an afterlife took on new urgency both for soldiers anxious about their own deaths and for bereaved kin speculating on the fate of the departed. And even if spirits and souls proved indeed immortal, there still remained the vexing question of bodies. The traditional notion that corporeal resurrection and restoration would accompany the Day of Judgment seemed increasingly implausible to many Americans who had seen the maiming and disfigurement inflicted by this war. Witnesses at field hospitals almost invariably commented with horror on the piles of limbs lying near the surgeon's table, dissociated from the bodies to which they had belonged, transformed into objects of revulsion instead of essential parts of people. These arms and legs seemed as unidentifiable—and unrestorable—as the tens of thousands of missing men who had been separated from their names. The integral relationship between the body and the human self it housed was as shattered as the wounded men.[8]

Bodies were in important ways the measure of the war—of its achievements and its impact; and indeed, bodies became highly visible in Civil War America. Commanders compared their own and enemy casualties as evidence of military success or failure. Soldiers struggled for the words to describe mangled corpses strewn across battlefields; families contemplated the significance of newspaper lists of wounds: "slightly, in the shoulder," "severely, in the groin," "mortally, in the breast." They nursed the dying and buried their remains. Letters and reports from the front rendered the physicality of injuries and death all but unavoidable. For the first time civilians directly confronted the reality of battlefield death rendered by the new art of photography. They found themselves transfixed by the paradoxically lifelike renderings of the slain of Antietam that Mathew Brady exhibited in his studio on Broadway. If Brady "has not brought bodies and laid them in our dooryards and along the streets, he has done something very like it," wrote the New York Times.[9]

This new prominence of bodies overwhelmingly depicted their destruction and deformation, inevitably raising the question of how they related to the persons who had once inhabited them. In the aftermath of battle survivors often shoveled corpses into pits as they would dispose of animals—"in bunches, just like dead chickens," one observer noted—dehumanizing both the living and the dead through their disregard. In Civil War death the distinction between men and animals threatened to disappear, just as it was simultaneously eroding in the doctrines of nineteenth-century science.[10]

The Civil War confronted Americans with an enormous task, one quite different from saving or dividing the nation, ending or maintaining slavery, or winning the military conflict—the demands we customarily understand to have been made of the Civil War generation. Americans North and South would be compelled to confront—and resist—the war's assault on their conceptions of how life should end, an assault that challenged their most fundamental assumptions about life's value and meaning. As they faced horrors that forced them to question their ability to cope, their commitment to the war, even their faith in a righteous God, soldiers and civilians alike struggled to retain their most cherished beliefs, to make them work in the dramatically altered world that war had introduced. Americans had to identify—find, invent, create—the means and mechanisms to manage more than half a million dead: their deaths, their bodies, their loss. How they accomplished this task reshaped their individual lives—and deaths—at the same time that it redefined their nation and their culture. The work of death was Civil War America's most fundamental and most demanding undertaking.

NOTES

1. [Stephen Elliott], *Obsequies of the Reverend Edward E. Ford, D.D., and Sermon by the Bishop of the Diocese* . . . (Augusta, Ga.: Augusta Chronicle and Sentinel, 1863), p.8.

2. James David Hacker, "The Human Cost of War: White Population in the United States, 1850–1880," Ph.D. diss. (University of Minnesota, 1999), pp. 1, 14. Hacker believes that Civil War death totals may be seriously understated because of inadequate estimates of the number of Confederate deaths from disease. Civil War casualty and mortality statistics are problematic overall, and the incompleteness of Confederate records makes them especially unreliable. . . . Maris A. Vinovskis concludes that about 6 percent of northern white males between ages thirteen and forty-five died in the war, whereas 18 percent of white men of similar age in the South perished. But because of much higher levels of military mobilization in the white South, mortality rates for southern soldiers were twice, not three times, as great as those for northern soldiers. James McPherson cites these soldiers' death rates as 31 percent for Confederate soldiers, 16 percent for Union soldiers. Gary Gallagher believes Vinovskis's overall death rate for the

South is too low; he estimates that closer to one in four rather than one in five white southern men of military age died in the conflict. I have cited the more conservative total. See Vinovskis, "Have Social Historians Lost the Civil War?" in Maris A. Vinovskis,. ed., *Toward a Social History of the American Civil War: Exploratory Essays* (New York: Cambridge University Press, 1990), pp. 3–7; James M. McPherson, personal communication to author, December 27, 2006; Gary Gallagher, personal communication to author, December 16, 2006.

3. James M. McPherson, *Crossroads of Freedom: Antietam* (New York: Oxford University Press, 2002), pp. 3, 177, n. 56.

4. [Francis W. Palfrey], *In Memoriam: H.L.A.* (Boston: Printed for private distribution, 1864), p. 5; Richard Shryock, "A Medical Perspective on the Civil War," *American Quarterly* 14 (Summer 1962): 164; H. Clay Trumbull, *War Memories of an Army Chaplain* (New York: C. Scribner's Sons, 1898), p. 67. Vital statistics for this period are very scarce, and the most complete cover only Massachusetts. I am grateful to historical demographer Gretchen Condran of Temple University for discussing these matters with me. See U.S. Bureau of the Census, *Historical Statistics of the United States, Part I* (Washington, D.C.: Government Printing Office, 1975), pp. 62–63. On the "untimely death of an adult child" as "particularly painful" in mid-nineteenth-century England, see Patricia Jalland, *Death in the Victorian Family* (New York: Oxford University Press, 1996), p. 39.

5. One notable appearance of the image of a harvest of death is in the title given Timothy O'Sullivan's photograph of a field of bodies at Gettysburg in Alexander Gardner, *Gardner's Photographic Sketchbook of the War* (1866; rpt. New York: Dover, 1959), plate 36; Kate Stone, *Brokenburn: The Journal of Kate Stone, 1861–1868*, ed. John Q. Anderson (Baton Rouge: Louisiana University Press, 1955), p. 264; C. W. Greene to John McLees, August 15, 1862, McLees Family Papers, South Carolina Library, University of South Carolina, Columbia.

6. [Frederick Law Olmsted], *Hospital Transports: A Memoir of the Embarkation of the Sick and Wounded from the Peninsula of Virginia in the Summer of 1862* (Boston: Ticknor & Fields, 1863), p. 115.

7. The general literature on death is immense and rich. [See] Thomas Lynch, *The Undertaking: Life Studies from the Dismal Trade* (New York: W. W. Norton, 1997); Thomas Lynch, *Bodies in Motion and at Rest: On Metaphor and Mortality* (New York: W. W. Norton, 2000); Sandra Gilbert, *Death's Door: Modern Dying and the Way We Grieve* (New York: W. W. Norton, 2006); Paul Monette, *Borrowed Time: An AIDS Memoir* (San Diego, Calif.: Harcourt Brace Jovanovich, 1988); Paul Monette, *Last Watch of the Night* (New York: Harcourt Brace, 1994); Jessica Mitford, *The American Way of Death* (New York: Simon & Schuster, 1963); Sherwin B. Nuland, *How We Die: Reflections On Life's Final Chapter* (New York: Alfred A. Knopf, 1994); Maurice Bloch and Jonathan Parry, eds., *Death and the Regeneration of Life* (New York: Cambridge University Press, 1982); Peter Metcalf and Richard Huntington, *Celebrations*

of Death: The Anthropology of Mortuary Ritual, 2nd ed. (New York: Cambridge University Press, 1991).

8. Mrs. Carson to R. F. Taylor, September 14, 1864, Carson Family Papers, South Caroliniana Library, University of South Carolina, Columbia. On changing notions of the self, see Charles Taylor, *Sources of the Self: The Making of Modern Identity* (Cambridge, Mass.: Harvard University Press, 1989), and Jerrold Seigel, *The Idea of the Self: Thought and Experience in Western Europe Since the Seventeenth Century* (New York: Cambridge University Press, 2005).

9. *New York Times,* October 20, 1862. See William A. Frassanito, *Antietam: The Photographic Legacy of America's Bloodiest Day* (New York: Charles Scribner's Sons, 1978); Franny Nudelman, *John Brown's Body: Slavery, Violence and the Culture of War* (Chapel Hill: University of North Carolina Press, 2004), pp. 103–31; and Alan Trachtenberg, *Reading American Photographs: Images as History: Mathew Brady to Walker Evans* (New York: Hill & Wang, 1989). Even as we acknowledge the impact of Civil War photography, it is important to recognize how few Americans would actually have seen Brady's or other photographs of the dead. Newspapers and periodicals could not yet reproduce photographs but could publish only engravings derived from them.

10. Maude Morrow Brown Manuscript, z/0907.000/S, Mississippi Department of Archives and History, Jackson, Miss.; on nineteenth-century science and the changed meaning of death, see Adam Phillips, *Darwin's Worms: On Life Stories and Death Stories* (New York: Basic Books, 2000).

17

GARY W. GALLAGHER

"The Net Result of the Campaign Was in Our Favor: Confederate Reaction to the Maryland Campaign"

1999

THE ROADS LEADING FROM SHARPSBURG to Boteler's Ford choked under the strain of men, vehicles, and animals during the night of September 18, 1862. Trudging through a sheltering fog that helped mask their movement toward the Potomac River, Confederates soldiers hoped that an enemy who had been quiescent all day would remain so for a few hours longer. A North Carolina chaplain, carried along through the pre-dawn Maryland darkness on this martial tide, left a vivid impression in his diary: "Though troops and wagons have been passing all night, still the roads and fields were full. Ram! Jam! Wagons and ambulances turned over! One man was killed by the overturning of an ambulance." An artillerist described a more orderly withdrawal, mentioning especially that Robert E. Lee "stood at the ford in Shepherdstown and gave directions to the teamsters and others, showing a wise attention to details which many men in less elevated positions would think beneath their notice." By eight o'clock on the morning of September 19, all were safely across the Potomac onto Virginia soil.[1]

Thus ended a fifteen-day campaign in Maryland that represented the final act of a drama begun eighty-five days earlier with Confederate assaults at the battle of Mechanicsville outside Richmond. These twelve momentous weeks had witnessed Lee's offensive victory over George B. McClellan in the Seven Days and an equally impressive thrashing of John Pope's Army of Virginia at Second Manassas, which together shifted the strategic focus in the Eastern Theater from Richmond to the Potomac River. Surging across the national frontier into Maryland less than a week after Second Manassas, Lee and his army had hoped to make the strategic reorientation even more striking. Dramatic events in the gaps of South Mountain, at Harpers Ferry, and amid the rolling countryside near Sharpsburg had punctuated Lee's foray north of the Potomac—and would dominate the thinking of most contemporary observers and later critics who sought to judge what the Army of Northern Virginia had won or lost.

Historians typically have assessed the Maryland campaign from the perspective of its long-term impact, looking back with later events in mind to label it a major turning point that foreshadowed Confederate defeat. Writing in the mid-1950s, Clement Eaton touched on the two factors most often mentioned in this connection—Lincoln's preliminary proclamation of emancipation and Europe's decision to back away from recognition of the Confederacy in the autumn of 1862. "The checking of the Confederate invasion at Antietam . . . was disastrous to the cause of Southern independence," wrote Eaton. "The retreat of Lee not only gave Lincoln a favorable opportunity to issue his Emancipation Proclamation but it also chilled the enthusiasm of the British government to recognize the independence of the Confederacy." Nearly two decades earlier, Robert Selph Henry had argued similarly in his widely read history of the Confederacy, pointing to Antietam and suggesting that "[o]n the seventeenth day of September in 1862 the decline of the Confederacy began." Clifford Dowdey, who in the 1950s and 1960s inherited Douglas Southall Freeman's mantle as the leading popular writer about Lee and his army, added his voice to this chorus, stating bluntly, "Politically, the war ended at Sharpsburg for the Confederacy. That was the last chance the Southern states had really to win independence."[2]

More recent historians have continued this interpretive tradition. James M. McPherson's magisterial history of the conflict reminded readers that the battle of Antietam "frustrated

Confederate hopes for British recognition and precipitated the Emancipation Proclamation. The slaughter at Sharpsburg therefore proved to have been one of the war's great turning points." In summary comments about Antietam from his overview of the Civil War era, Brooks D. Simpson asserted that "most people, North and South, American and European, interpreted a pitched battle followed by a Confederate withdrawal as a defeat." The result was diminished chances for European recognition and Lincoln's opening for the proclamation—a conclusion Charles P. Roland echoed in his insightful survey of the Civil War.[3]

A decade ago, I summarized the impact of the Maryland campaign on Confederate fortunes in similar terms: "Lee went north and fought, avoided a series of lurking disasters, and found refuge in the end along the southern bank of the Potomac River. But the military events of mid-September 1862 bore bitter political and diplomatic fruit for the Confederacy. The nature of the conflict changed because of Lee's Maryland campaign." No longer a contest to restore the status quo ante bellum, "the new war would admit of no easy reconciliation because the stakes had been raised to encompass the entire social fabric of the South. The war after Antietam would demand a decisive resolution on the battlefield, and that the Confederacy could not achieve."[4]

The understandable desire to highlight the broad implications of the Maryland campaign has left another important question relatively neglected, namely, how did Confederates at the time react to Lee's campaign in Maryland? Did the operations of September 1862 engender hope? Did they cause Confederates to lose heart at the thought that their struggle for independence had taken a grim turn downward? Did the campaign provoke a mixed reaction? In short, what impact did Lee's foray across the Potomac have on his men and on their fellow Confederates?

A survey of military and civilian testimony during the period following Lee's retreat from Maryland underscores the challenge of assessing the relationship between military events and popular will during the Civil War. Although any such survey is necessarily impressionistic, searching letters, diaries, and newspaper accounts for patterns of reaction is worthwhile.[5] Examined within the context of what people read and heard at the time, and freed from the powerful influence of historical hindsight, Confederate morale assumes a complex character. Rumors and inaccurate reports buffeted citizens long since grown wary of overblown prose in newspapers. Knowing they often lacked sound information, people nonetheless strove to reach satisfying conclusions about what had transpired.

As the autumn weeks went by, they groped toward a rough consensus that may be summed up briefly. The Maryland campaign did not represent a major setback for the Confederacy. Antietam was at worst a bloody standoff, at best a narrow tactical success for Confederates who beat back heavy Union assaults and then held the field for another day. Stonewall Jackson's capture of 12,000 Union soldiers and immense matériel at Harpers Ferry, as well as A. P. Hill's stinging repulse of Union forces at Shepherdstown on September 20, marked unequivocal high points of the campaign. McClellan's inaction throughout late September and October demonstrated how badly his army had been damaged, and Lincoln's emancipation proclamation betrayed Republican desperation and promised to divide northern society. Reconciled to the fact that the war would not end anytime soon, most Confederates looked to the future with a cautious expectation of success.[6]

NOTES

1. Jedediah Hotchkiss, *Make Me a Map of the Valley: The Civil War Journal of Stonewall Jackson's Topographer*, ed. Archie P. McDonald (Dallas, Tex.: Southern Methodist University Press, 1973), 83–84; Alexander D. Betts, *Experiences of a Confederate Chaplain, 1861–1865*, ed. W. A. Betts (190[?]; reprint, [Sanford, N.C.]: n.p., n.d.), 16–17; letter signed "A. B. C.," September 24, 1862, in Richmond *Weekly Dispatch*, September 30, 1862.

2. Clement Eaton, *A History of the Southern Confederacy*, (New York: Macmillan, 1954), 193; Robert Selph Henry, *The Story of the Confederacy*, rev. ed. (New York: Bobbs-Merrill, 1936), 191; Clifford Dowdey, *The Land They Fought For: The Story of the South as the Confederacy, 1832–1865* (Garden City, N.Y.: Doubleday, 1955), 218. In *The Confederacy* (Chicago: University of Chicago Press, 1960), 80–81, Charles P. Roland added Earl Van Dorn's defeat at Corinth and Braxton Bragg's retreat from Kentucky, both in October, to Lee's withdrawal from Maryland to make a similar point about Confederate fortunes in the fall of 1862: "These reverses spread demoralization

throughout the South and crippled the prestige of the administration. . . . Many Southerners began to doubt the ability of the Confederacy to win the war."

3. James M. McPherson, *Battle Cry of Freedom: The Civil War Era* (New York: Oxford University Press, 1988), 545; Brooks D. Simpson, *America's Civil War* (Wheeling, Ill.: Harlan Davidson, 1996), 86–87; Charles P. Roland, *An American Iliad: The Story of the Civil War* (Lexington: University Press of Kentucky, 1991), 83.

4. Gary W. Gallagher, "The Maryland Campaign in Perspective," in *Antietam: Essays on the 1862 Maryland Campaign*, ed. Gary W. Gallagher (Kent, Ohio: Kent State University Press, 1989), 94.

5. The conclusions in this essay rest on testimony from more than two hundred Confederates, including officers and soldiers within Lee's army, government officials, and men and women behind the lines. All major sections of the Confederacy are represented, and every effort was made to include people of various economic and social classes. As is often the case with Confederate witnesses, however, slaveholders are overrepresented, and the sample would not meet any social scientific standard.

6. In *The Road to Appomattox* (Memphis, Tenn.: Memphis State College Press, 1956), 60–61, Bell I. Wiley argued that a revival of Confederate spirits in the summer and early fall of 1862 "began to lose force with the coming of winter" and continued downward until reaching a crisis in the summer of 1863. The testimony examined for this essay does not sustain Wiley's conclusions.

PART 5

War and Freedom

Colored Troops Under General Wild Liberating Slaves in North Carolina,
from *Harper's Weekly*, January 3, 1864

The final conversation in the series concerns the most unanticipated outcome of the American Civil War: the immediate and uncompensated emancipation of four million people who had been held in slavery for over two centuries. The United States was the most powerful nation sustaining slavery in 1860, and few imagined the institution being abolished as rapidly as it was. Abraham Lincoln, in the first selection, tries to persuade a group of visiting African American clergymen to support his plan for colonizing freed blacks in Central America. Lincoln thinks, at this early point in the war, that it would be better for white and black alike if the two races were separated. Lincoln wanted to see slavery end but could not imagine that former slaves and former slave owners could manage to live together in peace. The remarkable determination and forbearance of the enslaved people of the South during the war itself, along with the widely respected heroism of African American troops—including men recently held in slavery—changed Lincoln's mind.

Even as Lincoln struggled with the issue, enslaved people were making themselves free in whatever ways they could find. James Washington, in a memoir written for his family in 1873 but published only recently, tells of his escape from slavery in Virginia in the midst of the war. Frederick Douglass, a decade after he despaired of the plight of African Americans in a United States that seemed determined to deprive them of their rights and of their humanity, urges black men to rush to the defense of the United States because that nation is now fighting for their freedom. Lincoln himself steadily broadens and deepens his commitment to emancipation, as two letters expressing his thinking reveal. In his 1863 letter to James C. Conkling, the president argues with those who want to end the war without driving it to its conclusion; in the letter to Albert Hodges the next year, Lincoln lays out why the war has to end slavery. While the Gettysburg Address, given in November 1863, does not speak of slavery directly, its potent language frames the purpose of the war as freedom understood in its broadest terms.

In just the two years after African American men were finally allowed, in 1863, to enlist for the United States, 200,000 black soldiers and sailors went into the service. The 1864 report from James Brisbin tells both of their valor and of the disrespect they often endured from their white compatriots. After it became clear that the United States would win the war and bring freedom with that victory, black Southerners struggled to secure the tools to protect that freedom. In early 1865, African Americans in Nashville petitioned the white leadership of the Union party—the name the Republicans briefly adopted in the midst of the war—for their rights as citizens in a free America. Their petition, presented here, is a powerful statement of the highest American ideals. There is no record of a response.

Emancipation was not a single event but a long and uneven series of struggles on plantations and farms, in cities and towns, all across the South. Margaret Walker, in a powerful 1966 novel, *Jubilee*, turned stories she'd heard from her grandmother into a novel about the coming of freedom. In her telling, freedom arrived in degrees of uncertainty, unclear in its reach or its ultimate meanings.

Leon Litwack's groundbreaking history of the end of slavery, *Been in the Storm So Long*, published in 1979, uses remarkable research to tell the story of freedom. In this excerpt, he chronicles the burning of Richmond in April 1865, almost exactly four years after the convention there voted to lead Virginia out of the Union. Abraham Lincoln would visit Richmond with his son only days later, soon after his inauguration for his second term. That second term, so much in doubt over the preceding four years, began with what is generally considered the greatest speech in American history, a brief reckoning with divine purpose and human frailty, a humble effort to find meaning in so much suffering. Six weeks after the speech and two weeks after his visit to Richmond, where newly freed men and women surrounded him, he was assassinated in Washington, D.C. Another chapter in American history began with his death.

As you read these selections, you will see why it has been difficult to comprehend entirely the role of emancipation in the Civil War. The white North certainly did not speak with one voice, and even Abraham Lincoln, whose leadership was crucial in bringing black freedom, spoke cautiously and inconsistently on the issue—in part, to help him achieve emancipation within a divided nation. African Americans themselves differed not on the desirability of freedom but on the best ways to win and cement that freedom.

How do we account for the emergence of emancipation in the Union cause? Are you struck more by the speed of that emergence or its delay, its thoroughness or its limitations? How did white Southerners, judging from other readings in this series, respond to black freedom?

To learn more about this complex issue, read Eric Foner, *Reconstruction: America's Unfinished Revolution* (1988) and see Edward Zwick's powerful film, *Glory* (1989).

18

ABRAHAM LINCOLN

Address on Colonization to a Deputation of Negroes

August 14, 1862

THIS AFTERNOON THE PRESIDENT OF the United States gave audience to a Committee of colored men at the White House. They were introduced by the Rev. J. Mitchell, Commissioner of Emigration. E. M. Thomas, the Chairman, remarked that they were there by invitation to hear what the Executive had to say to them. Having all been seated, the President, after a few preliminary observations, informed them that a sum of money had been appropriated by Congress, and placed at his disposition for the purpose of aiding the colonization in some country of the people, or a portion of them, of African descent, thereby making it his duty, as it had for a long time been his inclination, to favor that cause; and why, he asked, should the people of your race be colonized, and where? Why should they leave this country? This is, perhaps, the first question for proper consideration. You and we are different races. We have between us a broader difference than exists between almost any other two races. Whether it is right or wrong I need not discuss, but this physical difference is a great disadvantage to us both, as I think your race suffer very greatly, many of them by living among us, while ours suffer from your presence. In a word we suffer on each side. If this is admitted, it affords a reason at least why we should be separated. You here are freemen I suppose.

A VOICE: Yes, sir.

THE PRESIDENT: Perhaps you have long been free, or all your lives. Your race are suffering, in my judgment, the greatest wrong inflicted on any people. But even when you cease to be slaves, you are yet far removed from being placed on an equality with the white race. You are cut off from many of the advantages which the other race enjoy. The aspiration of men is to enjoy equality with the best when free, but on this broad continent, not a single man of your race is made the equal of a single man of ours. Go where you are treated the best, and the ban is still upon you.

I do not propose to discuss this, but to present it as a fact with which we have to deal. I cannot alter it if I would. It is a fact, about which we all think and feel alike, I and you. We look to our condition, owing to the existence of the two races on this continent. I need not recount to you the effects upon white men, growing out of the institution of Slavery. I believe in its general evil effects on the white race. See our present condition—the country engaged in war!—our white men cutting one another's throats, none knowing how far it will extend; and then consider what we know to be the truth. But for your race among us there could not be war, although many men engaged on either side do not care for you one way or the other. Nevertheless, I repeat, without the institution of Slavery and the colored race as a basis, the war could not have an existence.

It is better for us both, therefore, to be separated. I know that there are free men among you, who even if they could better their condition are not as much inclined to go out of the country as those, who being slaves could obtain their freedom on this condition. I suppose one of the principal difficulties in the way of colonization is that the free colored man cannot see that his comfort would be advanced by it. You may believe you can live in Washington or elsewhere in the United States the remainder of your life [as easily], perhaps more so than you can in any foreign country, and hence you may come to the conclusion that you have nothing to do with the idea of going to a foreign country. This is (I speak in no unkind sense) an extremely selfish view of the case.

But you ought to do something to help those who are not so fortunate as yourselves. There is an unwillingness on the part of our people, harsh as it may be, for you free colored people to remain with us. Now, if you could give a start to white people, you would open a wide door for many to be made free. If we deal with those who are not free at the beginning, and whose intellects are clouded by Slavery, we have very poor materials to start with. If intelligent colored men, such as are before me, would move in this matter, much might be accomplished. It is exceedingly important that we have men at the beginning capable of thinking as white men, and not those who have been systematically oppressed.

There is much to encourage you. For the sake of your race you should sacrifice something of your present comfort for the purpose of being as grand in that respect as the white people. It is a cheering thought throughout life that something can be done to ameliorate the condition of those who have been subject to the hard usage of the world. . . .

The colony of Liberia has been in existence a long time. In a certain sense it is a success. The old President of Liberia, Roberts, has just been with me—the first time I ever saw him. He says they have within the bounds of that colony between 300,000 and 400,000 people, or more than in some of our old States, such as Rhode Island or Delaware, or in some of our newer States, and less than in some of our larger ones. They are not all American colonists, or their descendants. Something less than 12,000 have been sent thither from this country. Many of the original settlers have died, yet, like people elsewhere, their offspring outnumber those deceased.

The question is if the colored people are persuaded to go anywhere, why not there? One reason for an unwillingness to do so is that some of you would rather remain within reach of the country of your nativity. I do not know how much attachment you may have toward our race. It does not strike me that you have the greatest reason to love them. But still you are attached to them at all events.

The place I am thinking about having for a colony is in Central America. It is nearer to us than Liberia—not much more than one-fourth as far as Liberia, and within seven days' run by steamers.

Unlike Liberia it is on a great line of travel—it is a highway. The country is a very excellent one for any people, and with great natural resources and advantages, and especially because of the similarity of climate with your native land—thus being suited to your physical condition.

The particular place I have in view is to be a great highway from the Atlantic or Caribbean Sea to the Pacific Ocean, and this particular place has all the advantages for a colony. On both sides there are harbors among the finest in the world. Again, there is evidence of very rich coal mines. A certain amount of coal is valuable in any country, and there may be more than enough for the wants of the country. Why I attach so much importance to coal is, it will afford an opportunity to the inhabitants for immediate employment till they get ready to settle permanently in their homes.

[...]

You are intelligent, and know that success does not as much depend on external help as on self-reliance. Much, therefore, depends upon yourselves. As to the coal mines, I think I see the means available for your self-reliance.

I shall, if I get a sufficient number of you engaged, have provisions made that you shall not be wronged. If you will engage in the enterprise I will spend some of the money intrusted to me. I am not sure you will succeed. The Government may lose the money, but we cannot succeed unless we try; but we think, with care, we can succeed.

The political affairs in Central America are not in quite as satisfactory condition as I wish. There are contending factions in that quarter; but it is true all the factions are agreed alike on the subject of colonization, and want it, and are more generous than we are here. To your colored race they have no objection. Besides, I would endeavor to have you made equals, and have the best assurance that you should be the equals of the best.

The practical thing I want to ascertain is whether I can get a number of able-bodied men, with their wives and children, who are willing to go, when I present evidence of encouragement and protection. Could I get a hundred tolerably intelligent men, with their wives and children, to "cut their own fodder," so to speak? Can I have fifty? If I could find twenty-five able-bodied men, with a mixture of women and children, good things in the family relation, I think I could make a successful commencement.

I want you to let me know whether this can be done or not. This is the practical part of my wish to see you. These are subjects of very great importance, worthy of a month's study, [instead] of a speech delivered in an hour. I ask you then to consider seriously not pertaining to yourselves merely, nor for your race, and ours, for the present time, but as one of the things, if successfully managed, for the good of mankind—not confined to the present generation, but as

> "From age to age descends the lay,
>   To millions yet to be,
>   Till far its echoes roll away,
>   Into eternity"

THE ABOVE IS MERELY GIVEN as the substance of the President's remarks.

The Chairman of the delegation briefly replied that "they would hold a consultation and in a short time give an answer." The President said: "Take your full time—no hurry at all."

The delegation then withdrew.

19

JOHN M. WASHINGTON

"Memorys of the Past"

1877

Chapter 7

January 1st 1861. I was sent to Richmond, Va to be hired out. I had long desired to go to Richmond. I had been told by my friends it was a good place to make money for myself and I wanted to go there.

So with a great many of old Friends I was placed in the Care of Mr Hay Hoomes, hireing agent, and (on the cars) started to Richmond where we arrived about 3 o,clock the same day, and I was hired to one Zetelle, An Eating Saloon keeper there was no liquors kept there.

I lived with him six months when he sold the place to a man named Wendlinger, both of these men were low, mean, and coarse. they treated their servants cruelly often whipping them their selves or sending them to the slave jail to be whipped where it was done fearfully for 50 cents.[1]

I got along unusally well with both men Especially the latter.

I was living there when the Southern Slave holders in open Rebellion fired on Fort Sumter, little did they then think, that they were Fireing the Death-knell of Slavery, and little did I think that my deliverence was so near at hand.

The fireing on Fort Sumter occurred April 12, 1861, and from that time forward Richmond became the seat of the Rebellion. Thousands of troops was sent to Richmond from all parts of the south on their way to Washington, as they said. and so many troops of all discription was landed there that it appeard to be an impossiability, to us, colord people, that they could ever by conquord.

In July 1861, the 21st day the Union Army, and the Rebels met at Bulls Run and a great Battle was fought and the union army was defeated. Already the slaves had been Escapeing into the union armys lines and many thereby getting of to the Free States. I could read the papers and Eagerly watched them for tidings of the war which had began in earnest. almost every day brought news of Battles. The Union troops was called "Yankees and the Southern "Rebs", It had now <u>become</u> a well known fact that slaves was daily making their Escape into the union lines. So at Christmas 1861 I left Richmond, having been provided with a pass and fare to Fredericksburg Va

I bid Mr Wendlinger and my fellow servants good-by They Expected me back the 1st of January again to live with them another year.

Soon after I arrived in Fredericksburg I sought and obtained a home for the year of 1862. at the "Shakespear House", Part of the time as "Steward," and the balance as Bar-keeper—My Master was not much pleased when he heard of my intention to remain in Fredericksburg that year; he seemed to think I wanted to remain too near the "Yankees", though he did not tell me these words.

The war was getting hoter Every day and the Yankees had approched within a few miles of the Town more than once. The later part of February 1862. the Rebs began to withdraw their forces from the Aquia Creek Landing which was then the terminus of the "Richmond Fredericksburg and Potomac Railroad", Early in March the Rebs began to fall back from the Potomack River;

The Town was now filled with Rebel Soilders, and their outrages and dastardly acts toward the colord people can not be told. It became dangerous to be out atal of nights.

The whites was hastening their slaves off to safeer places of refuge.

A great many slave men were sent into the Rebel Army as Drivers, Cooks, Hostlers, and any thing Else they could do.

The Firm of Payton & Mazine[2] who hired me were both officers in the Rebel Army. the first Captian in the 3oth Regiment of Virginia the later Was a Lieutanant in the same Regiment, was at home, on the sick list and ~~was~~ in charge of the Hotel.

About the last of March there was a good deal of talk about Evacuating Fredericksburg. Which was soon after, commenced. by the 15th of April. Most of the troops had been withdrawn. On the Night of the 15th or 16th, the Yankees advanced and had a Skirmish, and drove in the Rebel pickets with some of them wounded and the others most frightfully scared.

The Propietors of the Shakespear now told me the house would have to be closed very soon in consequence of the near approach of the Yankees. and that I would have to go to Saulsbury, North Carolina[3] to wait on Capt. Payton the balance of the year.

I could not very well make any objections as the Firm had always treated me well and paid me besides, for attending the Bar for them, when I was hired only for a Dining room servant.

I was easily induced to change from the Dining room for $37.00 and Extra money every week.

So When I was told that I would have to go to Saulsbery I became greatly alarmed and began to fear that the object in sending me down there, was to be done to get me out of the reach of the Yankees. and I secretly resolved not to go But I made them believe I was most anxious to go.

In fact I made them believe I was tereblely afred of the Yankees, any way.

My Master was well satisfied at my appearant disposition and told me I was quite Right, for if the Yankees were to catch me they would send me to Cuba or cut my hands off or otherwise maltreat me. I of course pretended to beleive all they said but knew they were lieing all the while. As soon as they told me When I had to start, I Intended to conceale myself and wait the approach of the Yankees and when once in the lines I intended to go to Detroit, Michigan where I had an uncle living.

Chapter 8

April 18th 1862. Was "Good-Friday". the Day was a mild pleasant one with the sun shining brightly, and everything unusally quite, the Hotel Was crowed with boarders who was seated at breakfast a rumor had been circulated amoung them that the Yankees was advancing but nobody seemed to beleive it, until Every body was startled by several reports of cannon.

Then in an instant all was wild confusion as a calvary man dashed into the Dining Room and said "The Yankees is in Falmouth." Every body was on their feet at once, no body finished but some ran to their rooms to get a few things, Officers and soldiers hurried to their Quarters Every where was hurried words and hasty foot steps.

Mr Mazene who had hurried to his room now came runing back called me out in the Hall and thrust a roll of Bank notes in my hand and hurriedly told me to pay off all the servants, and shut up the house and take charge of every thing.

"If the Yankees catch me they will kill me so I can't stay here," "said he", and was off at full speed like the wind. In less time than it takes me to write these lines, every white man was out the house. Every man servant[4] was out on the house top looking over the River at the Yankees for their glistening bayonets could Easily be seen I could not begin to Express my new born hopes for I felt already like I was certain of My freedom Now.

By this time the Two Bridges crossing the River here was on fire The match having been applied by the retreating rebels. 18 Vessels and 2 steamers at the wharf was all burnt In 2 hours from the firing of the First gun. Every store in town was closed. Every white man had run away or hid himself Every white woman had shut themselves in doors. No one could be seen on the streets but the colord people. and every one of them seemed to be in the best of humors Every rebel soilder had left the town and only a few of them hid in the woods west of the town watching. The Yankees turned out to be the 1st Brigade of "Kings Division", of McDowells Corpse, under Brigade Genl Auger[5] having advanced as far as Falmouth they had Stoped on Ficklins, Hill over looking the little town Genl Auger discovered a rebel Artillery on the oppisite Side of the river who, after setting fire to the Bridge was fireing at the Piers trying to knock them down. the "Yankees" soon turned several Peices loose on the

Rebels who after a few shots beat a hasty retreat; coming through Fredericksburg a a break neck speed as if the "Yankees," was at their heels Instead of across the river without a Ford, and all the Bridges burnt.

As soon as I had seen all things put to rights at the hotel and the Doors closed and shutters put up, I call all the servants in the Bar-Room and treated them all around plentifull and after drinking "the Yankees", healths" I paid each one according to Orders. I told them they could go, just where they pleased but be sure the "Yankees" have no trouble finding them.

I then put the keys into my pockets and proceeded to the Bank where my old mistress lived who was hurridly packing her silver-spoons to go out in the country to get away from the "Yankees". She asked me with tears in her Eyes what was I going to do. I replyed I am going back to the Hotel now. After you get throug" said she", child you better come and go out in the country with me. So as to keep away from the Yankees. Yes madam "I replyed" I will come right back directly. I proceeded down to where Mrs. Mazene lived (the propietiors Wife) and delivered the keys to her.

Safe in the Lines.

After delivering the hotel keys to Mrs Mazene I then walked up Water St above Coalters Bridge where I noticed a large crowd of the people standing Eagerly gazeing across the river at a small group of officers and soilders who was now approaching the river side and immediately raised a flag of Truce and called out for some one to come over to them. A white man named James Turner, stepped into a small boat and went over to them. and after a few minutes returned with Capt. Wood of Harris' Light Calvary," of New York. Who as soon as he had landed proceeded up the hill to the crowd amoung which was the Mayor. "Common Council", and the Corporation Attorney; Thomas Barton.

Capt. Wood then in the name of Genl Auger commanding the U.S. Troops on the Falmouth Heights demanded the unconditional surrender of the Town. Old Lawer Barton was bitterly opposed to surrendering saying "the Confederacy had a plenty of Troops yet at their command" Then why did they burn all the Bridges when we appeard on 'Fickling Heights"? demanded Capt Woods—Barton was silent. "The Orders are" continued Capt. Wood "that if any further attempt is made to burn cotton or any thing else, or if any Trains of cars Shall approach or attempt to leave the town without permission of Genl Auger the Town will be Immedialety fired upon.

The Mayor and "Common Council" hesitated no longer, notwithstanding Lawer Barton's objection, and Capt Wood then Informed the Mayor that he would be required to come over to Genl Augers Headquarters the next morning at 10 o,clock and sign the proper papers. He then bid them all good Evening and having again Entered the little Boat he was soon rowed across the River and in a few minutes thare after he was seen mounted on horse back and being joined by scores of other Horsemen, that had not been seen while he was on our side of the river. Evedently having been concealed in the woods near by.

As soon as the Officer had left the Constables was told to order the Negroes home which they did, but while we dispersed from thereabouts a great many did not go home Just then.[6] I hastened off in the direction of home and after making a circuitous route I, in company with James Washington, my first cusin and another free colord man left the town near the woolen mills and proceeded up the road leading to Falmouth our object being to get right oppisite the "Union Camp" and listen to the great number of "Bands" then playing those tuchinq tunes, "the Star Spangled Banner", "Red, White and Blue", &c.

We left the road just before we got to "Ficklin's Mill", and walked down to the river. The long line of sentnels on the other side doing duty colose to the water's Edge.

Very soon one, of a party of soilders, in a boat call out to the crowd standing arround me do any of you want to come over—Every body "said no," I hallowed out, "Yes I want to come over," "all right—Bully for you" was the response. and they was soon over to our side. I greeted them gladly and stepped into their Boat, as soon as James saw my determernation to go he joined me and the other young man who had come along with us—

After we had landed on the other side, a large crowd of the soilders off duty, gathered around us and asked all kinds of questions in reference to the where abouts of the "Rebels" I had stuffed my pockets full of rebel newspapers and, I distributed them around as far as they would go greatly to the delight of the men, and by this act won their good opinions right away. I told them I was most happy to see them all that I had been looking for them for a long time. Just here "one of them asked me I geuss you ain,t a "Secessish," then, me "said I know why colord people aint secessh, "Why you aint a colord man are you. "Said he," Yes Sir I am "I replyed," and a slave all my life—All of them seemed to utterly astonished. "do you want to be free inquired one" by all means "I answered." "Where Is your Master?" said another: In the Rebel Navy, "I said" well you don't belong to any body then. "said several at once." The District of Columbia is free now.[7] Emancapated 2 Days ago I did not know what to say for I was dumb with joy and could only thank God and laugh.

They insisted upon my going up to their camp on the Hill, and continued to ask all kind of questions about the "Rebs." I was conducted all over their camp and shown Every thing that could interest me most kind attention was shown me by a Corporal in Company H 21st New York State Volenteers.

He shared his meals and his bed with me and seemed to pity me with all his manly heart. His name was "Charles Ladd,"[8] But our acquaintance was of short duration a few weeks thereafter the army advanced and had several skirmishes and I never seen him again.

It was near night before I thought of returning home (for though there was not as yet any of the "Union Troops" in Fredericksburg.) the Town was right under their guns and a close watch was being kept on the Town.

When my friends (the soilders) and me arrived at the River side we found the Boat drawn out of the water and all intercourse forbidden for the night. My cousin and his friend had recrossed early in the afternoon.

So I found I should have to remain with my new found friends for the night. However I was well acquainted in Falmouth and soon found the soft side of a wooden Bench; at Mrs Butlers[9] who had given us an entire room for the use of some soilders and 3 or 4 of us. A good fire was Kept burning all night in an old fashiond fire-place.

A most memorable night that was to me the soilders assured me that I was now a free man and had nothing to do but to stay with. They told me I could soon get a situation waiting on some of the officers, I had already been offerd one or two, and had determined to take one or the other, as soon as I could go over and get my cloths and Some $30.00 of my own.

Before morning I had began to fee like I had truly Escaped from the hand of the slaves master and with the help of God, I never would be a slave no more. I felt for the first time in my life that I could now claim Every cent that I should work for as my own. I began now to feel that life had a new joy awaiting me. I might now go and come when I pleased So I wood remain with the army until I got Enough money to travel further North <u>This was the First Night</u> of my Freedom. It was good Friday indeed the Best Friday I had ever seen Thank God—xxxx——

NOTES

1. Washington's depiction of his "hiring out" experiences is one of the most revealing in any slave narrative, and this passage is indicative of how widely it was practiced in towns and cities. The tavern owners were a Greek immigrant, Speredone Zetelle, and a German immigrant, Caspar Wendlinger.

2. George Peyton and James Mazeen; both joined the 30th Virginia Infantry that winter or spring.

3. Salisbury, North Carolina.

4. Rather than the term "slave," Washington employs the more lofty label, "man servant," as if to give himself and his comrades a heightened ranking in this moment of imminent liberation.

5. Rufus King, former engineer, newspaper editor, and attorney general of New York; Union general, commander of the First Division, Pope's army, defeated at Groveton in Second Manassas campaign, August 28, 1862. Irvin McDowell, Union general, commander of the Union army at First Bull Run, July, 1861, and commander of the Third Corps of Pope's army, Second Manassas campaign. Christopher C. Augur, Union general, brigade commander, Army of Virginia, March–July, 1862, division commander wounded severely at the battle of Cedar Mountain, August 8, 1862. Washington's memory for the details of names, dates, and places is remarkably accurate.

6. Washington's sense of detail and drama in covering this scene demonstrates a remarkable example of his ambition as a writer and reflects his long-term residence in Fredericksburg. It also depicts a stunning example of how the nature of the war and the impending emancipation were realities no one could any longer hide from the slaves themselves.

7. The passage in Congress on April 16 of emancipation in the District of Columbia.

8. Washington may be misremembering Ladd's name. Ladd does not appear in the 21st New York's regimental history.

9. Eliza Butler, a free black laundress in Falmouth with eight children. Washington is surely aware by the time he wrote this that such a scene of white Union soldiers and a few freshly escaped freedmen bedding down together in a free black woman's humble house was a representation of the revolutionary character the war had taken on in 1862.

20

ABRAHAM LINCOLN

Emancipation Proclamation

January 1, 1863

WHEREAS, ON THE TWENTY-SECOND DAY of September, in the year of our Lord one thousand eight hundred and sixty-two, a proclamation was issued by the President of the United States, containing, among other things, the following, towit:

"That on the first day of January, in the year of our Lord one thousand eight hundred and sixty-three, all persons held as slaves within any State or designated part of a State, the people whereof shall then be in rebellion against the United States, shall be then, thenceforward, and forever free; and the Executive Government of the United States, including the military and naval authority thereof, will recognize and maintain the freedom of such persons, and will do no act or acts to repress such persons, or any of them, in any efforts they may make for their actual freedom.

"That the Executive will, on the first day of January aforesaid, by proclamation, designate the States and parts of States, if any, in which the people thereof, respectively, shall then be in rebellion against the United States; and the fact that any State, or the people thereof, shall on that day be, in good faith, represented in the Congress of the United States by members chosen thereto at elections wherein a majority of the qualified voters of such State shall have participated, shall, in the absence of strong countervailing testimony, be deemed conclusive evidence that such State, and the people thereof, are not then in rebellion against the United States."

Now, therefore I, Abraham Lincoln, President of the United States, by virtue of the power in me vested as Commander-in-Chief, of the Army and Navy of the United States in time of actual armed rebellion against the authority and government of the United States, and as a fit and necessary war measure for suppressing said rebellion, do, on this first day of January, in the year of our Lord one thousand eight hundred and sixty-three, and in accordance with my purpose so to do publicly proclaimed for the full period of one hundred days, from the day first above mentioned, order and designate as the States and parts of States wherein the people thereof respectively, are this day in rebellion against the United States, the following, towit:

Arkansas, Texas, Louisiana, (except the Parishes of St. Bernard, Plaquemines, Jefferson, St. John, St. Charles, St. James, Ascension, Assumption, Terrebonne, Lafourche, St. Mary, St. Martin, and Orleans, including the City of New Orleans) Mississippi, Alabama, Florida, Georgia, South-Carolina, North-Carolina, and Virginia, (except the fortyeight counties designated as West Virginia, and also the counties of Berkley, Accomac, Northampton, Elizabeth-City, York, Princess Ann, and Norfolk, including the cities of Norfolk & Portsmouth[)]; and which excepted parts, are for the present, left precisely as if this proclamation were not issued.

And by virtue of the power, and for the purpose aforesaid, I do order and declare that all persons held as slaves within said designated States, and parts of States, are, and henceforward shall be free; and that the Executive government of the United States, including the military and naval authorities thereof, will recognize and maintain the freedom of said persons.

And I hereby enjoin upon the people so declared to be free to abstain from all violence, unless in necessary self-defence; and I recommend to them that, in all cases when allowed, they labor faithfully for reasonable wages.

And I further declare and make known, that such persons of suitable condition, will be received into the armed service of the

United States to garrison forts, positions, stations, and other places, and to man vessels of all sorts in said service.

And upon this act, sincerely believed to be an act of justice, warranted by the Constitution, upon military necessity, I invoke the considerate judgment of mankind, and the gracious favor of Almighty God.

In witness whereof, I have hereunto set my hand and caused the seal of the United States to be affixed.

Done at the City of Washington, this first day of January, in the year of our Lord one thousand eight hundred and sixty three, and of the Independence of the United States of America the eighty-seventh.

By the President: ABRAHAM LINCOLN
WILLIAM H. SEWARD, Secretary of State.

21

FREDERICK DOUGLASS

"Men of Color, To Arms!"*

March 1863

A rallying cry that was reprinted in newspapers and in broadside form, "Men of Color, To Arms!" appeared in *Douglass' Monthly* in March 1863. In this address Douglass expressed his enthusiasm, echoed in speech after speech since the onset of the Civil War, for the engagement of the African American as a soldier in the cause of freedom. The assurances that Douglass the recruiter gave prospective black troops—that they would "receive the same wages, the same rations, the same equipments, the same protection, the same treatment, and the same bounty" as their white counterparts—turned out to be unreliable, not because Douglass misled his black followers, but because the United States government reneged on its promises to Douglass. Nevertheless, fervent appeals such as this to the patriotism and self-sacrifice of African Americans enabled Douglass to play a crucial role in attracting thousands of blacks to the Union Army. Through them he would finally deal a death blow to American slavery.

WHEN FIRST THE REBEL CANNON shattered the walls of Sumter, and drove away its starving garrison, I predicted that the war, then and there inaugurated would not be fought out entirely by white

---

* "Men of Color, to Arms!" by Frederick Douglass, from *The Oxford Frederick Douglass Reader*, edited with an introduction by William L. Andrews. Copyright ©1996 by Oxford University Press, Inc. Reprinted by permission of Oxford University Press, Inc.

men. Every month's experience during these two dreary years, has confirmed that opinion. A war undertaken and brazenly carried on for the perpetual enslavement of colored men, calls logically and loudly upon colored men to help suppress it. Only a moderate share of sagacity was needed to see that the arm of the slave was the best defence against the arm of the slaveholder. Hence with every reverse to the National arms, with every exulting shout of victory raised by the slaveholding rebels, I have implored the imperrilled nation to unchain against her foes her powerful black hand. Slowly and reluctantly that appeal is beginning to be heeded. Stop not now to complain that it was not heeded sooner. It may, or it may not have been best that it should not. This is not the time to discuss that question. Leave it to the future. When the war is over, the country is saved, peace is established, and the black man's rights are secured, as they will be, history with an impartial hand, will dispose of that and sundry other questions. Action! action! not criticism, is the plain duty of this hour. Words are now useful only as they stimulate to blows. The office of speech now is only to point out when, [w]here and how, to strike to the best advantage. There is no time for delay. The tide is at its flood that leads on to fortune. From East to West, from North to South, the sky is written all over "NOW OR NEVER." Liberty won by white men would lose half its lustre. Who would be free themselves must strike the blow. Better even to die free, than to live slaves. This is the sentiment of every brave colored man amongst us. There are weak and cowardly men in all nations. We have them amongst us. They tell you that this is the "white man's war";—that you will be no "better off after, than before the war"; that the getting of you into the army is to "sacrifice you on the first opportunity." Believe them not—cowards themselves, they do not wish to have their cowardice shamed by your brave example. Leave them to their timidity, or to whatever motive may hold them back.

I have not thought lightly of the words I am now addressing to you. The counsel I give comes of close observations of the great struggle now in progress—and of the deep conviction that this is your hour, and mine.

In good earnest then, and after the best deliberation, I now for the first time during this war feel at liberty to call and counsel you to arms. By every consideration which binds you to your enslaved fellow country-men, and the peace and welfare of your country; by every aspiration which you cherish for the freedom and equality of yourselves and your children; by all the ties of blood and identity which make us one with the brave black men, now fighting our battles in Louisiana, in South Carolina, I urge you to fly to arms, and smite with death the power that would bury the Government and your Liberty in the same hopeless grave. I wish I could tell you that the State of New York calls you to this high honor. For the moment her constituted authorities are silent on the subject. They will speak by and by, and doubtless on the right side; but we are not compelled to wait for her. We can get at the throat of treason and slavery, through the State of Massachusetts.

She was first in the war of Independence: first to break the chains of her slaves; first to make the black man equal before the law; first to admit colored children to her common schools, and she was first to answer with her blood the alarm cry of the nation— when its capital was menaced by rebels. You know her patriotic Governor, and you know Charles Sumner—I need not add more.

Massachusetts now welcomes you to arms as her soldiers. She has but a small colored population from which to recruit. She has full leave of the General Government to send one regiment to the war, and she has undertaken to do it. Go quickly and help fill up this first colored regiment from the North. I am authorized to assure you that you will receive the same wages, the same rations, the same equipments, the same protection, the same treatment and the same bounty secured to white soldiers. You will be led by able and skillful officers—men who will take especial pride in your efficiency and success. They will be quick to accord to you all the honor you shall merit by your valor—and see that your rights and feelings are respected by other soldiers. I have assured myself on these points— and can speak with authority. More than twenty years unswerving devotion to our common cause, may give me some humble claim to be trusted at this momentous crisis.

I will not argue. To do so implies hesitation and doubt, and you do not hesitate. You do not doubt. The day dawns—the morning star is bright upon the horizon! The Iron gate of our prison stands half open. One gallant rush from the North will fling it wide open, while four millions of our brothers and sisters, shall march out into Liberty! The chance is now given you to end in a day the bondage of centuries, and to rise in one bound from social degradation to the plane of common equality with all other varieties of men. Remember Denmark Vesey of Charleston.—Remember Nathaniel Turner of South Hampton, remember Shields Green, and Cope and who followed noble John Brown, and fell as glorious martyrs for the cause of the slave.—Remember that in a contest with oppression the Almighty has no attribute which can take sides with oppressors. The case is before you. This is our golden opportunity—let us accept it—and forever wipe out the dark reproaches unsparingly hurled against us by our enemies. Win for ourselves the gratitude of our Country—and the best blessings of our posterity through all time. The nucleus of this first regiment is now in camp at Readville, a short distance from Boston. I will undertake to forward to Boston all persons adjudged fit to be mustered into the regiment, who shall apply to me at any time within the next two weeks.

Frederick Douglass
Rochester, March 2d. 1863

22

ABRAHAM LINCOLN

Letters to James C. Conkling
and Albert G. Hodges

August 26, 1863 and April 4, 1864

To James C. Conkling

Hon. James C. Conkling   Executive Mansion, Washington
August 26, 1863

My Dear Sir.

Your letter inviting me to attend a mass-meeting of unconditional Union-men, to be held at the Capital of Illinois, on the 3d day of September, has been received.

It would be very agreeable to me, to thus meet my old friends, at my own home; but I can not, just now, be absent from here, so long as a visit there, would require.

The meeting is to be of all those who maintain unconditional devotion to the Union; and I am sure my old political friends will thank me for tendering, as I do, the nation's gratitude to those other noble men, whom no partizan malice, or partizan hope, can make false to the nation's life.

There are those who are dissatisfied with me. To such I would say: You desire peace; and you blame me that we do not have it. But how can we attain it? There are but three conceivable ways. First, to suppress the rebellion by force of arms. This, I am trying to do. Are you for it? If you are, so far we are agreed. If you are not for it, a second way is, to give up the Union. I am against this. Are you for it? If you are, you should say so plainly. If you are not for *force*, nor yet for *dissolution*, there only remains some imaginable *compromise*. I do not believe any compromise, embracing the maintenance of the Union, is now possible. All I learn, leads to a directly opposite belief. The strength of the rebellion, is its military—its army. That army dominates all the country, and all the people, within its range. Any offer of terms made by any man or men within that range, in opposition to that army, is simply nothing for the present; because such man or men, have no power whatever to enforce their side of a compromise, if one were made with them. To illustrate—Suppose refugees from the South, and peace men of the North, get together in convention, and frame and proclaim a compromise embracing a restoration of the Union; in what way can that compromise be used to keep Lee's army out of Pennsylvania? Meade's army can keep Lee's army out of Pennsylvania; and, I think, can ultimately drive it out of existence. But no paper compromise, to which the controllers of Lee's army are not agreed, can, at all, affect that army. In an effort at such compromise we should waste time, which the enemy would improve to our disadvantage; and that would be all. A compromise, to be effective, must be made either with those who control the rebel army, or with the people first liberated from the domination of that army, by the success of our own army. Now allow me to assure you, that no word or intimation, from that rebel army, or from any of the men controlling it, in relation to any peace compromise, has ever come to my knowledge or belief. All charges and insinuations to the contrary, are deceptive and groundless. And I promise you, that if any such proposition shall hereafter come, it shall not be rejected, and kept a secret from you. I freely acknowledge myself the servant of the people, according to the bond of service—the United States constitution; and that, as such, I am responsible to them.

But, to be plain, you are dissatisfied with me about the negro. Quite likely there is a difference of opinion between you and myself upon that subject. I certainly wish that all men could be free, while

I suppose you do not. Yet I have neither adopted, nor proposed any measure, which is not consistent with even your view, provided you are for the Union. I suggested compensated emancipation; to which you replied you wished not to be taxed to buy negroes. But I had not asked you to be taxed to buy negroes, except in such way, as to save you from greater taxation to save the Union exclusively by other means.

You dislike the emancipation proclamation; and, perhaps, would have it retracted. You say it is unconstitutional—I think differently. I think the constitution invests its commander-in-chief, with the law of war, in time of war. The most that can be said, if so much, is, that slaves are property. Is there—has there ever been—any question that by the law of war, property, both of enemies and friends, may be taken when needed? And is it not needed whenever taking it, helps us, or hurts the enemy? Armies, the world over, destroy enemies' property when they can not use it; and even destroy their own to keep it from the enemy. Civilized belligerents do all in their power to help themselves, or hurt the enemy, except a few things regarded as barbarous or cruel. Among the exceptions are the massacre of vanquished foes, and non-combatants, male and female.

But the proclamation, as law, either is valid, or is not valid. If it is not valid, it needs no retraction. If it is valid, it can not be retracted, any more than the dead can be brought to life. Some of you profess to think its retraction would operate favorably for the Union. Why better after the retraction, than *before* the issue? There was more than a year and a half of trial to suppress the rebellion before the proclamation issued, the last one hundred days of which passed under an explicit notice that it was coming, unless averted by those in revolt, returning to their allegiance. The war has certainly progressed as favorably for us, since the issue of the proclamation as before. I know as fully as one can know the opinions of others, that some of the commanders of our armies in the field who have given us our most important successes, believe the emancipation policy, and the use of colored troops, constitute the heaviest blow yet dealt to the rebellion; and that, at least one of those important successes, could not have been achieved when it was, but for the aid of black

232 · america's war

soldiers. Among the commanders holding these views are some who have never had any affinity with what is called abolitionism, or with republican party politics; but who hold them purely as military opinions. I submit these opinions as being entitled to some weight against the objections, often urged, that emancipation, and arming the blacks, are unwise as military measures, and were not adopted, as such, in good faith.

You say you will not fight to free negroes. Some of them seem willing to fight for you; but, no matter. Fight you, then, exclusively to save the Union. I issued the proclamation on purpose to aid you in saving the Union. Whenever you shall have conquered all resistance to the Union, if I shall urge you to continue fighting, it will be an apt time, then, for you to declare you will not fight to free negroes.

I thought that in your struggle for the Union, to whatever extent the negroes should cease helping the enemy, to that extent it weakened the enemy in his resistance to you. Do you think differently? I thought that whatever negroes can be got to do as soldiers, leaves just so much less for white soldiers to do, in saving the Union. Does it appear otherwise to you? But negroes, like other people, act upon motives. Why should they do any thing for us, if we will do nothing for them? If they stake their lives for us, they must be prompted by the strongest motive—even the promise of freedom. And the promise being made, must be kept.

The signs look better. The Father of Waters again goes unvexed to the sea. Thanks to the great North-West for it. Nor yet wholly to them. Three hundred miles up, they met New-England, Empire, Key-Stone, and Jersey, hewing their way right and left. The Sunny South too, in more colors than one, also lent a hand. On the spot, their part of the history was jotted down in black and white. The job was a great national one; and let none be banned who bore an honorable part in it. And while those who have cleared the great river may well be proud, even that is not all. It is hard to say that anything has been more bravely, and well done, than at Antietam, Murfreesboro, Gettysburg, and on many fields of lesser note. Nor must Uncle Sam's Web-feet be forgotten. At all the watery margins they have been present. Not only on the deep sea, the broad bay, and the rapid river, but also up the narrow muddy bayou, and wherever the ground was a little damp, they have been, and made their tracks. Thanks to all. For the great republic—for the principle it lives by, and keeps alive—for man's vast future,—thanks to all.

Peace does not appear so distant as it did. I hope it will come soon, and come to stay; and so come as to be worth the keeping in all future time. It will then have been proved that, among free men, there can be no successful appeal from the ballot to the bullet; and that they who take such appeal are sure to lose their case, and pay the cost. And then, there will be some black men who can remember that, with silent tongue, and clenched teeth, and steady eye, and well-poised bayonet, they have helped mankind on to this great consummation; while, I fear, there will be some white ones, unable to forget that, with malignant heart, and deceitful speech, they have strove to hinder it.

Still let us not be over-sanguine of a speedy final triumph. Let us be quite sober. Let us diligently apply the means, never doubting that a just God, in his own good time, will give us the rightful result. Yours very truly

To Albert G. Hodges

A. G. Hodges, Esq   Executive Mansion, Washington
Frankfort, Ky.
April 4, 1864

My dear Sir: You ask me to put in writing the substance of what I verbally said the other day, in your presence, to Governor Bramlette and Senator Dixon. It was about as follows:

"I am naturally anti-slavery. If slavery is not wrong, nothing is wrong. I can not remember when I did not so think, and feel. And yet I have never understood that the Presidency conferred upon me an unrestricted right to act officially upon this judgment and feeling. It was in the oath I took that I would, to the best of my ability, preserve, protect, and defend the Constitution of the United States. I could not take the office without taking the oath. Nor was it my view that I might take an oath to get power, and break the oath in using the power. I understood, too, that in ordinary civil adminis-tration this oath even forbade me to practically indulge my primary abstract judgment on the moral question of slavery. I had publicly declared this many times, and in many ways. And I aver that, to this day, I have done no official act in mere deference to my abstract judg-ment and feeling on slavery. I did understand however, that my oath to preserve the constitution to the best of my ability, imposed upon me the duty of preserving, by every indispensable means, that gov-ernment—that nation—of which that constitution was the organic law. Was it possible to lose the nation, and yet preserve the constitu-tion? By general law life *and* limb must be protected; yet often a limb must be amputated to save a life; but a life is never wisely given to save a limb. I felt that measures, otherwise unconstitutional, might become lawful, by becoming indispensable to the preservation of the constitution, through the preservation of the nation. Right or wrong, I assumed this ground, and now avow it. I could not feel that, to the best of my ability, I had even tried to preserve the con-stitution, if, to save slavery, or any minor matter, I should permit the wreck of government, country, and Constitution all together. When, early in the war, Gen. Fremont attempted military emancipa-tion, I forbade it, because I did not then think it an indispensable necessity. When a little later, Gen. Cameron, then Secretary of War, suggested the arming of the blacks, I objected, because I did not yet think it an indispensable necessity. When, still later, Gen. Hunter attempted military emancipation, I again forbade it, because I did not yet think the indispensable necessity had come. When, in March, and May, and July 1862 I made earnest, and successive appeals to the border states to favor compensated emancipation, I believed the indispensable necessity for military emancipation, and arming the blacks would come, unless averted by that measure. They declined the proposition; and I was, in my best judgment, driven to the alternative of either surrendering the Union, and with it, the Constitution, or of laying strong hand upon the colored element. I chose the latter. In choosing it, I hoped for greater gain than loss; but of this, I was not entirely confident. More than a year of trial now shows no loss by it in our foreign relations, none in our home popular sentiment, none in our white military force,—no loss by it any how or any where. On the contrary, it shows a gain of quite a hundred and thirty thousand soldiers, seamen, and laborers. These are palpable facts, about which, as facts, there can be no cavilling. We have the men; and we could not have had them without the measure.

["] And now let any Union man who complains of the measure, test himself by writing down in one line that he is for subduing the rebellion by force of arms; and in the next; that he is for taking these hundred and thirty thousand men from the Union side, and placing them where they would be but for the measure he condemns. If he can not face his case so stated, it is only because he can not face the truth. ["]

I add a word which was not in the verbal conversation. In telling this tale I attempt no compliment to my own sagacity. I claim not to have controlled events, but confess plainly that events have controlled me. Now, at the end of three years struggle the nation's condition is not what either party, or any man devised, or expected. God alone can claim it. Whither it is tending seems plain. If God now wills the removal of a great wrong, and wills also that we of the North as well as you of the South, shall pay fairly for our complicity in that wrong, impartial history will find therein new cause to attest and revere the justice and goodness of God. Yours truly

23

ABRAHAM LINCOLN

Gettysburg Address

November 19, 1863

FOUR SCORE AND SEVEN YEARS ago our fathers brought forth on this continent, a new nation, conceived in liberty, and dedicated to the proposition that all men are created equal.

Now we are engaged in a great civil war, testing whether that nation, or any nation so conceived and so dedicated, can long endure. We are met on a great battle-field of that war. We have come to dedicate a portion of that field, as a final resting place for those who here gave their lives that that nation might live. It is altogether fitting and proper that we should do this.

But, in a larger sense, we can not dedicate—we can not consecrate—we can not hallow—this ground. The brave men, living and dead, who struggled here, have consecrated it, far above our poor power to add or detract. The world will little note, nor long remember what we say here, but it can never forget what they did here. It is for us the living, rather, to be dedicated here to the unfinished work which they who fought here have thus far so nobly advanced. It is rather for us to be here dedicated to the great task remaining before us—that from these honored dead we take increased devotion to that cause for which they gave the last full measure of devotion—that we here highly resolve that these dead shall not have died in vain—that this nation, under God, shall have a new birth of freedom—and that government of the people, by the people, for the people, shall not perish from the earth.

24

JAMES S. BRISBIN AND THOMAS J. MORGAN

Reports on U.S. Colored Cavalry in Virginia

October 20, 1864 and November 23, 1864

Superintendent of the Organization of Kentucky Black Troops to the Adjutant General of the Army

Lexington Ky Oct 20 /64

General   I have the honor to forward herewith a report of the operations of a detachment of the 5th U.S. Colored Cavalry during the late operations in Western Virginia against the Salt Works.

After the main body of the forces had moved, Gen'l Burbridge Comdg District was informed I had some mounted recruits belonging to the 5th. U.S. Colored Cavalry, then organizing at Camp Nelson and he at once directed me to send them forward.

They were mounted on horses that had been only partly recruited and that had been drawn with the intention of using them only for the purpose of drilling. Six hundred of the best horses were picked out, mounted and Col Jas. F. Wade 6th. U.S.C. Cav'y was ordered to take command of the Detachment.

The Detachment came up with the main body at Prestonburg Ky and was assigned to the Brigade Commanded by Colonel R. W. Ratliff 12th O.V. Cav.

On the march the Colored Soldiers as well as their white Officers were made the subject of much ridicule and many insulting remarks by the White Troops and in some instances petty outrages such as the pulling off the Caps of Colored Soldiers, stealing their horses etc was practiced by the White Soldiers. These insults as well as the jeers and taunts that they would not fight were borne by the Colored Soldiers patiently or punished with dignity by their Officers but in no instance did I hear Colored soldiers make any reply to insulting language used toward [them] by the White Troops.

On the 2d of October the forces reached the vicinity of the Salt Works and finding the enemy in force preparations were made for battle. Col Ratliffs Brigade was assigned to the left of the line and the Brigade dismounted was disposed as follows. 5th U.S.C. Cav. on the left. 12th O.V.C. in the centre and 11th Mich. Cav. on the right. The point to be attacked was the side of a high mountain, the Rebels being posted about half way up behind rifle pits made of logs and stones to the height of three feet. All being in readiness the Brigade moved to the attack. The Rebels opened upon them a terrific fire but the line pressed steadily forward up the steep side of the mountain until they found themselves within fifty yards of the Enemy. Here Col. Wade ordered his force to charge and the Negroes rushed upon the works with a yell and after a desperate struggle carried the entire line killing and wounding a large number of the enemy and capturing some prisoners   There were four hundred black soldiers engaged in the battle. one hundred having been left behind sick and with broken down horses on the march, and one hundred having been left in the Valley to hold horses. Out of the four hundred engaged, one hundred and fourteen men and four officers fell killed or wounded. Of this fight I can only say that men could not have behaved more bravely. I have seen white troops fight in twenty-seven battles and I never saw any fight better. At dusk the Colored Troops were withdrawn from the enemies works, which they had held for over two hours, with scarcely a round of ammunition in their Cartridge Boxes.

On the return of the forces those who had scoffed at the Colored Troops on the march out were silent.

Nearly all the wounded were brought off though we had not an Ambulance in the command. The negro soldiers preferred present suffering to being murdered at the hands of a cruel enemy. I saw one man riding with his arm off another shot through the lungs and another shot through both hips.

Such of the Colored Soldiers as fell into the hands of the Enemy during the battle were brutally murdered. The Negroes did not retaliate but treated the Rebel wounded with great kindness, carrying them water in their canteens and doing all they could to alleviate the sufferings of those whom the fortunes of war had placed in their hands.

Col. Wade handled his command with skill bravery and good judgement, evincing his capacity to command a much larger force. I am General Very Respectfully Your Obedt. Servant

JAMES S BRISBIN

Col. James S. Brisbin to Brig. Gen. L. Thomas, 20 Oct. 1864, vol. 39, Union Battle Reports, ser. 729, War Records Office, RG 94 [HH-9]. The 5th and 6th U.S. Colored Cavalry regiments were both recruited in Kentucky.

Order by the Commander of a Tennessee Black Regiment

Chattanooga Tenn Nov 23rd 1864

General Order No 50   The Colonel commanding desires to express to the Officers and men of the 14" U.S.C.I. his entire satisfaction with their conduct during the 27" 28" 29 and 30" days of October, in the defense of Decatur Ala— On the march, on the skirmish line, in the charge, they proved themselves Soldiers— Their conduct has gained for the regiment an enviable reputation in the Western army, noted for its fighting qualities— The blood of those who fell has hushed the mouths of our Enemies while the conduct of those who live Elicited praises and cheers from *all* who witnessed it— It is no small event for a black regiment to receive three hearty cheers from a regiment of white men; and yet the 14th deserved the compliment. It is sad to lose the Officers and men who have been so long intimately connected with the regiment, but it had been better for *all* to have gone with them to honorable graves, than for the regiment to have failed to do its duty— There were many instances of personal bravery and devotion shown by the Regiment shown by the Enlisted men— The Colonel was especially pleased with these and will not forget those who thus distinguished themselves—Sergeant Major, George Griffith, 1st Serg't Thos Mc-Clellan, Serg't King, Serg't Graffenberg, Corp'l Seuter and those who bore and stood by the Colors did admirably— Companies F and G. never before been under fire and yet they behaved, like Veteran Soldiers— One year ago the regiment was unknown, and it was considered by most of the army and a large number of the people of the United States very doubtful whether Negroes would make good soldiers and it was esteemed no honor to be an Officer in a black regiment— Today the regiment is known throughout the army and the North and is honored— The Col commanding is proud of the regiment and would not [*exchange*] its command for that of the best white regiment in the U.S. service— He again thanks the men for their bravery and the earnestness they have manifested in their work and the Officers for their ready co-operation with him in advancing the interests of the Command, but he cautions them that very much remains to be done

By Order of Thomas J. Morgan Col 14" U.S.C. Infantry—

General Order No. 50, H'd. Q'r's. 14th U.S. Col'd. Infantry, 23 Nov. 1864, General Orders, 14th USCI, Regimental Books & Papers USCT, RG 94 [G-252].

25

COLORED CITIZENS OF NASHVILLE, TENNESSEE

Petition to the Union Convention of Tennessee Assembled in the Capitol at Nashville

January 9, 1865

During the waning months of the war, efforts to inaugurate political reconstruction prompted intense debate about slavery and freedom, loyalty and treason, and the rights of citizens. Active in that debate were Americans of African descent, who argued that their services to the nation had entitled them not only to freedom but also to civil and political rights. Black Tennesseans petitioned a convention of white unionists that was considering reorganization of the state government and the abolition of slavery. Among the many arguments they advanced for the fitness of black men to exercise the suffrage and other privileges of citizenship, they especially emphasized the role of black soldiers in saving the Union. In the months and years to come, this theme would reappear in countless demands by former slaves for full citizenship.

WE THE UNDERSIGNED PETITIONERS, AMERICAN citizens of African descent, natives and residents of Tennessee, and devoted friends of the great National cause, do most respectfully ask a patient hearing of your honorable body in regard to matters deeply affecting the future condition of our unfortunate and long suffering race.

First of all, however, we would say that words are too weak to tell how profoundly grateful we are to the Federal Government for the good work of freedom which it is gradually carrying forward; and for the Emancipation Proclamation which has set free all the slaves in some of the rebellious States, as well as many of the slaves in Tennessee.

After two hundred years of bondage and suffering a returning sense of justice has awakened the great body of the American people to make amends for the unprovoked wrongs committed against us for over two hundred years.

Your petitioners would ask you to complete the work begun by the nation at large, and abolish the last vestige of slavery by the express words of your organic law.

Many masters in Tennessee whose slaves have left them, will certainly make every effort to bring them back to bondage after the reorganization of the State government, unless slavery be expressly abolished by the Constitution.

We hold that freedom is the natural right of all men, which they themselves have no more right to give or barter away, than they have to sell their honor, their wives, or their children.

We claim to be men belonging to the great human family, descended from one great God, who is the common Father of all, and who bestowed on all races and tribes the priceless right of freedom. Of this right, for no offence of ours, we have long been cruelly deprived, and the common voice of the wise and good of all countries, has remonstrated against our enslavement, as one of the greatest crimes in all history.

We claim freedom, as our natural right, and ask that in harmony and co-operation with the nation at large, you should cut up by the roots the system of slavery, which is not only a wrong to us, but the source of all the evil which at present afflicts the State. For slavery, corrupt itself, corrupted nearly all, also, around it, so that it has influenced nearly all the slave States to rebel against the Federal Government, in order to set up a government of pirates under which slavery might be perpetrated.

In the contest between the nation and slavery, our unfortunate people have sided, by instinct, with the former. We have little fortune to devote to the national cause, for a hard fate has hitherto forced us to live in poverty, but we do devote to its success, our hopes, our toils, our whole heart, our sacred honor, and our lives.

We will work, pray, live, and, if need be, die for the Union, as cheerfully as ever a white patriot died for his country. The color of our skin does not lesson in the least degree, our love either for God or for the land of our birth.

We are proud to point your honorable body to the fact, that so far as our knowledge extends, not a negro traitor has made his appearance since the beginning of this wicked rebellion.

Whether freeman or slaves the colored race in this country have always looked upon the United States as the Promised Land of Universal freedom, and no earthly temptation has been strong enough to induce us to rebel against it. We love the Union by an instinct which is stronger than any argument or appeal which can be used against it. It is the attachment of a child to its parent.

Devoted as we are to the principles of justice, of love to all men, and of equal rights on which our Government is based, and which make it the hope of the world. We know the burdens of citizenship, and are ready to bear them. We know the duties of the good citizen, and are ready to perform them cheerfully, and would ask to be put in a position in which we can discharge them more effectually. We do not ask for the privilege of citizenship, wishing to shun the obligations imposed by it.

Near 200,000 of our brethren are to-day performing military duty in the ranks of the Union army. Thousands of them have already died in battle, or perished by a cruel martyrdom for the sake of the Union, and we are ready and willing to sacrifice more. But what higher order of citizen is there than the soldier? or who has a greater trust confided to his hands? If we are called on to do military duty against the rebel armies in the field, why should we be denied the privilege of voting against rebel citizens at the ballot-box? The latter is as necessary to save the Government as the former.

The colored man will vote by instinct with the Union party, just as uniformly as he fights with the Union army.

This is not a new question in Tennessee. From 1796 to 1835, a period of thirty-nine years, free colored men voted at all her elections without question. Her leading politicians and statesmen asked for and obtained the suffrages of colored voters, and were not ashamed of it. Such men as *Andrew Jackson*, President of the United States, Hon. *Felix Grundy*, John Bell, Hon. *Hugh L. White, Cave Johnson,* and *Ephraim H. Foster,* members of the United States Senate and of the Cabinet, *Gen. William Carroll, Samuel Houston,* Aaron V. Brown, and, in fact, all the politicians and candidates of all parties in Tennessee solicited colored free men for their votes at every election.

Nor was Tennessee alone in this respect, for the same privileges was granted to colored free men in North Carolina, to-day the most loyal of all the rebellious States, without ever producing any evil consequences.

If colored men have been faithful and true to the Government of the United States in spite of the Fugitive Slave Law, and the cruel policy often pursued toward them, will they not be more devoted to it now than ever, since it has granted them that liberty which they desired above all things? Surely, if colored men voted without harm to the State, while their brethren were in bondage, they will be much more devoted and watchful over her interests when elevated to the rank of freemen and voters. If they are good law-abiding citizens, praying for its prosperity, rejoicing in its progress, paying its taxes, fighting its battles, making its farms, mines, work-shops and commerce more productive, why deny them the right to have a voice in the election of its rulers?

This is a democracy—a government of the people. It should aim to make every man, without regard to the color of his skin, the amount of his wealth, or the character of his religious faith, feel personally interested in its welfare. Every man who lives under the Government should feel that it is his property, his treasure, the bulwark and defence of himself and his family, his pearl of great price, which he must preserve, protect, and defend faithfully at all times, on all occasions, in every possible manner.

This is not a Democratic Government if a numerous, law-abiding, industrious, and useful class of citizens, born and bred on the soil, are to be treated as aliens and enemies, as an inferior degraded class, who must have no voice in the Government which they support, protect and defend, with all their heart, soul, mind, and body, both in peace and war.

This Government is based on the teachings of the Bible, which prescribes the same rules of action for all members of the human family, whether their complexion be white, yellow, red or black. God no where in his revealed word, makes an invidious and degrading distinction against his children, because of their color. And happy is that nation which makes the Bible its rule of action, and obeys principle, not prejudice.

Let no man oppose this doctrine because it is opposed to his old prejudices. The nation is fighting for its life, and cannot afford to be controlled by prejudice. Had prejudice prevailed instead of principle, not a single colored soldier would have been in the Union army to-day. But principle and justice triumphed, and now near 200,000 colored patriots stand under the folds of the national flag, and brave their breasts to the bullets of the rebels. As we are in the battlefield, so we swear before heaven, by all that is dear to men, to be at the ballot-box faithful and true to the Union.

The possibility that the negro suffrage proposition may shock popular prejudice at first sight, is not a conclusive argument against its wisdom and policy. No proposition ever met with more furious or general opposition than the one to enlist colored soldiers in the United States army. The opponents of the measure exclaimed on all hands that the negro was a coward; that he would not fight; that one white man, with a whip in his hand could put to flight a regiment of them; that the experiment would end in the utter rout and ruin of the Federal army. Yet the colored man has fought so well, on almost every occasion, that the rebel government is prevented, only by its fears and distrust of being able to force him to fight for slavery as well as he fights against it, from putting half a million of negroes into its ranks.

The Government has asked the colored man to fight for its preservation and gladly has he done it. It can afford to trust him with a vote as safely as it trusted him with a bayonet.

How boundless would be the love of the colored citizen, how intense and passionate his zeal and devotion to the government, how enthusiastic and how lasting would be his gratitude, if his white brethren were to take him by the hand and say, "You have been ever loyal to our government; henceforward be voters." Again, the granting of this privilege would stimulate the colored man to greater exertion to make himself an intelligent, respected, useful citizen. His pride of character would be appealed to this way most successfully; he would send his children to school, that they might become educated and intelligent members of society. It used to be thought that ignorant negroes were the most valuable, but this belief probably originated from the fact that it is almost impossible to retain an educated, intelligent man in bondage. Certainly, if the free colored man be educated, and his morals enlightened and improved, he will be a far better member of society, and less liable to transgress its laws. It is the brutal, degraded, ignorant man who is usually the criminal.

One other matter we would urge on your honorable body. At present we can have only partial protection from the courts. The testimony of twenty of the most intelligent, honorable, colored loyalists cannot convict a white traitor of a treasonable action. A white rebel might sell powder and lead to a rebel soldier in the presence of twenty colored soldiers, and yet their evidence would be worthless so far as the courts are concerned, and the rebel would escape. A colored man may have served for years faithfully in the army, and yet his testimony in court would be rejected, while that of a white man who had served in the rebel army would be received.

If this order of things continue, our people are destined to a malignant persecution at the hands of rebels and their former rebellious masters, whose hatred they may have incurred, without precedent even in the South. Every rebel soldier or citizen whose arrest in the perpetration of crime they may have effected, every white traitor whom they may have brought to justice, will torment and persecute them and set justice at defiance, because the courts will not receive negro testimony, which will generally be the only possible testimony in such cases. A rebel may murder his former slave and defy justice, because he committed the deed in the presence of half a dozen respectable colored citizens. He may have the dwelling of his former slave burned over his head, and turn his wife and children out of doors, and defy the law, for no colored man can appear against him. Is this the fruit of freedom, and the reward of our services in the field? Was it for this that colored soldiers fell by hundreds before Nashville, fighting under the flag of the Union? Is it for this that we have guided Union officers and soldiers, when escaping from the cruel and deadly prisons of the South through forests and swamps, at the risk of our own lives, for we knew that to us detection would be death? Is it for this that we have concealed multitudes of Union refugees in caves and cane-brakes, when flying from the conscription officers and tracked by bloodhounds, and divided with them our last morsal of food? Will you declare in your revised constitution that a pardoned traitor may appear in court and his testimony be heard, but that no colored loyalist shall be believed even upon oath? If this should be so, then will our last state be worse than our first, and we can look for no relief on this side of the grave. Has not the colored man fought, bled and died for the Union, under a thousand great disadvantages and discouragements? Has his fidelity ever had a shadow of suspicion cast upon it, in any matter of responsibility confided to his hands?

There have been white traitors in multitudes in Tennessee, but where, we ask, is the black traitor? Can you forget how the colored man has fought at Fort Morgan, at Milliken's Bend, at Fort Pillow, before Petersburg, and your own city of Nashville?

When has the colored citizen, in this rebellion been tried and found wanting?

In conclusion, we would point to the fact that the States where the largest measure of justice and civil rights has been granted to the colored man, both as to suffrage and his oath in court, are among the most rich, intelligent, enlightened and prosperous. Massachusetts, illustrious for her statesmen and her commercial and manufacturing enterprises and thrift, whose noble liberality has relieved so many loyal refugees and other sufferers of Tennessee, allows her colored citizens to vote, and is ever jealous of their rights. She has never had reason to repent the day when she gave them the right of voting.

Had the southern states followed her example the present rebellion never would have desolated their borders.

Several other Northern States permit negro suffrage, nor have bad effects ever resulted from it. It may be safely affirmed that Tennessee was quite as safe and prosperous during the 39 years while she allowed negro suffrage, as she has been since she abolished it.

In this great and fearful struggle of the nation with a wicked rebellion, we are anxious to perform the full measure of our duty both as citizens and soldiers to the Union cause we consecrate ourselves, and our families, with all that we have on earth. Our souls burn with love for the great government of freedom and equal rights. Our white brethren have no cause for distrust as regards our fidelity, for neither death nor life, nor angels, nor principalities, nor powers, nor things present, nor things to come, nor height, nor depth, nor any other creature, shall be able to separate us from the love of the Union.

Praying that the great God, who is the common Father of us all, by whose help the land must be delivered from present evil, and before whom we must all stand at last to be judged by the rule of eternal justice, and not by passion and prejudice, may enlighten your minds and enable you to act with wisdom, justice, and magnanimity, we remain your faithful friends in all the perils and dangers which threaten our beloved country.

[*59 signatures*]
And many other colored citizens of Nashville[1]

The convention adopted an amendment to the state constitution abolishing slavery, which was ratified on February 22, 1865. The delegates took no action to extend the rights of suffrage or testimony to black Tennesseans.

NOTE

1. Unidentified newspaper clipping of Andrew Tait et al. to the Union Convention of Tennessee, 9 Jan. 1865, *Black Military Experience*, pp. 811–16.

26

MARGARET WALKER

Excerpt from *Jubilee*

1966

Chapter 36
A Noise Like Thunder . . . a Cloud of Dust

January 1, 1865, the Emancipation Proclamation was repeated in
Georgia. But the telegraph poles and wires had all been damaged or
cut by Sherman's men in their march to Savannah and the sea, so
there was no news, and the people in the backwoods knew nothing.
The first three or four months passed without any news from the
eastern war front and with little news from Tennessee where the
last western battles were being fought around Nashville.

Vyry persuaded Caline and May Liza as well as Miss Lillian that
they should try to plant some kind of crop.

"What for?" asked May Liza. "Big Missy never could get the last
harvest."

"We got to eat," said Vyry, "and we got the younguns to feed.
Leastwise Miss Lillian got hern, and I got mine."

Vyry took the initiative, and to the amazement of the whole
household she set the plow in the field and made more than a dozen
long furrows in one day. When the other women saw her determination they grudgingly helped her plant corn, collards, pease, okra,
mustard and turnip salad, tomato plants, potatoes, and onions.
Miss Lillian seemed to pay less attention to what was going on

around her as the days passed, but she smiled and gave her approval to their plans.

The first green shoots were in the fields by the middle of May and Vyry looked at their "crop" with pride and pleasure. Life on the plantation was no longer pure drudgery, with every hour one of hard driving labor. Things were not so hard, but an almost deserted farm with no men was not easy either. Vyry's children were growing. Minna was a quiet one, docile, obedient, and easily controlled, but Vyry was having difficulty trying to train Jim to work.

Early one morning, about the third week in May, Vyry was in the kitchen cooking when all the children came running to alarm the house. They could hear a noise like thunder and the sky was black. Caline and May Liza closed the upstairs windows against a possible thunder storm. But as the rumbling noise grew louder and the black sky obscured the sunlight, they heard voices singing with drums and bugles sounding and in a few minutes they saw that the black cloud was dust from the horses hooves of a great army of men riding and singing:

> Hurrah, hurrah, we bring the jubilee
> Hurrah, hurrah, the flag to make you free
> . . . .
> While we go marching through Georgia!

They rode up to the steps, and in less than fifteen minutes soldiers and horses were over-running the place. They came like a crowd of locusts and the noise was so great that suddenly there was bedlam. Miss Lillian had only just finished dressing and, as Caline said, "I don't believe she ever got her shoes buttoned, and her hair was still hanging down her back in one long yellow plait like she went to bed."

The commanding officer, a major-general, came to the front door and knocked. When May Liza saw for the first time the Union blue uniform, she was so flustered and excited she kept curtseying and bobbing up and down saying, "Come in sir, come right in sir, and make yourself at home."

He smiled and said, "Is your mistress home?"

"Yassah, yassah, she'll be down terreckly. Won't you have a seat in the parlor sir? That's where gentlemens generally goes."

"I'll wait here till she comes, thank you."

Miss Lillian came down the long stairs slowly, her skirts trailing, her blue eyes looking more calm than stricken, and only her husky voice sounding a little startled.

"Good morning, sir."

"Good morning, madam, are you the mistress of this place?" Miss Lillian looked around as though expecting Big Missy to answer and then again at the soldier, his hat in his hand.

"Yes. I reckon I am. I'm the only one left."

"The only one left?" He was puzzled.

"Of my family. My mother and my father, my husband and my brother are all out there." And she pointed vaguely toward the cemetery.

He still looked puzzled and seeing his bewilderment she hastened to say with more alertness than usual but with no asperity, "They're dead."

He saw her agitation because she was ringing her hands. Now he fully understood.

"I'm sorry ma'am. How many slaves do you have on the place?"

"Slaves?"

"Yes, servants?"

"Oh, about five, I guess. Vyry and Caline and May Liza and Vyry's children. I think the rest must have all run away."

"Well ma'am, I am ordered to have all your slaves appear in the yard, and in the presence of you and the witnessing soldiers, hear me read the proclamation freeing them from slavery."

"Oh." Her voice trembled only ever so slightly. "Mister Lincoln's proclamation? I told Mama he had set the slaves free." And then she turned toward the cord to ring the parlor bell, but seeing May Liza and Caline standing gaping in the inner door, she called instead.

"Liza, call Vyry and tell her to get her children and you and Caline come out on the porch. This gentleman has something he wants to tell you."

Vyry would never forget the scene of that morning of the front veranda as long as she lived. Miss Lillian stood in the door with her two children, Bob and Susan, and her arms were around their shoulders. Standing beside Vyry were Caline and May Liza, their faces working though they were trying to look solemn while the man read the paper. Vyry scarcely heard a word he said. It was all she could do to keep Jim still because he wanted to dance a jig before the reading was over. Minna stood quietly beside her mother, holding a corner of Vyry's apron in her hand and, like Miss Lillian's children, she stared curiously at the soldiers. Vyry caught snatches of the long document as the man's voice droned on, "Shall be . . . forever free" and she was caught up in a reverie hearing that magic word. Could it be possible that the golden door of freedom had at last swung open? She mused further, watching the long lines of soldiers standing on Marse John's plantation, and still coming in long lines from the big road, and she was thinking, *There must be no end of them.*" Her ears caught the words:

> And I hereby enjoin upon the people so declared to be free
> to abstain from all violence, unless in necessary self-defense;
> and I recommend to them that, in all cases when allowed,
> they labor faithfully for reasonable wages.

He was folding the paper before Vyry realized that the tears were running down her face. Then she turned to go back inside to her kitchen and her cooking.

Jim could restrain himself no longer. The ten-year-old little boy grabbed his six-year-old sister and, lifting her in his arms, began to dance his jig and sing,

> You is free, you is free!
> Minna you is free!
> You free as a jaybird setting on a swinging limb.
> Jubilee, you is free!
> Jubilee, you is free!

And Minna, who was puzzled but excited, smiled and tried to catch some of the contagion of her brother's wild spirits. She laughed and clapped her hands and said, "Free? Free? Free?"

When Vyry got back to her kitchen she found it overrun with soldiers. They had eaten her pan of biscuits and the ham she had cooked for breakfast and the big coffee pot was empty. They were, moreover, all over the barnyard catching the chickens and wringing their necks and hollering, "Fried chicken for breakfast! Come and get it! Fried chicken!" And they took a big black wash pot and made a fire under it in the backyard and inside the kitchen they were breaking open the cabinets taking food out and emptying the flour bin and getting out the lard. Vyry stepped back in amazement. "Scuse me ma'am," then seeing she wasn't the young missus they began to beg her to cook some more food, saying they were hungry.

"If yall will just get outa my way, I'll fix some more food."

Perhaps, if she had known what she was saying, and getting herself into that day, she might have gone out of the kitchen and let them have it. But instinctively she ran them out of the kitchen and began to make pans of biscuits and fry chicken. She fried chicken all day long. She stood so long, cooking as fast as they could scald the chickens and pick the feathers off and dress them, that at last she was too numb to feel anything and she lost track of the time and how late the day was getting.

In the meantime the soldiers were ransacking everything. They broke open the smokehouse and emptied it of all hams and shoulders and middlings, the sides of beef, and the dried mutton. They gathered basketsful of eggs, cleaned out the springhouse of milk and butter and cream and cheese; loaded the corn into wagons, gathered up all the ducks and geese and turkeys and tied them with strings and ropes. Vyry heard a great yell go up when they found Marse John's liquor. They drank up or carted away all the whiskey, brandy, rum, and wine that was left on the place. They turned loose all the horses and ran some away while they hitched others to all the wagons on the place, the carriage, barouche, and buggy. They found two new calves and took these and all others with the cows. They left an old pesky bull in the pasture. They gave the hogs and pigs a merry chase with sticks and they ran through muddy pig sties catching the slippery, slimy, squealing animals, mud, slops and all, in their arms and boxing them into pens. They set the gin house, that was full of cotton, on fire and burned it to the ground. They took molasses and started strewing it all over the place, in and out of the Big House, up and down stairs and through the parlors making trickling streams all over Big Missy's fine scarlet carpets. They yanked down the heavy silk and velvet portieres and broke up half the furniture.

Behind the soldiers came still another motley lot, more than a mile of freed slaves following the army. They had bundles of rags and some had pots and pans and squawking chickens and other fowl. They were in wagons and on foot, riding mules and driving little oxcarts. There were gray-haired men and women, young mothers with their babies at the breast and streaming lines of children walking. These people were also hungry, and some were sick and diseased with running sores. One poor old gray-haired woman was driving a cart pulled by a team of goats and she had in the cart every possible thing she could carry, such as sacks of seed and meal, squawking chickens, geese, ducks, and a shoat, iron cooking pots and skillets, a wash pot, quilts and croker sacks, and a big tin coffee pot. One of the soldiers observing her said, "Hey, Auntie, where'd you get all this stuff? You look like the children of Israel coming out of Egypt!" The soldiers laughed but the old black woman answered indignantly, "I buyed it."

"You buyed it? Buyed it with what? Worthless Confederate specie?" And they laughed again.

"Nossah. I buyed it with myself. I work for Marster nigh on to fifty years; ever since I been big enough to hold the hoe. I ain't never even much had enough to eat, had to scrounge around for scraps half the time. When we come away to freedom everything turn wrong-side-outwards. I just took what was mine, cause I buyed it with myself."

Somewhere among the motley crowd was Jim, the houseboy. When Caline and May Liza appeared in the kitchen with him, Vyry was flabbergasted.

"Vyry, look who's here?" said May Liza, much more gaily than usual, although she had been bubbling over with joy all day.

"And he come to take me away!"

This was the most surprising news of all to Vyry. All these years she had never thought of Jim and May Liza as sweethearts, but they had worked all their lives in the Big House and Jim was a man in his forties. Come to think of it, May Liza had to be near the same age. Caline was much older. Vyry had never known exactly how old Caline was, but when she was a child and Aunt Sally was cooking in the Big House, Caline was a much younger woman than Aunt Sally. Caline was a middle-aged woman now, more than twice the age of Vyry. Vyry was twenty-eight years old, now that freedom had come to her, but she had not let her mind wander past the business of the morning. It was the middle of the afternoon when Jim appeared. May Liza had her few things tied in a bundle and so did Caline.

"Yall ain't gwine now, is you?"

"Yes we is. We's gwine right now," said May Liza, "Jim says our best bet is to follow the army and they'll be all getting away from here by sundown."

"Why don't you come, too, Vyry?" said Jim. "Me and May Liza is getting married today and Caline gwine live with us soon as we can find a place to stay."

"Where yall gwine, and whichaway is the army headed?"

"We's gwine down in Alabamy. The army is headed that-away now. And Vyry, you might as well, cause I seen the last of Randall Ware."

Vyry's heart lurched painfully at the mention of Randall Ware's name. Her voice was unsteady as she answered Jim.

"What you mean, you seen the last of him, and whereabouts was he at?"

"Last I seen he was sick in Atlanta. Too sick to follow Uncle Billy when he came through Georgia marching to the sea. I seen him on a litter. He was wasted until he was too poor to stand on his feets and he had the fever so bad I doubt he coulda lasted another week. They was sending all the sick and wounded back to Chattanooga and I reckon thereabouts is where they brung him. He bound to be in his grave now. You better come with us."

Vyry felt so weak she had to sit down, and then she trembled so for a moment she couldn't speak. When she did find her voice she was surprised to hear herself saying, "Naw. I don't believe he's dead.

I feel like he mighta been sick and couldn't get here by now, but he told me to wait here for him until the war was over . . ."

"Well the war's over now. Mister Lincoln's dead and buried. . . .

"Aw, naw he ain't!"

"Yeah, and Lee had done surrendered to Grant before ever Mister Lincoln got shot."

"Who shot him? The Confederate soldiers?"

"Naw, but it was a southern white man what shot him. He say some kind of gibberish in a foreign tongue bout Mister Lincoln was a tyrant."

"What is that?"

"I think it means a overbearing ruler like a king."

"Lawd, ain't that a pity! I reckon he done it cause Mister Lincum was trying to help the poor colored peoples."

"Yeah, it just like Brother Zeke said that time, Mister Lincoln sure enough the colored peoples' Moses. He make old Pharaoh get up and git!"

"Where you seen Brother Zeke?"

"He died in the Union camp where me and your free man Randall Ware was before Randall Ware taken sick. I was right there when Brother Zeke died and I helped to bury him."

"Lawd, I sure hates to hear that. He sure was a good man."

"That's just what we says. Now, is you gwine with us?"

"Naw, Jim, I ain't leaving here now. I gotta feeling he ain't dead and I'm duty bound to wait. But I sure hates to see yall go, and I thanks you just the same."

"Wellum we gwine," said Caline. "I been here all my life and I ain't never seen nothing but this here piece of Georgia woods and I'm sick to my stomach of this here place. I wants to travel and see some more of the world before I die. I had me a husband once, Big Boy, but they sold him away and I think they sold him down in Alabamy. Course that was years ago and I don't know where he's at now, living or dead. I ain't got no where to go, but I'm gwine. I'm free, and I ain't staying here no more."

"I ain't heard tell nothing from Randall Ware but once until today. My youngun, Minna, were a young nursing baby when he went away and she nigh on to seven summers old. I got his younguns and I prays to Gawd to see they daddy one more time in this life. I feels like something down deep inside of me would tell me was he dead. I ain't got nowhere to go, neither, but I'm duty bound to wait."

The sun was still high in the sky when Jim and May Liza and Caline left Marse John's plantation and Vyry told them goodbye. She was still working in the kitchen. Miss Lillian and Bob and Susan came in the kitchen where she was cooking, saying they were hungry, and she fed them fried chicken and bread and went to the back door to call Jim and Minna.

"Maw, ain't we gwine with the soldiers?" asked Jim as he stuffed his mouth full of chicken.

"Whoever give you that notion?" asked Vyry.

"Aw Maw, everybody what's anybody is gwine with the soldiers. We's free ain't we? We ain't got to stay here and work no more is we?"

"Yes, son, we's free and we ain't got to stay, but being free don't mean we ain't gotta work, and anyhow I promise your daddy I'd wait here for him."

Jim was crestfallen, but slightly mollified with the promise of his own father. He was excited, however, over the prospect of going with the soldiers and secretly he had been getting a bundle of rags together, too, to follow the army.

Vyry really hadn't promised Randall Ware to wait, but she had promised so long in her mind to stay where he could find her that now it did not make sense for her to go. In the first place, where would they go? She knew that sometime in the future, unless Randall Ware was really dead, he would make it back to his blacksmith shop and grist mill in nearby Dawson. He could make money and make a living for them and give her and their children a home. Maybe her children would even learn to read and write, as he could, and cipher on their hands. She wasn't ready to leave the plantation, not yet.

Jim went outside to tell a newly found friend, a man who was among the contraband freedmen, "My Maw says naw, we ain't gwine with the army. She waiting here for us daddy."

"Oh, I see. How long your daddy been gone?"
"I dunno. I can't hardly remember him. I musta been real little."
"And your sister were a baby?"
"Yassah, I reckon so."

Jim was sharing his fried chicken with his new friend, and the man ate awhile and said nothing. But he was still with the children around the back door of the kitchen when Vyry finally quit cooking and made ready to go to her old cabin for the night.

27

LEON F. LITWACK

Excerpt from *Been in the Storm So Long*

1979

Chapter Four
Slaves No More

Slavery chain done broke at last!
Broke at last! Broke at last!
Slavery chain done broke at last!
Gonna praise God till I die!

Way up in that valley,
Pray-in' on my knees,
Tell-in' God a-bout my troubles,
And to help me if He please.

I did tell him how I suffer,
In the dungeon and the chain;
And the days I went with head bowed down,
An' my broken flesh and pain.

I did know my Jesus heard me,
'Cause the spirit spoke to me,
An' said, 'Rise, my chile, your children
An' you too shall be free."

I done 'p'int one mighty captain
For to marshal all my hosts;
An' to bring my bleeding ones to me,
An' not one shall be lost.

Now no more weary trav'lin;
'Cause my Jesus set me free,
An' there's no more auction block for me
Since He give me liberty.[1]

ON THE NIGHT OF APRIL 2, 1865, Confederate troops abandoned Richmond. The sudden decision caught Robert Lumpkin, the well-known dealer in slaves, with a recently acquired shipment which he had not yet managed to sell. Desperately, he tried to remove them by the same train that would carry Jefferson Davis out of the Confederate capital. When Lumpkin reached the railway station, however, he found a panic-stricken crowd held back by a line of Confederate soldiers with drawn bayonets. Upon learning that he could not remove his blacks, the dealer marched them back to Lumpkin's Jail, a two-story brick house with barred windows, located in the heart of Richmond's famous slave market—an area known to local blacks as "the Devil's Half Acre." After their return, the slaves settled down in their cells for still another night, apparently unaware that this would be their last night of bondage. For Lumpkin, the night would mark the loss of a considerable investment and the end of a profession. Not long after the collapse of the Confederacy, however, he took as his legal wife the black woman he had purchased a decade before and who had already borne him two children.[2]

With Union soldiers nearing the city, a Confederate official thought the black residents looked as stunned and confused as the whites. "The negroes stand about mostly silent," he wrote, "as if wondering what will be their fate. They make no demonstrations of joy." Obviously he had not seen them earlier that day emerging from a church meeting with particular exuberance, "shaking hands and exchanging congratulations upon all sides." Nor had he heard, probably, that familiar refrain with which local blacks occasionally regaled themselves: "Richmond town is burning down, High diddle diddle inctum inctum ah." Whatever the origins of the song, the night of the evacuation must have seemed like a prophetic fulfillment. Explosions set off by the retreating Confederates left portions of the city in flames and precipitated a night of unrestrained looting and rioting, in which army deserters and the impoverished residents of Richmond's white slum shared the work of expropriation and destruction with local slaves and free blacks. Black and white women together raided the Confederate Commissary, while the men rolled wheelbarrows filled with bags of flour, meal, coffee, and sugar toward their respective shanties. Along the row of retail stores, a large black man wearing a bright red sash around his waist directed the looting. After breaking down the doors with the crowbar he carried on his shoulder, he stood aside while his followers rushed into the shops and emptied them of their contents. He took nothing for himself, apparently satisfied to watch the others partake of commodities long denied them. If only for this night, racial distinctions and customs suddenly became irrelevant.[3]

Determined to reap the honors of this long-awaited triumph, white and black Yankees vied with each other to make the initial entry into the Confederate capital. The decision to halt the black advance until the white troops marched into the city would elicit some bitter comments in the northern black press. "History will show," one editor proclaimed, "that they [the black troops] were in the suburbs of Richmond long before the white soldiers, and but for the untimely and unfair order to halt, would have triumphantly planted their banner first upon the battlements of the capital of 'ye greate confederacie.'" Many years later, a former Virginia slave still brooded over this issue. "Gawdammit, 'twas de nigguhs tuk Richmond," he kept insisting. "Ah ain't nevuh knowed nigguhs—even all uh dem nigguhs—could mek such uh ruckus. One huge sea uh black faces filt de streets fum wall tuh wall, an' dey wan't nothin' but nigguhs in sight."

Regardless of who entered Richmond first, black newspapers and clergymen perceived the hand of God in this ironic triumph. The moment the government reversed its policy on black recruitment it had doomed the Confederacy. And now, "as a finishing touch, as though He would speak audible words of approval to the nation," God had delivered Richmond—"that stronghold of treason and wickedness"— into the hands of black soldiers. This is an admonition to which men, who make war on God would do well to take heed."[4]

To the black soldiers, many of them recently slaves, this was the dramatic, the almost unbelievable climax to four years of war that had promised at the outset to be nothing more than a skirmish to preserve the Union. Now they were marching into Richmond as free men, amidst throngs of cheering blacks lining the streets. Within hours, a large crowd of black soldiers and residents assembled on Broad Street, near "Lumpkin Alley," where the slave jails, the auction rooms, and the offices of the slave traders were concentrated. Among the soldiers gathered here was Garland H. White, a former Virginia slave who had escaped to Ohio before the war and now returned as chaplain of the 28th United States Colored Troops.

> I marched at the head of the column, and soon I found myself called upon by the officers and men of my regiment to make a speech, with which, of course, I readily complied. A vast multitude assembled on Broad street, and I was aroused amid the shouts of ten thousand voices, and proclaimed for the first time in that city freedom to all mankind.

From behind the barred windows of Lumpkin's Jail, the imprisoned slaves began to chant:

> *Slavery chain done broke at last!*
> *Broke at last! Broke at last!*
> *Slavery chain done broke at last!*
> *Gonna praise God till I die!*

The crowd outside took up the chant, the soldiers opened the slave cells, and the prisoners came pouring out, most of them shouting, some praising God and "master Abe" for their deliverance. Chaplain White found himself unable to continue with his speech.

"I became so overcome with tears, that I could not stand up under the pressure of such fulness of joy in my own heart. I retired to gain strength." Several hours later, he located his mother, whom he had not seen for some twenty years.[5]

The white residents bolted their doors, remained inside, and gained their first impressions of Yankee occupation from behind the safety of their shutters. "For us it was a requiem for buried hopes," Sallie P. Putnam conceded. The sudden and ignominious Confederate evacuation had been equaled only by the humiliating sight of black soldiers patrolling the city streets. For native whites, it was as though the victorious North had conspired to make the occupation as distasteful as possible. Few of them could ever forget the long lines of black cavalry sweeping by the Exchange Hotel, brandishing their swords and exchanging "savage cheers" with black residents who were "exulting" over this dramatic moment in their lives. After viewing such spectacles from her window, a young white woman wondered, "Was it to this end we had fought and starved and gone naked and cold? To this end that the wives and children of many dear and gallant friends were husbandless and fatherless? To this end that our homes were in ruins, our state devastated?" Understandably, then, local whites boycotted the military band concerts on the Capitol grounds, even after Federal authorities, in a conciliatory gesture, had barred blacks from attendance.[6]

Four days after the entry of Union troops, Richmond blacks assembled at the First African Church on Broad Street for a Jubilee Meeting. The church, built in the form of a cross and scantily furnished, impressed a northern visitor as "about the last place one would think of selecting for getting up any particular enthusiasm on any other subject than religion." On this day, some 1,500 blacks, including a large number of soldiers, packed the frail structure. With the singing of a hymn, beginning "Jesus my all to heaven is gone," the congregation gave expression to their newly won freedom. After each line, they repeated with added emphasis, "I'm going to join in this army; I'm going to join in this army of my Lord." But when they came to the verse commencing, "This is the way I long have sought," the voices reached even higher peaks and few of the blacks could suppress the smiles that came across their faces. Meanwhile, in the Hall of Delegates, where the Confederate Congress had only recently deliberated and where black soldiers now took turns swiveling in the Speaker's chair, T. Morris Chester, a black war correspondent, tried to assess the impact of these first days of liberation: the rejoicing of the slaves and free blacks, the tumultuous reception accorded President Lincoln when he visited the city, the opening of the slave pens, and the mood of the black population. They declare that they cannot realize the change; though they have long prayed for it, yet it seems impossible that it has come."[7]

It took little time for the "grapevine" to spread the news that Babylon (as some blacks called it) had fallen. When black children attending a freedmen's school in Norfolk heard the news, they responded with a resounding chorus of "Glory Hallelujah." Reaching the line "We'll hang Jeff Davis to a sour apple tree," one of the pupils inquired if Davis had, indeed, met that fate. The teacher told her that Davis was still very much alive. At this news, the pupil expressed her dismay "by a decided pout of her lips, such a pout as these children only are able to give." Still, the news about Richmond excited them. Most of the children revealed that they had relatives there whom they now hoped to see, several looked forward to reunions with fathers and mothers "dat dem dere Secesh carried off," and those who had neither friends nor relatives in the city were "mighty glad" anyway because they understood the news to mean that "cullud people free now."[8]

When the news reached a plantation near Yorktown, the white family broke into tears, not only over the fall of Richmond but over the rumor that the Yankees had captured Jefferson Davis. Overhearing the conversation, a black servant rushed through the preparation of the supper, asked another servant to wait on the table for her, and explained to the family that she had to fetch water from the "bush-spring." She walked slowly until no one could see her and then ran the rest of the way. Upon reaching the spring, she made certain she was alone and then gave full vent to her feelings.

> I jump up an' scream, "Glory, glory, hallelujah to Jesus! I's free! I's free! Glory to God, you come down an' free us; no big

man could do it." An' I got sort o' scared, afeared somebody
hear me, an' I takes another good look, an' fall on de groun',
an' roll over, an' kiss de groun' fo' de Lord's sake, I's so full
o' praise to Masser Jesus. He do all dis great work. De soul
buyers can neber take my two chillen lef' me; no, neber can
take 'em from me no mo'.

Several years before, her husband and four children had been
sold to a slave dealer. Her thoughts now turned to the possibility of
a reunion.[9]

Only a few miles from the Appomattox Courthouse, Fannie
Berry, a house servant, stood in the yard with her mistress, Sarah
Ann, and watched the white flag being hoisted in the Pamplin village
square. "Oh, Lordy," her mistress exclaimed, "Lee done surrendered!"
Richmond had fallen the previous week, but for Fannie Berry this
was the day she would remember the rest of her life.

Never was no time like 'em befo' or since. Niggers shoutin'
an' clappin' hands an' singin'! Chillun runnin' all over de
place beatin' tins an' yellin'. Ev'ybody happy. Sho' did some
celebratin'. Run to de kitchen an' shout in de winder:

Mammy, don't you cook no mo'
You's free! You's free!

Run to de henhouse an' shout:

Rooster, don't you crow no mo'
You's free! You's free!
Ol' hen, don't you lay no mo' eggs,
You's free! You's free!

Go to de pigpen an' tell de pig:

Ol' pig, don't you grunt no mo'
You's free! You's free!

Tell de cows:

Ol' cow, don't you give no mo' milk,
You's free! You's free!

Meanwhile, she recalled, some "smart alec boys" sneaked up under her mistress's window and shouted, "Ain't got to slave no mo'.
We's free! We's free!" The day after the celebration, however, Fannie
Berry went about her usual duties, as if she hadn't understood the
full implications of what had transpired. And as before, she permitted her mistress to hire her out. Finally, the woman for whom she
was working told her she was now free, there was no need to return
to her mistress, and she could stay and work for room and board. "I
didn't say nothin' when she wuz tellin' me, but done 'cided to leave
her an' go back to the white folks dat furst own me."[10]

Unlike many of their rural brethren, who evinced a certain
confusion about the implications of freedom and when to claim it,
the blacks in Richmond had little difficulty in appreciating the significance of this event. And they could test it almost instantly. They
promenaded on the hitherto forbidden grounds of Capitol Square.
They assembled in groups of five or more without the presence or
authorization of a white man. They sought out new employers at
better terms. They moved about as they pleased without having to
show a pass upon the demand of any white person. "We-uns kin go
jist anywhar," one local black exulted, "don't keer for no pass—go
when yer want'er. Golly! de kingdom hab kim dis time for sure—dat
ar what am promised in de generations to dem dat goes up tru great
tribulations." And they immediately seized upon the opportunity to
educate themselves and their children, to separate their church from
white domination, and to form their own community institutions.[11]

Less than two years after the fall of Richmond, a Massachusetts
clergyman arrived in the city with the intention of establishing a
school to train black ministers. But when he sought a building for
his school, he encountered considerable resistance, until he met
Mary Ann Lumpkin, the black wife of the former slave dealer. She
offered to lease him Lumpkin's Jail. With unconcealed enthusiasm,

black workers knocked out the cells, removed the iron bars from the windows, and refashioned the old jail as a school for ministers and freedmen alike. Before long, children and adults entered the doors of the new school, some of them recalling that this was not their first visit to the familiar brick building.[12]

NOTES

1. Irwin Silber (ed.), *Soldier Songs and Home-Front Ballads of the Civil War* (New York, 1964), 41; Work Projects Adm. (WPA), *The Negro in Virginia* (New York, 1940), 212; Charles L. Perdue, Jr., Thomas E. Barden, and Robert K. Phillips (eds.), *Weevils in the Wheat: Interview with Virginia Ex-Slaves* (Charlottesville, 1976), 117.

2. WPA, *Negro in Virginia, 164–65,* 201.

3. John B. Jones, *A Rebel War Clerk's Diary at the Confederate States Capital* (2 vols.; Philadelphia, 1866; repro in one volume, ed. Earl Schenck Miers, 1958), 528–30; Allan Nevins, *The War for the Union: The Organized War to Victory 1864–1865* (New York, 1971), 294; Henry L. Swint (ed.), *Dear Ones at Home: Letters from Contraband Camps* (Nashville, 1966), 90; Rembert W. Patrick, *The Fall of Richmond* (Baton Rouge, 1960), 41–58; Katharine M. Jones (ed.), *Heroines of Dixie: Confederate Women Tell Their Story of the War* (Indianapolis, 1955), 398; Sallie A. Putnam, *In Richmond During the Confederacy* (New York, 1867; repr. 1961), 363–64.

4. *Christian Recorder,* April 8, 15, 22, 1865; George P. Rawick (ed.), *The American Slave: A Composite Autobiography* (19 vols.; Westport, Conn., 1972), 35–37; Perdue et al. (eds.), *Weevils in the Wheat,* 103, 145–46. See also *New York Tribune,* April 6, 1865.

5. *Christian Recorder,* April 22, 1865. See also *Black Republican,* May 20, 1865; WPA, *Negro in Virginia,* 212; Jones, *Rebel War Clerk's Diary,* 530.

6. Putnam, *Richmond During the Confederacy,* 367; Patrick, *Fall of Richmond,* 68–69; Phoebe Yates Pember, *A Southern Woman's Story: Life in Confederate Richmond* (Jackson, Tenn., 1959), 135.

7. *New York Times,* April 11, 1865; James M. McPherson, *The Negro's Civil War* (New York, 1965), 67–68; Patrick, *Fall of Richmond,* 115. See also *Christian Recorder,* April 22, 1865.

8. Hope R. Daggett to Rev. George Whipple, April 1865; Mary E. Watson to Rev. George Whipple, May 1, 1865; Miss Frances Littlefield to Rev. George Whipple, May I, 1865, American Missionary Assn. Archives.

9. Laura S. Haviland, *A Woman's Life-Work: Labors and Experiences* (Cincinnati, 1881), 414–15.

10. WPA, *Negro in Virginia,* 205, 210; Rawick (ed.), *American Slave,* XVI: Va. Narr., 3, 5–6; Perdue et al. *(eds.), Weevils in the Wheat, 36–39.*

11.   Patrick, *Fall of Richmond*, 117–18; *New York Times*, April 30, 1865.
12.   WPA, *Negro in Virginia*, 266.

28

ABRAHAM LINCOLN

Second Inaugural Address

March 4, 1865

[FELLOW COUNTRYMEN:]

At this second appearing to take the oath of the presidential office, there is less occasion for an extended address than there was at the first. Then a statement, somewhat in detail, of a course to be pursued, seemed fitting and proper. Now, at the expiration of four years, during which public declarations have been constantly called forth on every point and phase of the great contest which still absorbs the attention, and engrosses the enerergies [sic] of the nation, little that is new could be presented. The progress of our arms, upon which all else chiefly depends, is as well known to the public as to myself; and it is, I trust, reasonably satisfactory and encouraging to all. With high hope for the future, no prediction in regard to it is ventured.

On the occasion corresponding to this four years ago, all thoughts were anxiously directed to an impending civil-war. All dreaded it—all sought to avert it. While the inaugeral address was being delivered from this place, devoted altogether to *saving* the Union without war, insurgent agents were in the city seeking to *destroy* it without war—seeking to dissol[v]e the Union, and divide effects, by negotiation. Both parties deprecated war; but one of them would *make* war rather than let the nation survive; and the other would *accept* war rather than let it perish. And the war came.

One eighth of the whole population were colored slaves, not distributed generally over the Union, but localized in the Southern part of it. These slaves constituted a peculiar and powerful interest. All knew that this interest was, somehow, the cause of the war. To strengthen, perpetuate, and extend this interest was the object for which the insurgents would rend the Union, even by war; while the government claimed no right to do more than to restrict the territorial enlargement of it. Neither party expected for the war, the magnitude, or the duration, which it has already attained. Neither anticipated that the *cause* of the conflict might cease with, or even before, the conflict itself should cease. Each looked for an easier triumph, and a result less fundamental and astounding. Both read the same Bible, and pray to the same God; and each invokes His aid against the other. It may seem strange that any men should dare to ask a just God's assistance in wringing their bread from the sweat of other men's faces; but let us judge not that we be not judged. The prayers of both could not be answered; that of neither has been answered fully. The Almighty has His own purposes. "Woe unto the world because of offences! for it must needs be that offences come; but woe to that man by whom the offence cometh!" If we shall suppose that American Slavery is one of those offences which, in the providence of God, must needs come, but which, having continued through His appointed time, He now wills to remove, and that He gives to both North and South, this terrible war, as the woe due to those by whom the offence came, shall we discern therein any departure from those divine attributes which the believers in a Living God always ascribe to Him? Fondly do we hope—fervently do we pray—that this mighty scourge of war may speedily pass away. Yet, if God wills that it continue, until all the wealth piled by the bondman's two hundred and fifty years of unrequited toil shall be sunk, and until every drop of blood drawn with the lash, shall be paid by another drawn with the sword, as was said three thousand years ago, so still it must be said "the judgments of the Lord, are true and righteous altogether."

With malice toward none; with charity for all; with firmness in the right, as God gives us to see the right, let us strive on to finish the work we are in; to bind up the nation's wounds; to care for him who shall have borne the battle, and for his widow, and his orphan—to do all which may achieve and cherish a just, and a lasting peace, among ourselves, and with all nations.

PART 6
....

Images of War

Firsthand Drawings and
Printed Engravings

Thousands of images were produced during the Civil War to satisfy the craving of the American public to consume war news as fully and as quickly as possible. Most of the original drawings were created by artists who expected, or at least hoped, that their work would become the basis of engravings that would be published in one of the three recently founded American illustrated newspapers. *Frank Leslie's Illustrated Newspaper*, *Harper's Weekly*, and the *New York Illustrated News* had been established in the 1850s to use images that artist-reporters had drawn as observers present at newsworthy events. Between 1861 and 1865, these newspapers sent artist-correspondents, called Special Artists, to travel with the Union armies to make drawings of what they saw. Although American draftsmen had begun documenting combat during the War of 1812,[1] embedding artists within the armies was a new practice, and newspaper readers eagerly studied the engravings that accompanied war stories.

During the war years, these American illustrated weekly newspapers published 2,096 engravings of the Civil War based on firsthand drawings by their thirteen most prolific Special Artists[2], including Henri Lovie, James E. Taylor, and Alfred R. Waud. This number accounts for only a fraction of the drawings that these artists actually made and sent to their employers in New York City, since many of the drawings never found their way into print. These newspapers employed additional Special Artists on a more occasional basis and sometimes utilized the drawings of amateur artists, generally military personnel. In total, more than three thousand illustrations of the Civil War appeared in print, but many more drawings were produced on the battlefields and in the camps, fortresses, towns, cities, and surrounding countryside through which the armies moved. From our vantage point, the original firsthand drawings that survived the vagaries of battle, transport, and editorial whim are the most concrete and telling artifacts of the Civil War.

Unlike contemporary photographers—whose cumbersome, costly, and fragile equipment required stillness and safety—Special Artists could record action in the midst of battle, and often did so under life-threatening conditions. Francis (Frank) Schell, a Special Artist working for *Leslie's*, demonstrated such composure under fire that a major in the Ninth New York Regiment noted the following in a letter to Frank Leslie (b. Henry Carter, 1821-80), owner and editor of *Leslie's*:

I noticed, and so did the whole of the Ninth Regiment, Mr. Schell, your artist, sitting on a log sketching under the hottest fire from Fort Defiance. His nonchalance and coolness did as much toward inspiring our troops as the enthusiasm and bravery of any of the officers.[3]

Confederate troops captured John Hillen, also a Special Artist working for *Leslie's*, at the Battle of Chickamauga during the summer of 1863, and the following year he was severely wounded during General William Tecumseh Sherman's campaign to capture Atlanta.[4]

Special Artist Henri Lovie of *Leslie's* first ironically, then poignantly, described his harrowing experiences on and off the battlefield. In 1861, his hometown newspaper, the *Cincinnati Daily Gazette*, reported, "Henri Lovie was a running target for Union sentries who mistook him for an enemy scout," and added, "fortunately their aim was not too good."[5] The article quotes Lovie, commenting that he had "no objections to running reasonable risks from the enemy, but to be killed by mistake would be damnably unpleasant." By the following year, Lovie's gallows humor had evolved into distress when the hardships of daily life weighed ever more heavily on him, as he communicated to Leslie in a letter:

I shall not annoy you with a detail of my *petites miseres*, but, believe me, I have never encountered so many and great difficulties since I joined McClellan's army in Western Virginia, now nearly a year ago. Riding from 10 to 15 miles daily, through mud and underbrush, and then working until midnight by the dim light of an attenuated tallow 'dip', are among the least of my *desagremens* [sic] and sorrows. To use an indigenous but expressive phrase, I am nearly 'played out'. . . I am deranged about the stomach, ragged, unkempt and unshorn, and need the conjoined skill and services of the apothecary, the tailor and the barber, and above all the attentions of home and the cheerful prattle of children.[6]

In a series of drawings called *Adventures of a Special Artist*,[7] Lovie encapsulated the debilitating effects of these hardships.

Alfred Waud, Special Artist for *Harper's Weekly*, recorded his harrowing experience of making a drawing during the siege of Petersburg:

This sketch was made at the request of General Meade, for his use—from a tree used by the Signal officers. It took over an hour and a half—rebel sharpshooters kept up a fire at me the whole time.[8]

Waud, Theodore Davis, who was also on the staff of *Harper's Weekly*, and *Leslie's* William Crane were the only Special Artists to travel with the Union armies from the earliest troop movements to the war's end. After the war, Davis described the qualities that the artist-correspondent needed:

Total disregard for personal safety and comfort; an owl-like propensity to sit up all night and a hawky style of vigilance during the day; capacity for going on short food, willingness to ride any number of miles on horseback for just one sketch, which might have to be finished at night by no better light than that of a fire—this may give an inkling of some of it, and will, I trust, be sufficient to convince my readers that the frequently supposed mythical special [artist] was occasionally "on the spot."[9]

In spite of the hardships of the job, the Civil War artists understood the unique nature of their work. As Harry Katz, former head curator in the Prints and Photographs Division at the Library of Congress, states: "Special Artists were in their glory: At that time, they were the only graphic journalists capable of depicting the action and drama of newsworthy events as they happened."[10]

Photographers sent to document the war, Katz adds, couldn't keep up with the Special Artists.

Photographic processes had been refined since their first successes of the late 1830s but were still slow, and the equipment was cumbersome. The exposure time needed for light to be recorded in a camera was too long to capture motion. The fragile glass plates had to be dipped in a light-sensitive emulsion and exposed before the emulsion dried. After exposure, the plate had to be dipped into a second emulsion bath to fix the image. Of course, the glass plates had to be protected from breakage. Furthermore, the technology of half-tone printing that was required to reproduce photographs directly in newspapers would not be invented until the turn of the century. Thus, it was the draftsman, rather than the photographer, who could most effectively capture the life of the war, but the nature of the publishing process inevitably compromised the vibrancy of the firsthand drawing.

By the time a drawing appeared as a printed engraving in an illustrated newspaper, it had undergone a subtle but significant transformation that began in the editor's office. Once a drawing arrived at the New York City offices of the publisher, the editor would decide if it would be a candidate for immediate use, later use, or indefinite archiving. If it was to be used immediately to depict a recent event, the editor would decide what, if any, changes were needed to convey the visual information most clearly or to suggest a particular editorial perspective.[11] Sometimes, several drawings were combined to depict one event. Once the composition was decided, a complex process was set in motion using the hands of many artists and technicians to turn the original drawing into an engraving.

The illustrated newspapers converted drawings into printed images through wood engravings carved onto Turkish boxwood blocks.[12] Turkish boxwood is very hard, enabling engravers to incise very fine lines, but the tree grows extremely slowly and typical blocks are only a few inches square. To engrave a large drawing, as Frank Leslie explained, several small blocks had to be bolted together. A single engraver would spend approximately two weeks carving one large engraving. Leslie turned this impediment to his advantage, giving his newspaper the competitive edge in the constant contest among the illustrated newspapers to "scoop" the competition on a news story.

Leslie adapted assembly-line methods to the production of the engraved image. Once an edited drawing was finalized and traced onto a woodblock composed of as many as sixteen boxwood sections, the block was taken apart and the separate pieces were distributed to different engravers to carve. Each engraver could complete the task in as few as two days, occasionally overnight. The individual blocks were then refastened, and the unified block was electrotyped and copied onto metal plates to be printed on the newspaper's rotary presses. The turn-around time for the publication of an illustration, which had been roughly four weeks in 1861, was reduced to a few days by the later war years.

Leslie had utilized the division of labor to publish news images faster than the competition could, and soon, all three illustrated newspapers were using the same procedure to bring the latest news to their readers.

The result was a flood of images and information that swamped the original sources of the published material: the Special Artist's drawing. Today, many viewers mistakenly believe that the printed engraving and the original firsthand drawing are one and the same. Yet the differences are significant. Multiple engravers were required to follow uniform protocols for incising their boxwood blocks in order to ensure that the final image would appear unified. All areas of shading and line gradation had to be reduced to uniform, repeated lines and even light or dark shadow. Figures became stiff and generalized, their features set in rigid and stylized expressions. Subtle detail was usually eliminated, and emphasis was changed to suit the editorial policy of the newspaper where necessary.[13] The artists' subtlety and curiosity gave way in the newspaper images to clarity, certainty, and uniformity.

The Special Artists whose works are included in this anthology transcended circumstances that would have thwarted less determined artists in order to create often riveting, insightful, and beautiful drawings. Many of them brought prior art experience to their work as

Special Artists, which made their draftsmanship subtle and elegant and their compositions expressive. Their sensitivity, honed in the war, resulted in drawings that speak less of victory or defeat and more of the complexity and cost of the conflict. These drawings, perceived as artworks, constitute the most enduring legacy of the Special Artists.

Judith Bookbinder, Co-Director
The Becker Collection, Boston College

NOTES

1. Harry L. Katz, "Special Artists of the Civil War: America's First 'Photojournalists'," in Judith Bookbinder and Sheila Gallagher, editors, *First Hand: Civil War Era Drawings from* the Becker Collection (Chestnut Hill, Mass.: McMullen Museum of Art, 2009), p. 43.

2. William P. Campbell, *Civil War: A Centennial Exhibition of Eyewitness Drawings* (Washington, D.C.: National Gallery of Art, 1961), p. 14.

3. Letter to the Editor, *Frank Leslie's Illustrated Newspaper* XIII (March 15, 1862), 258, quoted in Campbell, *Civil War*, pp. 39-40.

4. Joshua Brown, *Beyond the Lines: Pictorial Reporting, Everyday Life, and the Crisis of Gilded Age America* (Berkeley, Calif.: University of California Press, 2002), p. 53.

5. *Cincinnati Daily Gazette* (June 29, 1861), quoted in J. Cutler Andrews, *The North Reports the Civil War* (Pittsburgh, Pa.: University of Pittsburgh Press, 1955), pp. 103-104.

6. Henri Lovie, letter to the editor, *Frank Leslie's Illustrated Newspaper* XIV (May 17, 1862), 66, quoted in Campbell, *Civil War*, pp. 33-34.

7. Published in *Frank Leslie's Illustrated Newspaper* XIV (February 17, 1863), p. 332.

8. Alfred Waud, *In Front of Petersburg*, sketch, Library of Congress, Prints and Photographs Division.

9. Theodore R. Davis, "How a Battle is Sketched," *St. Nicholas Magazine*, July 1889.

10. Katz, "Special Artists of the Civil War," p. 43.

11. The significant impact of the editorial perspective on Civil War era newspaper images is revealed in the comparison of the artists' original drawings with the published engravings, a rich area of investigation that the Becker Collection of over 600 Civil War-era original drawings, now available online, has, along with other sources, made easier.

12. Frank Leslie, "How Illustrated Newspapers are Made," *Frank Leslie's Illustrated Newspaper*, August 2, 1856, as cited in Natasha Seaman,

"Authenticity, the Master Author, and the Missing Hand: Drawings by the Civil War Special Artists in *Frank Leslie's Illustrated Newspaper*," in Bookbinder and Gallagher, *First Hand*, p. 124.

13. See Judith Bookbinder, "Civil War Drawings as Art," Bookbinder and Gallagher, *First Hand*, p. 19. A comparison of Henri Lovie's drawings of the Battle of Shiloh and the engravings derived from those drawings and published in *Frank Leslie's Illustrated Newspaper*, May 1862, reveals that the editor and engravers obscured some of the horrific detail and chaotic atmosphere that Lovie depicted.

ARTIST: JAMES E. TAYLOR

**Dedication of a Monument to the
Memory of the Heroes of the
New Hampshire Regiment
Killed in the Battle of Winchester,
April 10, 1865**

ARTIST: UNKNOWN

United States Hospital at Georgetown, D.C., formerly the Union Hotel

ARTIST: HENRI LOVIE

Squirrel Rifles:
Sketch at the Depot in Xenia, Ohio
September 5, 1862

**Battle of Pittsburgh Landing,
Shiloh, Tennessee:
Centre, Sunday Morning
April 6, 1862**

No. 2

Ricketts' Battery, Capt. Ramsay commanding...
Desperate Retreat

I mes'd 48 horses killed & many wounded

Upon the repeated attack
still bent in the spot till the
killed & horses remained all the position
and these dragoons they previously wounded
killed

Gen. McDowell's
Head quarters

ARTIST: ALFRED R. WAUD

**Citizen volunteers assisting
wounded in the field of battle,
September 17, 1862**

ARTIST: UNKNOWN

Colored Troops Under General Wild Liberating Slaves in North Carolina

sources

ALL POSSIBLE CARE HAS BEEN taken to trace ownership and secure reprint permission for each selection in this anthology. The American Library Association and National Endowment for the Humanities wish to thank the following authors, publishers, and representatives for providing reprint permission and source material for the following selections:

Text Sources

Journal kept at the hospital, Georgetown, D.C., 1862, by Louisa May Alcott, from *Louisa May Alcott: Her Life, Letters, and Journals,* edited by Ednah D. Cheney. Boston: Roberts Brothers, 1889.

"What To the Slave Is the Fourth of July?" and "Men of Color, To Arms!" by Frederick Douglass, from *The Oxford Frederick Douglass Reader*, edited with an introduction by William L. Andrews. Copyright © 1996 by Oxford University Press Inc. Reprinted by permission of Oxford University Press Inc.

"A Plea for Captain John Brown," by Henry David Thoreau, from *Henry D. Thoreau Reform Papers,* edited by Thomas F. Glick. Copyright ©

Image Sources

COVER: Henri Lovie, *Feeding the Squirrel Rifles in Cincinnati, Ohio,* September 6, 1862. Reprinted courtesy of the Becker Collection, Boston, MA.

FRONTISPIECE: James E. Taylor, *Dedication of a Monument to the Memory of the Heroes of the New Hampshire Regiment Killed in the Battle of Winchester,* April 10, 1865. Reprinted courtesy of the Becker Collection, Boston, MA.

PART I: *United States Hospital at Georgetown, D.C., formerly the Union Hotel,* from the book, *Official Portfolio of War and Nation,* edited by General Marcus F. Wright. Copyright © 1907 by C. J. Stanley. First appearing in *Frank Leslie's Illustrated Newspaper,* July 6, 1861. Courtesy of Collections of Maine Historical Society. Item #5263.

PART II: Henri Lovie, *Squirrel Rifles: Sketch at the Depot in Xenia, Ohio,* September 5, 1862. Reprinted courtesy of the Becker Collection, Boston, MA.

PART III: Henri Lovie, *Battle of Pittsburgh Landing, Shiloh, Tennessee: Centre, Sunday Morning,* April 6, 1862. Reprinted courtesy of the Becker Collection, Boston, MA.

PART IV: Alfred R. Waud, *Citizen volunteers assisting the wounded in the field of battle,* September 17, 1862. From the Morgan Collection of Civil War Drawings, Library of Congress, Prints and Photographs Division, Washington, D.C. Reproduction #LC-USZ62-1059.

PART V: *Colored Troops Under General Wild Liberating Slaves in North Carolina,* from *Harper's Weekly,* January 3, 1864, p. 52. Reprinted by permission of HarpWeek.

EDWARD L. AYERS assumed the presidency of the University of Richmond in July, 2007. Previously Dean of Arts and Sciences at the University of Virginia, where he began teaching in 1980, Ayers was named the National Professor of the Year by the Carnegie Foundation for the Advancement of Teaching in 2003.

A historian of the American South, Ayers has written and edited ten books. *The Promise of the New South: Life After Reconstruction* was a finalist for both the National Book Award and the Pulitzer Prize. *In the Presence of Mine Enemies: Civil War in the Heart of America* won the Bancroft Prize for distinguished writing in American history and the Beveridge Prize for the best book in English on the history of the Americas since 1492. A pioneer in digital history, Ayers created *The Valley of the Shadow: Two Communities in the American Civil War*, a website that has attracted millions of users and won major prizes in the teaching of history.

Ayers has received a presidential appointment to the National Council on the Humanities, served as a Fulbright professor in the Netherlands, and been elected to the American Academy of Arts and Sciences. He currently serves as the national project scholar for "Let's Talk About It: Making Sense of the American Civil War," a reading and discussion program for public audiences, developed in cooperation with the American Library Association's Public Programs Office, with funding from the National Endowment for the Humanities.